D0834060

Discover

Britain's historic houses

The Borders

Discover **Britain's**

Published by Reader's Digest Association Ltd
London • New York • Sydney • Montreal

The Borders

historic houses

Simon Jenkins & Hamish Scott

Contents

6 The best in Britain
8 Introduction
9 Star ratings and accessibility
10 Architectural timeline and houses in brief
14 **Berkshire**
32 **London Central**
82 **London East**
110 **London West**
162 **Surrey**
186 Glossary and Simon Jenkins' sources
188 Contact details
190 Index
192 Picture credits and acknowledgements

4 DUMFRIES & GALLOWAY

Page	House	
136	8	Caerlaverock Castle ★★★
138	1	Drumlanrig Castle ★★★★
142	4	Ecclefechan: Carlyle's Birthplace ★
143	2	Ellisland Farm ★
144	9	Kirkcudbright: Broughton House ★
146	10	Kirkcudbright: MacLellan's Castle ★
147	3	Rammerscales ★
148	7	Shambellie House ★
149	5	Threave House ★
150	6	Threave Castle ★★

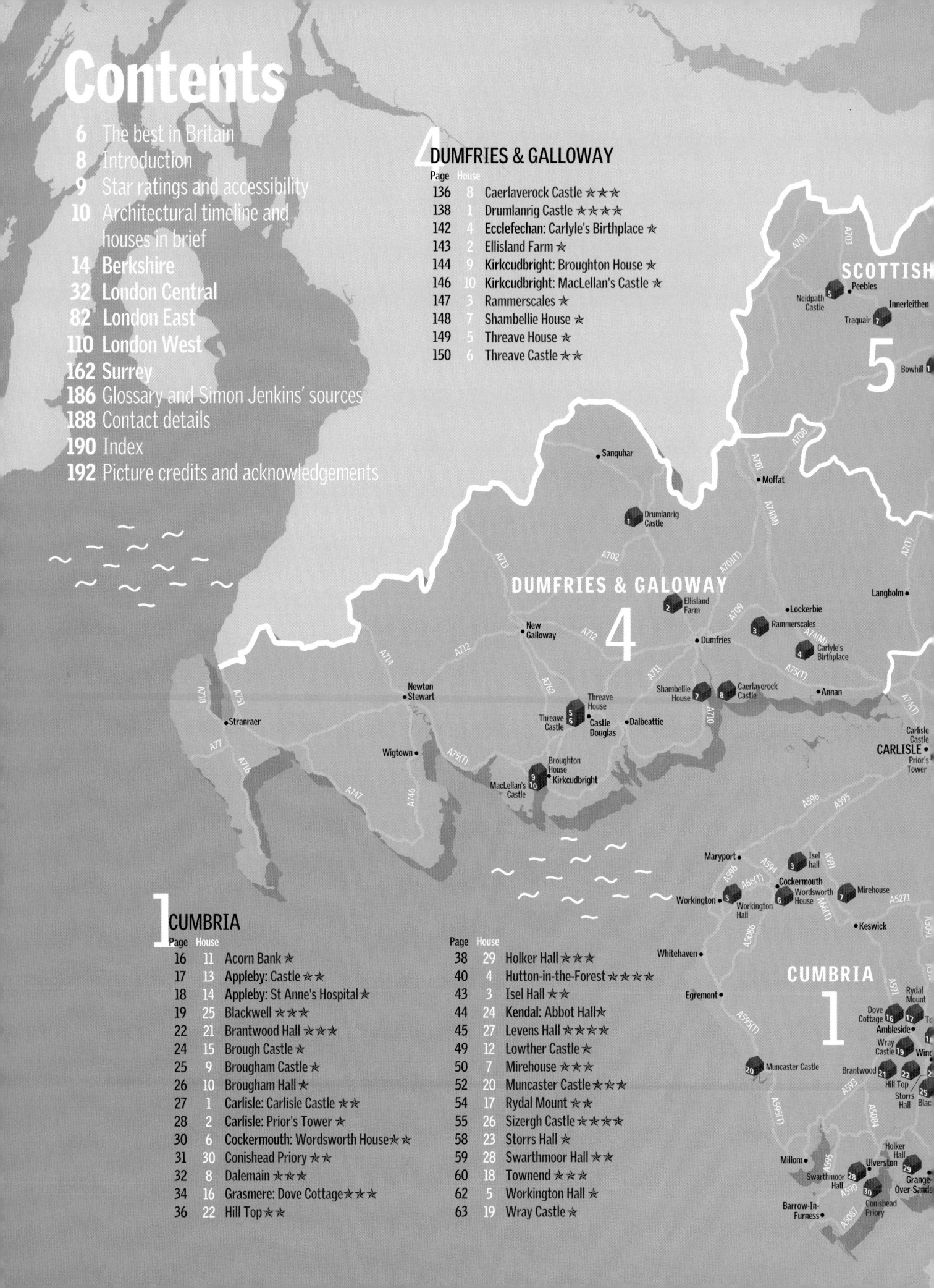

1 CUMBRIA

Page	House	
16	11	Acorn Bank ★
17	13	Appleby: Castle ★★
18	14	Appleby: St Anne's Hospital ★
19	25	Blackwell ★★★
22	21	Brantwood Hall ★★★
24	15	Brough Castle ★
25	9	Brougham Castle ★
26	10	Brougham Hall ★
27	1	Carlisle: Carlisle Castle ★★
28	2	Carlisle: Prior's Tower ★
30	6	Cockermouth: Wordsworth House ★★
31	30	Conishead Priory ★★
32	8	Dalemain ★★★
34	16	Grasmere: Dove Cottage ★★★
36	22	Hill Top ★★
38	29	Holker Hall ★★★
40	4	Hutton-in-the-Forest ★★★★
43	3	Isel Hall ★★
44	24	Kendal: Abbot Hall ★
45	27	Levens Hall ★★★★
49	12	Lowther Castle ★
50	7	Mirehouse ★★★
52	20	Muncaster Castle ★★★
54	17	Rydal Mount ★★
55	26	Sizergh Castle ★★★★
58	23	Storrs Hall ★
59	28	Swarthmoor Hall ★★
60	18	Townend ★★★
62	5	Workington Hall ★
63	19	Wray Castle ★

SCOTTISH BORDERS

Page	House	
154		Abbotsford ★★★★
157		Ayton Castle ★★
158		Bowhill ★★★
160		Dryburgh Abbey ★★
161		Ferniehirst Castle ★
162		Floors Castle ★★★
164		Hermitage Castle ★★★
166		Jedburgh: Jedburgh Castle Jail ★★
167		Jedburgh: Mary, Queen of Scots' House ★
168		Manderston ★★★★
172		Mellerstain ★★★★
175		Neidpath Castle ★
176		Old Gala House ★
177		Paxton House ★★★
179		Smailholm Tower ★
180		Thirlestane Castle ★★★★
183		Traquair ★★★★

NORTHUMBERLAND

Page	House	
100		Alnwick Castle ★★★★
104		Aydon Castle ★★★
106		Bamburgh Castle ★★
108		Belford Hall ★
109		Belsay Castle ★
110		Belsay Hall ★★
112		Chillingham Castle ★★★★
115		Chipchase Castle ★★
116		Cragside ★★★★
120		Langley Castle ★★
121		Lindisfarne Castle ★★★
123		Newcastle upon Tyne: Bessie Surtees House ★
124		Newcastle upon Tyne: Castle ★★
125		Preston Tower ★
126		Seaton Delaval Hall ★★
128		Wallington Hall ★★★★
132		Warkworth Castle ★★
133		Warkworth Hermitage ★

DURHAM

Page	House	
66	12	Barnard Castle: Blagraves Bouse ★
67	9	Barnard Castle: Bowes Museum ★★
68	8	Barnard Castle: The Castle ★
70	3	Beamish: Beamish Museum ★/★★
74	15	Bishop Auckland: Auckland Castle ★★★
77	4	Chester-le-Street: Anker's House ★
78	11	Croxdale Hall ★★
79	10	Durham: Castle ★★★
80	7	Durham: Crook Hall ★★
83	6	Finchale Priory ★
84	13	Harperley Camp ★★
86	17	Headlam Hall ★
87	1	Hylton Castle ★
88	5	Lumley Castle ★★★
89	19	Preston Hall ★
90	16	Raby Castle ★★★★
94	18	Rokeby Park ★★★
96	2	Washington Old Hall ★★
97	14	Witton Castle ★

The best in Britain

SCOTLAND

- 114 Abbotsford, Melrose *
- 127 Blair Castle
- 130 Cawdor Castle
- 128 Craigievar Castle
- 112 Drumlanrig Castle *
- 131 Dunrobin Castle
- 129 Dunvegan Castle
- 126 Glamis Castle
- 120 Hill House
- 121 Hopetoun House
- 124 Inveraray Castle
- 117 Manderston *
- 115 Mellerstain *
- 118 Mount Stuart
- 119 New Lanark
- 122 Palace of Holyroodhouse
- 125 Scone Palace
- 132 Skara Brae
- 123 Stirling Castle
- 116 Thirlestane Castle *
- 113 Traquair House *

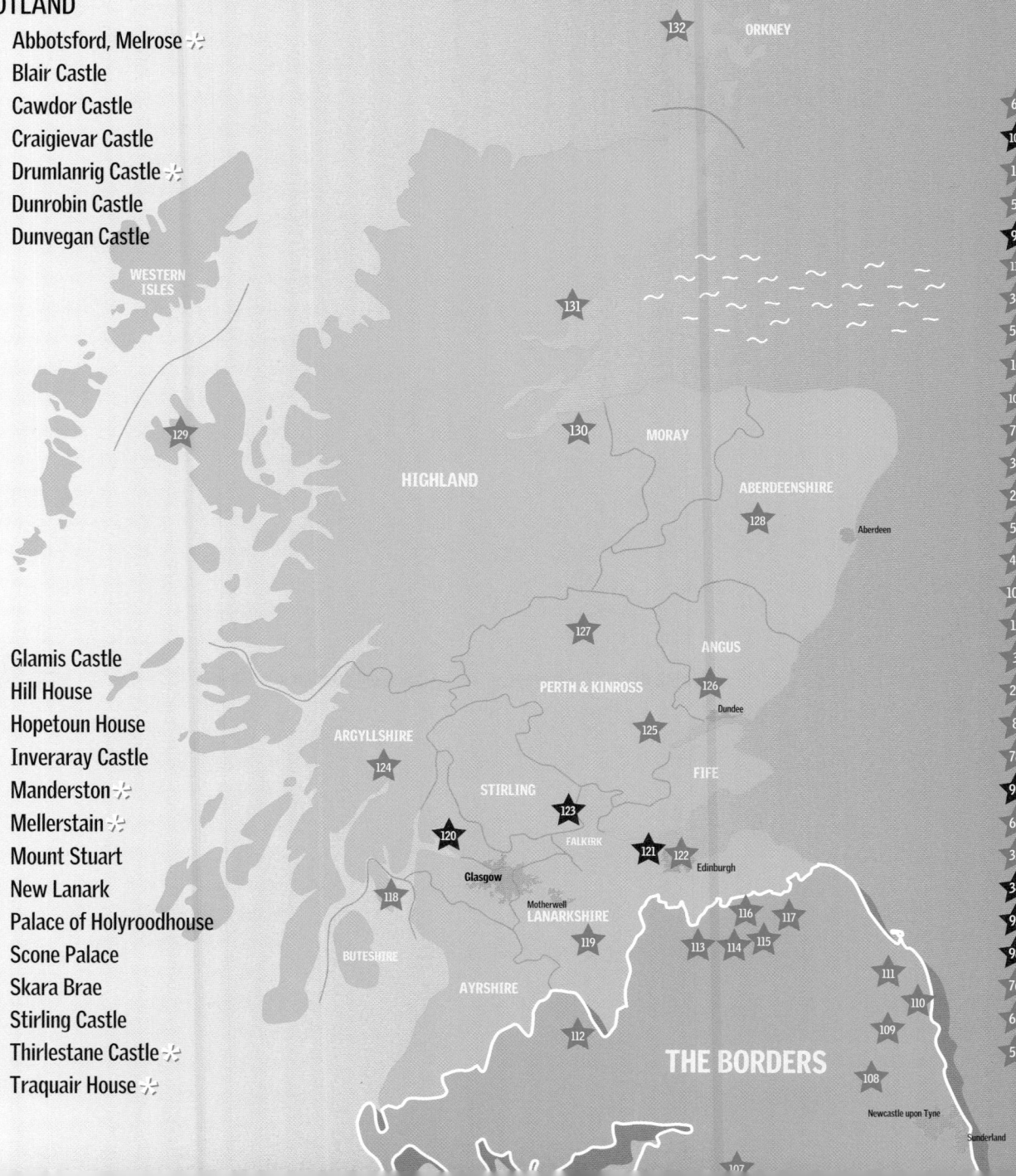

- 61 Canons Ashby
- 102 Castle Howard
- 14 Charleston
- 54 Chastleton
- 91 Chatsworth House
- 111 Chillingham Castle *
- 36 Chiswick House
- 56 Claydon House
- 16 Cothay Manor
- 109 Cragside *
- 70 Deene Park
- 38 Dennis Severs House
- 28 Dyrham Park
- 52 Eastnor Castle
- 40 Eltham Palace
- 100 Fairfax House
- 13 Firle Place
- 3 Forde Abbey
- 27 Godinton Park
- 8 Goodwood House
- 78 Grimsthorpe Castle
- 90 Haddon Hall
- 66 Hagley Hall
- 35 Ham House
- 34 Hampton Court
- 93 Hardwick Hall
- 98 Harewood House
- 76 Harlaxton Manor
- 65 Harvington Hall
- 51 Hatfield House
- 22 Hever Castle
- 80 Holkham Hall
- 37 Home House
- 79 Houghton Hall
- 107 Hutton-in-the-Forest *
- 25 Ightham Mote
- 74 Kedleston Hall
- 21 Kensington Palace
- 5 Kingston Lacy
- 50 Knebworth House
- 24 Knole
- 29 Lacock Abbey
- 1 Lanhydrock
- 26 Leeds Castle
- 104 Levens Hall *
- 19 Longleat
- 89 Lyme Park
- 53 Madresfield Court
- 48 Magdalen College
- 17 Montacute House
- 101 Newby Hall
- 94 Newstead Abbey
- 96 Nostell Priory
- 6 Osborne House
- 32 Osterley Park
- 72 Oxburgh Hall
- 10 Parham House
- 23 Penshurst Place
- 9 Petworth House
- 106 Raby Castle *
- 59 Ragley Hall
- 41 Restoration House

WALES

- 84 Beaumaris Castle
- 82 Caernarfon Castle
- 43 Caerphilly Castle
- 42 Castell Coch
- 86 Conwy Castle
- 87 Erddig
- 85 Plas Mawr
- 83 Plas Newydd
- 73 Powis Castle
- 45 Raglan Castle
- 44 Tredegar House

ENGLAND

- 110 Alnwick Castle ✢
- 62 Althorp
- 68 Arbury Hall
- 11 Arundel Castle
- 95 Astley Hall
- 4 Athelhampton House
- 58 Audley End
- 15 Bateman's
- 77 Belton House
- 75 Belvoir Castle
- 99 Beningbrough Hall
- 46 Berkeley Castle
- 47 Blenheim Palace
- 81 Blickling Hall
- 92 Bolsover Castle
- 69 Boughton House
- 12 Brighton Pavilion
- 55 Broughton Castle
- 71 Burghley House
- 103 Burton Agnes Hall
- 97 Burton Constable Hall

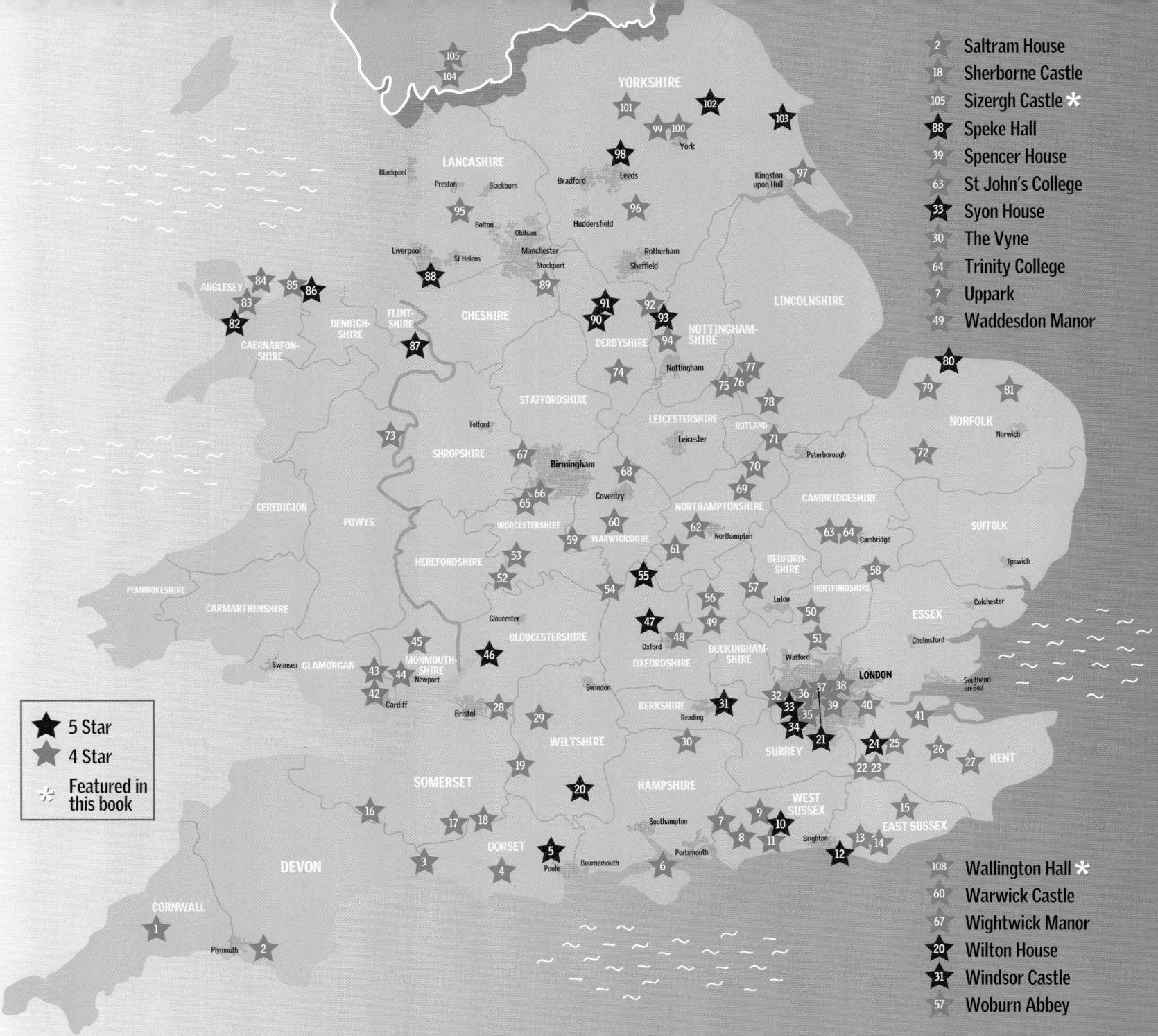

- 2 Saltram House
- 18 Sherborne Castle
- 105 Sizergh Castle ✢
- 88 Speke Hall
- 39 Spencer House
- 63 St John's College
- 33 Syon House
- 30 The Vyne
- 64 Trinity College
- 7 Uppark
- 49 Waddesdon Manor

- 108 Wallington Hall ✢
- 60 Warwick Castle
- 67 Wightwick Manor
- 20 Wilton House
- 31 Windsor Castle
- 57 Woburn Abbey

I visited these buildings after writing a book on English churches and the experience was as moving as it was different. While places of worship were built according to the authority and liturgy of the Church, people built houses for themselves. A house was useful first and beautiful second, and from this derives the joy of visiting houses. They are a conversation between utility and beauty down the ages.

In defining the word 'house' I soon found that I could not sensibly distinguish castle from palace, house from hut, roof from ruin. My list embraces any structure in which men and women have laid their heads, provided that they are in some degree accessible to public view. The selection is a personal list and the commentary is a personal vision, warts and all.

Simon Jenkins

Historic houses of the Borders

From the Roman Conquest to the reign of James I, **Cumbria** was a land under threat. Houses were either fortified or they were seized by marauding Scots. The commonest building type was the keep, evolving into the pele or tower house. An exceptional stock of castles include royal Carlisle and the curtain-walled peles of the Cliffords. Even Elizabethan houses such as Levens and Hutton have peles at their cores.

The arrival of Lady Anne Clifford in 1649 initiated the restoration of her castles at Appleby, Brough and Brougham. Classicism ventured into Cumbria in the 17th century at Hutton and Appleby. In the 18th century came the cladding of Dalemain and Carr of York's embellishment of Workington.

The medieval revival saw Salvin refurbish Hutton and rebuild Muncaster. Spectacular sites led to spectacular architecture at Smirke's Lowther Castle and Philip Wyatt's astonishing Conishead. Romantic poets and their followers made Cumbria a cradle of the Picturesque at Wordsworth's Cockermouth, Grasmere and Rydal. They were followed by Ruskin at Brantwood and Beatrix Potter at Hill Top.

The charms of Windermere were no less appealing to the Merseyside and Mancunian plutocracy who left houses as diverse as Storrs Hall, Wray Castle and Baillie Scott's Arts and Crafts Blackwell.

Durham was a handsome county of rolling hills and high moors until the coming of King Coal. Few English landscapes have been so ravaged by industrial development. Yet Durham has its corners of delight. Castles predominate among the earlier buildings, with fine examples at Raby and Durham. The Tudors left the impressive hilltop profile of Lumley Castle and its sadder neighbour, Hylton. There is little from the Georgian era apart from Croxdale and the Palladian villa at Rokeby, the latter an exquisite touch of Italy in the North.

The Gothic revival is represented by Wyatt's alterations to Auckland Castle and the refashioning of Raby and Witton. Vernacular buildings, from medieval Crook Hall and Jacobean Washington to Beamish, offer unspectacular but rewarding houses of all periods.

Northumberland is a wild and little-visited place. There are some 500 fortified buildings, castles and pele towers, relics of a time when the Percys, Greys, Fenwicks, Herons and Forsters ruled what were, in effect, buffer statelets. Almost all houses contain fragments of defensive pele towers as at Chipchase, Langley and at Warkworth, where the pele is a full palace-keep.

Not until the union of the English and Scottish crowns in 1603 did owners feel secure enough to build conventional mansions. James I's progress south was greeted with Great Halls and new state rooms, as at Chillingham. The old families began to fade away and new money rebuilt the county in the 18th century. The result was the Georgian rooms at Wallington and Salvin's redecoration of Alnwick for the Percys, while Norman Shaw produced Cragside, his masterpiece, for Lord Armstrong.

In the **Scottish Borders** warriors, cattle-thieves and rogues have shaped both history and architecture. A general lawlessness required any wealthy house to be a stronghold. When the Union of the Crowns brought peace, some old towers such as Hermitage and Smailholm fell into ruin while others such as Traquair were restyled for a gentler way of life. Grandiose new mansions, such as the baroque Thirlestane reflected their owners' wealth and power. In the 18th century classical influences produced Paxton and Mellerstain. Sir Walter Scott's Abbotsford was as influential as his writings in giving Scotland a new, Romantic image. Baronial mansions such as Ayton Castle became the norm while the neo-Georgian extravagance of Manderston is an Edwardian swansong to the history of the British country house.

Dumfries & Galloway were independent of the Scottish crown until the 11th century and of doubtful later allegiance. Close by the Solway shore, Caerlaverock is an early castle, whilst Threave is a testament to the great medieval power of the 'Black' Douglases. Another, more lastingly successful branch of the family built Drumlanrig Castle, remodelled in the 1670s as a vast Baroque palace. But some of the houses to be seen are very modest, including Robert Burns's Ellisland cottage, while Kirkudbright's Broughton House, was the home of artist E.A. Hornel, drawn to the picturesque coastline.

Hamish Scott

☆ STAR RATINGS AND ACCESSIBILITY ☆☆☆☆☆

The 'star' ratings are entirely my personal choice (but see note below). They rate the overall quality of the house as presented to the public, and not gardens or other attractions. On balance I scaled down houses, however famous, for not being easily accessible or for being only partly open.

The top rating, five stars, is given to those houses that qualify as 'international' celebrities. Four stars are awarded to houses of outstanding architectural quality and public display. Three-star houses comprise the run of good historic houses, well displayed and worthy of national promotion. Two and one-star houses are of more local interest, are hard to visit, or have just one significant feature.

Accessibility varies greatly, from buildings that are open all year to houses that can only be visited 'by appointment' (rarely, I have broken my rule and included a private property that is not open at all, but is viewable from nearby walks or public gardens). Opening hours tend to alter from year to year, but an indication of how accessible a house is to visitors is given at the start of each entry, together with brief information on location and ownership. Many of the houses are National Trust or English Heritage properties, some are now museums or hotels, others are privately owned by families who open to the public for part of the year (English Heritage grant requirements insist on 28 days minimum). Some owners may, understandably, seek to cluster visitors on particular days. More details for each house are given at the back of this book, and readers are advised to check before visiting.

A final note, houses are, or should be, living things subject to constant change and how we view them is bound to be a subject of debate. I welcome any correction or comment, especially from house owners, sent to me c/o the publisher.

NOTE: On the UK map (pages 6-7) the 4 and 5-star houses in England and Wales were selected by Simon Jenkins. Those in Scotland were selected by Hamish Scott and the editors of Reader's Digest.

Architectural timeline
and Borders houses in brief

Abbotsford
Sir Walter Scott's house, designed by the author, with architect William Atkinson, it reflects his taste for romance, history and legend.

Acorn Bank
A house of two sides: a Georgian front with a 16th- and 17th- century façade at the rear. Traces of a pele tower remain.

Alnwick Castle
Ancient seat of the Dukes of Northumberland with an outer bailey enclosing a shell keep. The interior was transformed by Robert Adam in the 18th century and Anthony Salvin in the 19th.

Appleby Castle
Cumbrian stronghold of Lady Anne Clifford. Jacobean house, with Northern Baroque façade, and Norman keep, with Georgianized top floor.

Appleby: St Anne's Hospital
Almshouses built under the walls of Appleby Castle by Lady Anne Clifford in the 1650s. There are 12 houses in pink-hued Penrith stone.

Aydon Castle
A hall house, dating from the late 13th century and fortified in the early 14th, enclosed by a wall for extra protection. Interesting interiors.

Ayton Castle
Built in the 1830s by James Gillespie Graham in Scots-baronial style. Enlarged in the 1860s by David Bryce and then James Wardrop.

Bamburgh Castle
Coastal fortress of Saxon origin, set on a rocky promontory. Rescued from ruin and much altered at the end of the 19th century.

Barnard Castle: Blagraves House
A town house dating back to the Middle Ages. The façade features a four-storey bay that projects out into the street.

Barnard Castle: Bowes Museum
Elaborate mansion, designed by Jules Pellechet in 1869 in imitation of the Le Havre town hall to house John Bowes' art and artefacts.

Barnard Castle: The Castle
A 12th-century castle; the Great Hall, Great Chamber with oriel window and Round Tower survive. The remains are in ruins, the inner and outer wards transformed into gardens.

Beamish Museum
A museum of England's industrial past. Pit cottages have been restored and a town centre reconstructed as they would have been in 1913.

Belford Hall
A Palladian house of 1756, designed by James Paine. The Newcastle architect, John Dobson, gave the Hall a new rear entrance in 1817.

Belsay Castle
The ruins of a 15th-century castle with pele tower. The surviving façade of a Jacobean house stands nearby.

Belsay Hall
A neo-classical mansion in strict Greek style, inspired by the Theseion at Athens. Each floor of the two-storeyed central hall is colonnaded.

Bishop Auckland: Auckland Castle
Palace of the Bishops of Durham, restored and adapted in Gothick style by James Wyatt in the late 18th century.

Blackwell
Designed by M.H. Baillie Scott in Arts-and-Crafts style, as a Lakeland holiday home. Restored by Modernist architects Allies and Morrison.

Bowhill
Built around an earlier villa, by the 4th Duke of Buccleuch. It was extended over several decades from 1812.

Brantwood
Lakeside house bought by Ruskin in 1872 and much expanded and adapted by him to make the most of the surrounding landscape.

Brough Castle
Ruined castle with Norman origins, built on site of a Roman fort. Owned by the Cliffords and restored by Lady Anne in the 1660s.

Brougham Castle
A Norman castle, fortified in the Middle Ages. Another Clifford fortress, restored by Lady Anne but fallen to ruin again.

Brougham Hall
Great Cumbrian house of ancient origin, converted in the 19th century and known as the 'Windsor of the North'. Now a ruin in process of renovation.

Caerlaverock Castle
A medieval 'castle of enclosure' dating back to the 1270s and built on a triangular plan, unique in Scotland. Transformed in the 1600s into a Renaissance-style house, it is now a ruin.

Carlisle Castle
Once a mighty fortress, of great strategic importance, protecting the English from the Scots; with Norman keep and medieval interiors.

Carlisle: Prior's Tower
Part of a priory and once an ancient pele tower on Carlisle's ramparts. Contains remains of the prior's solar with a 16th-century painted roof.

Chester-le-Street: Anker's House
An anchorage attached to a church, home to a hermit who was walled up inside the building with only two apertures, one for food and water, the other offering a view inside the church.

Chillingham Castle
A medieval castle with pele tower still in evidence. New additions were made to both interior and exterior in the 17th century to honour visits by King James I.

Chipchase Castle
A Jacobean mansion built on the site of an earlier house – the substantial pele tower remains. The house was Georgianized both inside and out during the 1780s.

Cockermouth: Wordsworth House
William Wordsworth's birthplace, a comfortable Georgian town house awarded to Wordsworth's father when he was agent to Sir James Lowther.

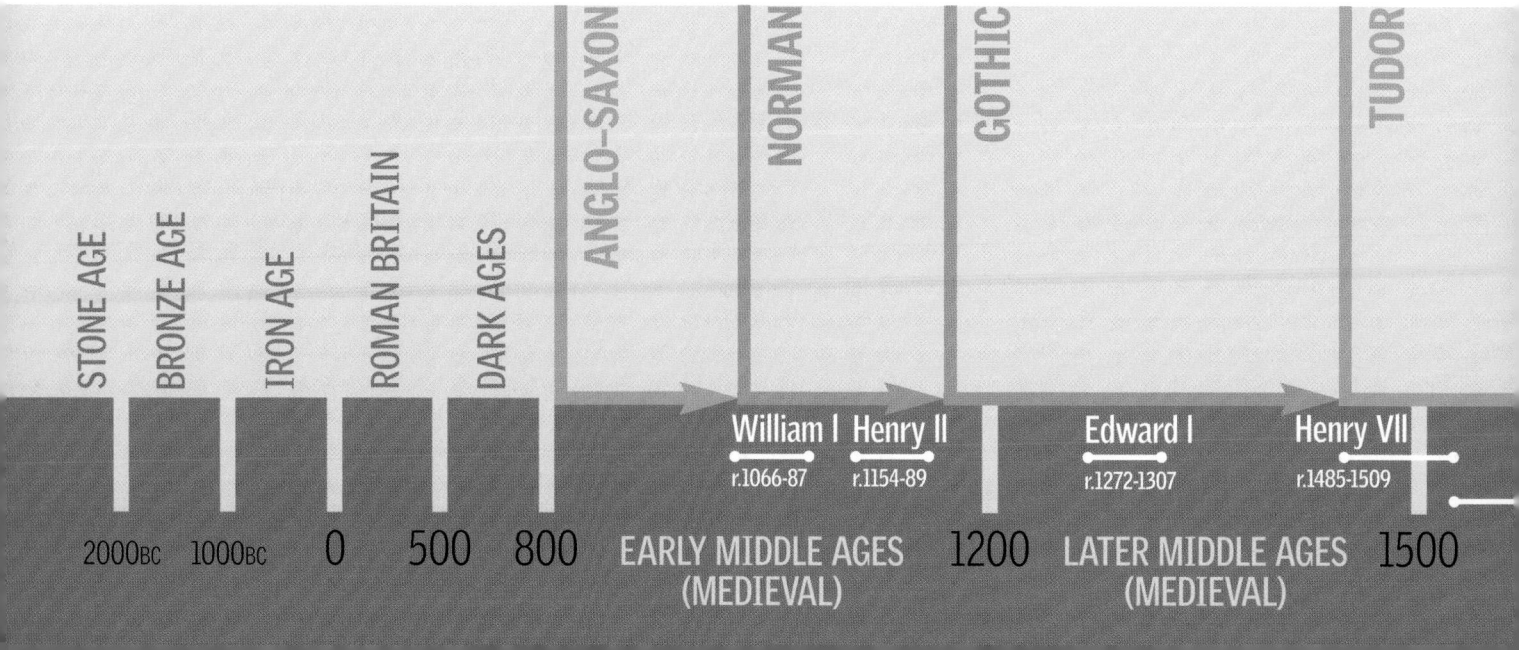

Conishead Priory
An early 19th-century eccentric mansion with many turrets, pinnacles and gables, typical of the Gothick style; based on a design by Philip Wyatt.

Cragside
The masterpiece of Richard Norman Shaw who combined medieval, Tudor and Jacobean styles to create the Victorian ideal house.

Croxdale Hall
A Georgian house, built over an earlier, possibly Tudor, house. A private, Catholic chapel in the Gothick style is found in the north wing.

Dalemain
At the rear are the remains of two medieval pele towers and medieval buildings with Tudor additions; at the front is a Georgian façade.

Drumlanrig Castle
Seat of one of the oldest Scottish families since the 14th century. The first castle was replaced in the 1500s, and rebuilt palatially in 1675.

Dryburgh Abbey
The ruins of an old abbey with many rooms still intact. It became a picturesque feature in an ideal landscape, created in the 18th century in the grounds of Dryburgh House.

Durham: Durham Castle
A Norman castle of great strategic importance. Once the seat of the Prince Bishops of Durham, now home to Durham University.

Durham: Crook Hall
A medieval hall house, mostly 14th-century but with some walls dating back to the 13th century. The hall is linked to a Georgian house.

Ecclefechan: Carlyle's Birthplace
Birthplace of the Victorian writer Thomas Carlyle. One of a pair of simple village cottages built by Carlyle's father and uncle in the local vernacular.

Ellisland Farm
The farmhouse where Robert Burns lived for some years and where he wrote some of his most famous poetry. The house is much altered since Burns had it rebuilt, in 1788.

Ferniehirst Castle
A Kerr-family home, built at the end of the 16th century from the ruins of an earlier castle. The staircases rise counter-clockwise to allow for the Kerr's left-handed fighting techniques.

Norman architecture

After 1066, as the Normans consolidated their control over Britain, there was an increase in building. Castles went up around the country, symbols of the power of the new ruling elite. As the Norman bishops exerted their authority over hearts and minds, new cathedrals, abbeys and churches were built. The new castles were a development of the motte and bailey type – a Norman innovation that had been introduced into Britain before the Conquest – with a stone keep replacing the wooden tower on top of the 'motte', or mound. Churches were cruciform with a square tower over the crossing. The dominant style used for these buildings was Romanesque, the architecture prevalent in Europe at the time; translated to Britain, it eventually became known as Norman architecture. The style was in use in Britain before the Conquest; elements were used in Edward the Confessor's rebuilding at Westminster Abbey.

Norman architecture was characterized by its massive proportions. Walls and pillars were hollow, faced with stone and filled with rubble, and had to be thick in order to be strong enough. Buttressing was used for further support and windows remained small to avoid further weakening the walls. Ceilings were vaulted – Norman architecture used barrel, rib and cross vaults. Probably the most typical feature of the style was the Norman arch, found on both doorways and windows. These arches receded into the thickness of the wall and could be highly decorated. Decoration was carved and incised and featured geometric patterns, such as chevrons and diamond shapes.

A Norman arch

Finchale Priory
Remains of a priory, created in the 13th century on the site of St Godric's hermitage. The prior's house, refectory and undercroft can be seen.

Floors Castle
An early 18th-century mansion designed by William Adam and remodelled in 1837 by William Playfair, who transformed the Palladian palace with extravagant architectural details.

Grasmere: Dove Cottage
A tiny cottage, once an inn, that was home to William Wordsworth and his family from 1799 to 1809. The interiors are preserved as they would have been in the poet's time.

Harperley Camp
The remains of a POW camp, built in 1943. The camp was made up of huts of brick, wood and breeze-block that served as sleeping quarters and living areas for the inmates.

Headlam Hall
A manor house with a 17th-century front; the rear façade is classically Georgian. A Jacobean chimneypiece survives inside.

Hermitage Castle
A castle built in the late 14th century to control a strategic cross-border route. An earlier courtyard house was integrated into the fortress when defensive measures were added.

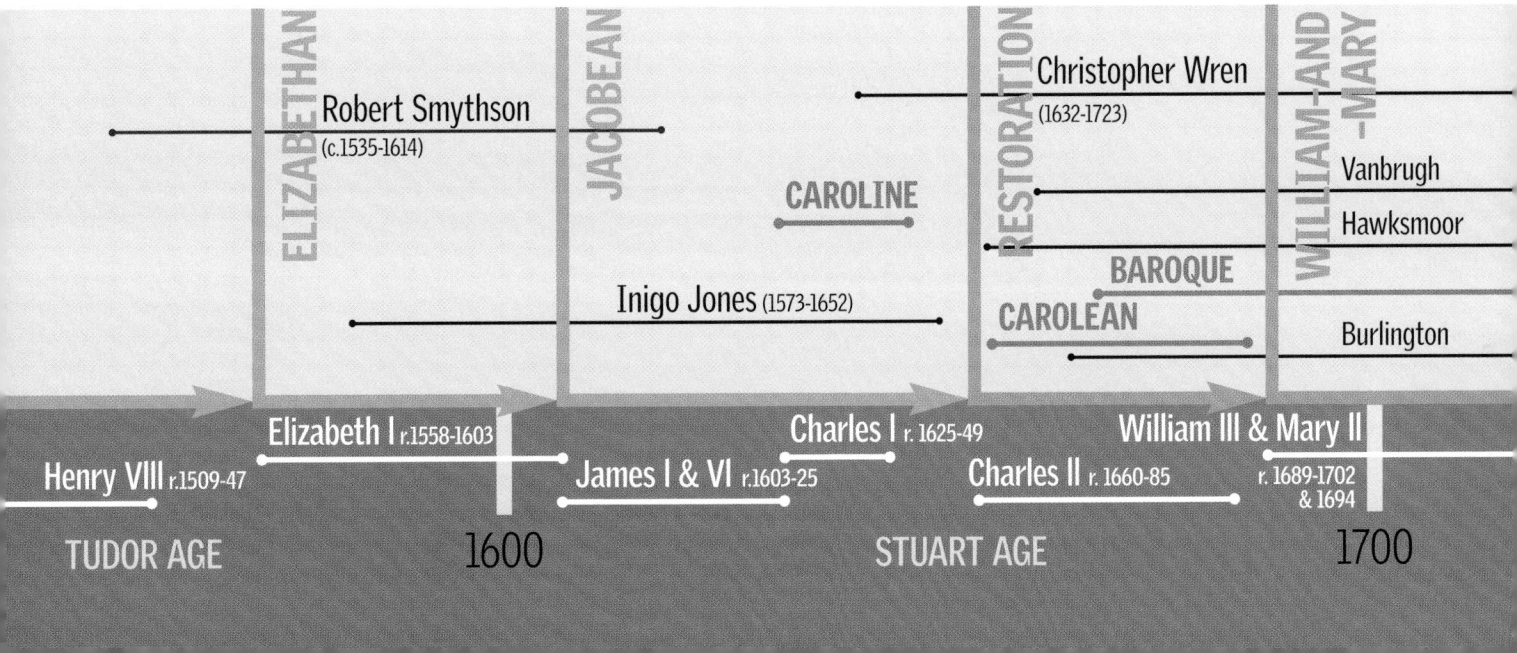

John Dobson (1787–1864)

John Dobson was born in North Shields in 1787. At the age of 15 he was apprenticed to Newcastle architect and builder David Stephenson. After a time in London, he returned to Newcastle and established his own practice. During his career, Dobson was responsible for close to 100 houses and more than 50 churches. His designs were neo-classical in style, but built with modern engineering techniques. He believed that the new buildings of the industrial age should be as much about great architecture as about function. He put his principles into practice with his plans for Newcastle Central railway station.

Dobson's greatest achievement was probably Newcastle itself. Between 1834 and 1839, he collaborated with builder Richard Grainger and Town Clerk John Clayton to redesign and rebuild the city centre on classical lines. The new streets were admired around the world and Grey Street, in particular, was praised. It was, according to W.E. Gladstone in 1862, 'the finest street in modern times'. More recently, it was voted Britain's most beautiful street by Radio 4 listeners.

John Dobson died in 1864 and was buried in Newcastle General Cemetery, designed by Dobson himself in 1834–6.

Hill Top
Lake District 17th-century farmhouse bought by Beatrix Potter with the profits on her first books. She never lived there but used it as a source of inspiration for her writing and illustrations.

Holker Hall
Rebuilt in the 1870s in Elizabethan style, includes a neo-Jacobean wing from the 1830s.

Hutton-in-the-Forest
Originally two pele towers, linked with a Great Hall. Added to in the 17th and 18th centuries; remodelled in a medieval revival style by Salvin.

Hylton Castle
A 15th century tower house, Hylton was refashioned in Victorian Gothic style after 1869. Now a ruin, the upper floors and roof gone.

Isel Hall
House with an early medieval pele tower, with a pink lime-harling. Great Hall linked to the tower in the 16th century to form a courtyard range.

Jedburgh Castle Jail
An 1823 prison, designed by Archibald Elliot and based on the ideas of penal reformers. Turrets and crenellation give it the look of a castle.

Jedburgh: Mary, Queen of Scots House
A 16th-century tower house built on a T-shaped plan. Mary, Queen of Scots, is reputed to have stayed there for a month in 1566.

Kendal: Abbot Hall
A Georgian mansion in ochre stone, reputedly by Carr of York. Inside, the main hall runs from front to back; it houses a fine art collection.

Kirkcudbright: Broughton House
An 18th-century town house adapted by the artist E.A. Hornel, one of the 'Glasgow Boys'. He added a studio and magnificent gallery space.

Kirkcudbright: MacLellan's Castle
The ruins of an impressive town house, built in the 1570s. Despite the towers and gun loops, the building was never a castle.

Langley Castle
A 14th-century hall keep, restored in the late 19th century. There is one chamber on each floor with smaller chambers in the corner towers.

Levens Hall
A 13th-century pele tower and hall, converted in the Elizabethan age. The late-17th century topiary garden is one of the oldest in England.

Lindisfarne Castle
An Elizabethan island castle transformed by Edwin Lutyens in 1902. He modernized it while maintaining its medieval features.

Lowther Castle
A Regency mansion of 1809 by Robert Smirke. Designed in the style of a medieval castle and with a dramatic façade, it is now mainly a ruin.

Lumley Castle
Built in the 1390s, it was altered by Vanbrugh in the 1720s. He created a range of state rooms, and transformed the undercroft into a library.

Manderston
An Edwardian mansion in Georgian style built around an 18th century house. The opulent interiors include a magnificent silver staircase.

Mellerstain
Started by William Adam and finished by his son Robert. The interiors are among his finest and have been maintained over the centuries.

Mirehouse
A 17th-century manor house, extended in the 19th. Home to the Spedding brothers and visited by the poets and writers who were their friends.

Muncaster Castle
Created in 1862 by Anthony Salvin around a medieval core. He remodelled the interiors, including a Great Hall and octagonal library.

Neidpath Castle
An L-shaped tower house dating from the 14th century, an outpost of the Lords of Tweedale, expanded during the 17th century.

Newcastle-upon-Tyne: Bessie Surtees House
A five-storeyed, timber-framed house with windows stretching the width of three floors. Two 17th-century rooms survive inside.

Newcastle-upon-Tyne: Castle
The keep of one of the most important Norman castles, built over the remains of a Roman fort, complete with dungeons, Great Hall and solars.

Old Gala House
A late 16th-century bastle (fortified farmhouse) enlarged in the 17th century.

Paxton House
A country villa above the River Tweed, built in the 18th century to perfect Palladian proportions by John Adam, Robert's elder brother.

Preston Hall
An 1820s villa, built in brick but with later 19th-century stone additions. A Victorian 'street' has been recreated in part of the service wing.

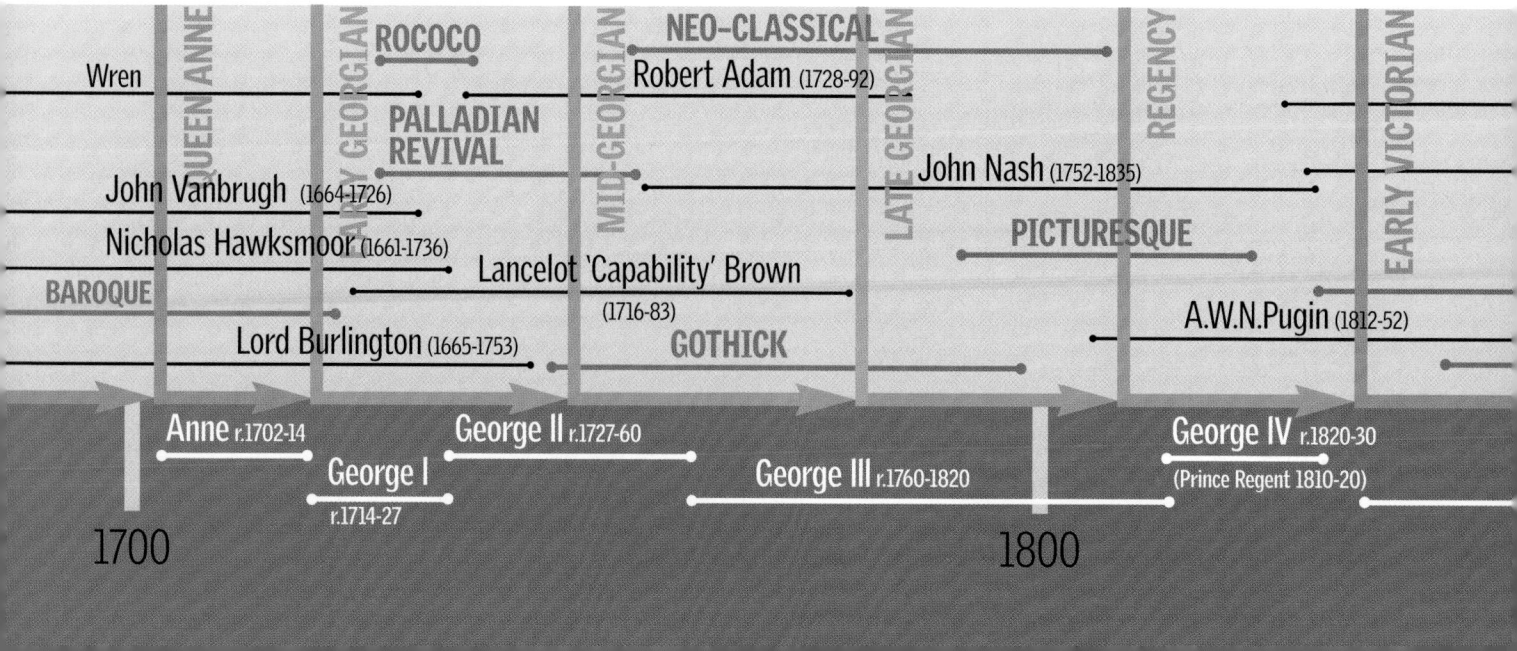

Pele towers

These fortified structures are peculiar to the North of England and Scottish borders. They were built in response to the many conflicts that played out in the region between c1200 and c1750 but can be hard to date accurately. In England, most pele towers were put up in the 16th and 17th centuries; in Scotland this was during the 17th and 18th centuries. Around 100 towers were built and about 75 have survived in some form or another. Most pele towers were situated in small settlements and have been described as 'poormen's castles'. They were designed to protect the family who had built the tower and their retainers from attack but were not intended to withstand a prolonged siege.

A typical pele tower looked like a small square or rectangular stone keep (although some were made from wood). The walls were thick – between 3 and 10 feet – and there were usually three storeys. The windowless ground floor was used for storage and as a refuge for livestock during a raid. On the first floor was a hall and kitchen; living and sleeping quarters were found on the second. Windows on the upper floors were deliberately small and few in number. The flat battlemented roof provided the ideal vantage point for defence, as well as a look-out post and site for a signal beacon.

Preston Tower
Part of a pele tower built in 1392. Half of the tower was demolished in the 17th century and the stone used to build an attached house. This was taken down in the 19th century.

Raby Castle
A medieval fortress of nine towers, all dating from different periods, linked by a curtain wall and once surrounded by an outer wall.

Rammerscales
A Georgian house built on simple classical lines. A Victorian owner created a massive library, running the full length of the top floor.

Rokeby Park
A Palladian mansion built in 1725 by and for Sir Thomas Robinson. The central range is topped by two towers and flanked by two wings.

Rydal Mount
The last home of William Wordsworth. Originally a 16th-century cottage, the house was a comfortable residence by the early 19th century.

Seaton Delaval Hall
A mansion designed by Vanbrugh in 1718, ruined in a fire some 100 years later. The shell reveals the architecture's baroque splendour.

Shambellie House
A Victorian house designed in 1850 by David Bryce in the Scots-baronial style. Today, it houses Scotland's National Museum of Costume.

Sizergh Castle
Built around a medieval pele tower and hall complex. Two wings were added in the 1550s and a Georgian façade in the late 18th century.

Smailholm Tower
A 15th century fortified home, enclosed by a barmkin, or defensive wall. Traces of a 17th-century house and earlier structure remain.

Storrs Hall
A stucco-clad classical villa overlooking Lake Windermere, created out of an early Georgian house in 1808; designed by J.M. Gandy, Soane's assistant

Swarthmoor Hall
An Elizabethan house, home in the mid-17th century of influential early Quakers. George Fox is reputed to have preached from the unusual balcony over the door.

Thirlestane Castle
A Scottish palace, built in 1587 and improved in the 17th and 19th centuries. It has many towers and turrets, topped with soaring roofs.

Threave Castle
A Scots-baronial shooting lodge, designed in 1871 by Edinburgh architects Peddie & Kinnear. The decor of the house dates back to the 1930s and has recently been restored.

Threave House
A fortress stronghold built on an island in the River Dee in 1369. The wall that surrounds it was built in the 1450s as a defence against artillery attack, the first of its kind in Britain.

Townend
An ancient Lakeland farmhouse with traditional Cumbrian features; the kitchen is the 'Down House', the main parlour is the 'Fire House', the screens passage the 'Hallan'.

Traquair
Believed to have origins in a 10th-century thatched hall, it has grown over the centuries; remains of a medieval tower can still be seen.

Wallington Hall
An 18th-century house built in Palladian style with some Georgian Rococo interiors. Much of the house was remodelled in the 19th century – the covered courtyard is by John Dobson.

Washington: Old Hall
The reputed home of George Washington's ancestors. A 17th-century E-plan house, the interiors presented in Jacobean style.

Warkworth Castle
In the care of the Dukes of Northumberland since 1332. The traditional keep, surrounded by a curtain wall was palatial inside; partly restored by Anthony Salvin in the 19th century.

Warkworth Hermitage
A riverside hermitage carved form the rock. The hermit had a hall, kitchen and latrine as his living quarters, as well as a chapel, complete with Gothic windows and rib vaulting.

Witton Castle
A castle with origins dating back to the early 15th century but much rebuilt and altered over time; what remains to day is mainly Victorian.

Workington Hall
The ruin of a once-great house. A medieval pele tower, gatehouse and range remain; the Elizabethan wings were once Georgianized by Carr of York.

Wray Castle
An early Victorian castle designed in a baronial neo-Romantic style by H.P. Horner, who gave his creation extravagant battlemented turrets and a massive porte-cochère.

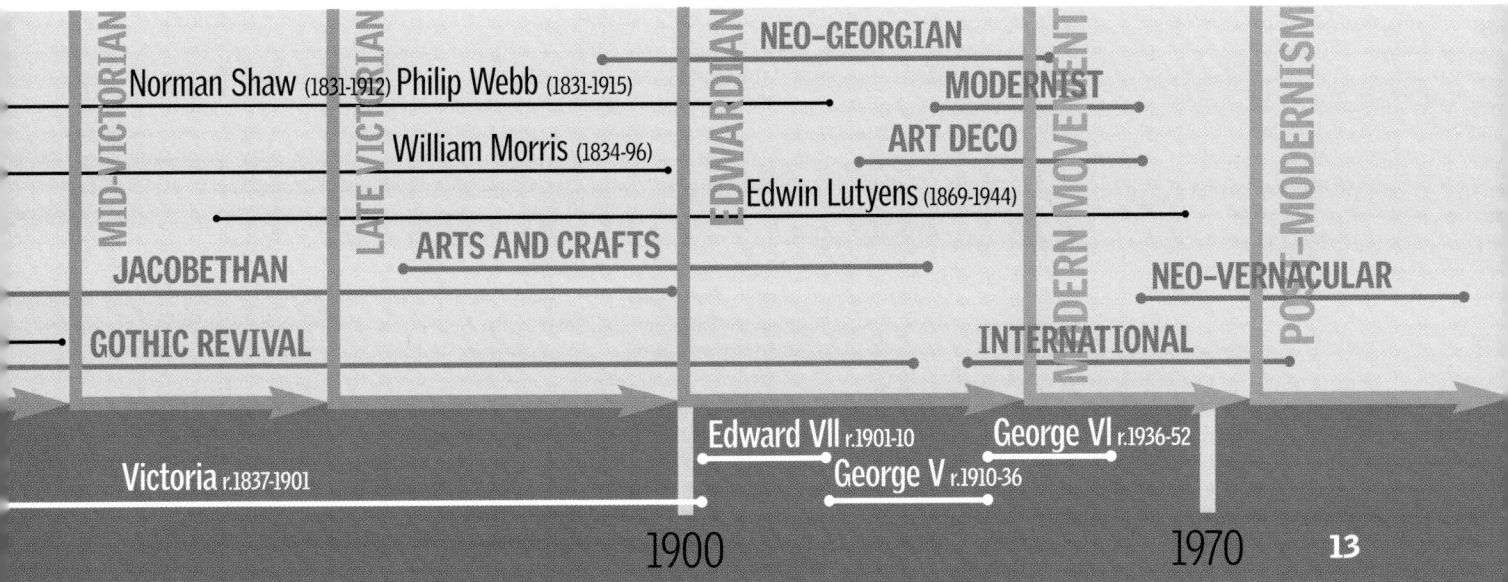

Cumbria

Hill Top

Acorn bank

☆ The remains of an earlier house with a Georgian façade

Near Temple Sowerby, 6 miles E of Penrith; National Trust, gardens open part year

Acorn Bank is a leading centre for medicinal and culinary herbs. Aconite and arnica flourish in the lee of the Pennines in a garden created in the 1930s by the travel writer and botanist Dorothy Una Ratcliffe. The house is being restored by the National Trust to allow public access but the exterior can already be perambulated on a visit to the garden. On an autumn day, with the sun bright on the house and storm clouds on the hills behind, this is a dramatic spot.

The house has clearly been extended as and when resources permitted. To the rear are traces of a pele tower and much 16th- and 17th-century stonework. This façade offers a jagged ridge of gables looking out through fine iron gates down to a stream. From here Acorn looks like a traditional, modified E-plan Jacobean structure.

But that is the back. The more prominent new entrance front is quite different. In the 1740s the ancestral owners, the Dalstons, added a completely new façade. Apparently short of money, they contrived little more than a stage set. The style is Georgian, but many windows are false and Venetian windows are scattered almost at random. The right-hand wing is the stable block, its windows painted on stone. The composition looks splendid from the distant road, which was doubtless the intention.

At Acorn Bank, the health-and-safety fanatics not only warn visitors that every step they take is dangerous but that the smell of some plants is poisonous. Who knows but that the Cumbrian air is also lethal? Nothing is too absurd for these people.

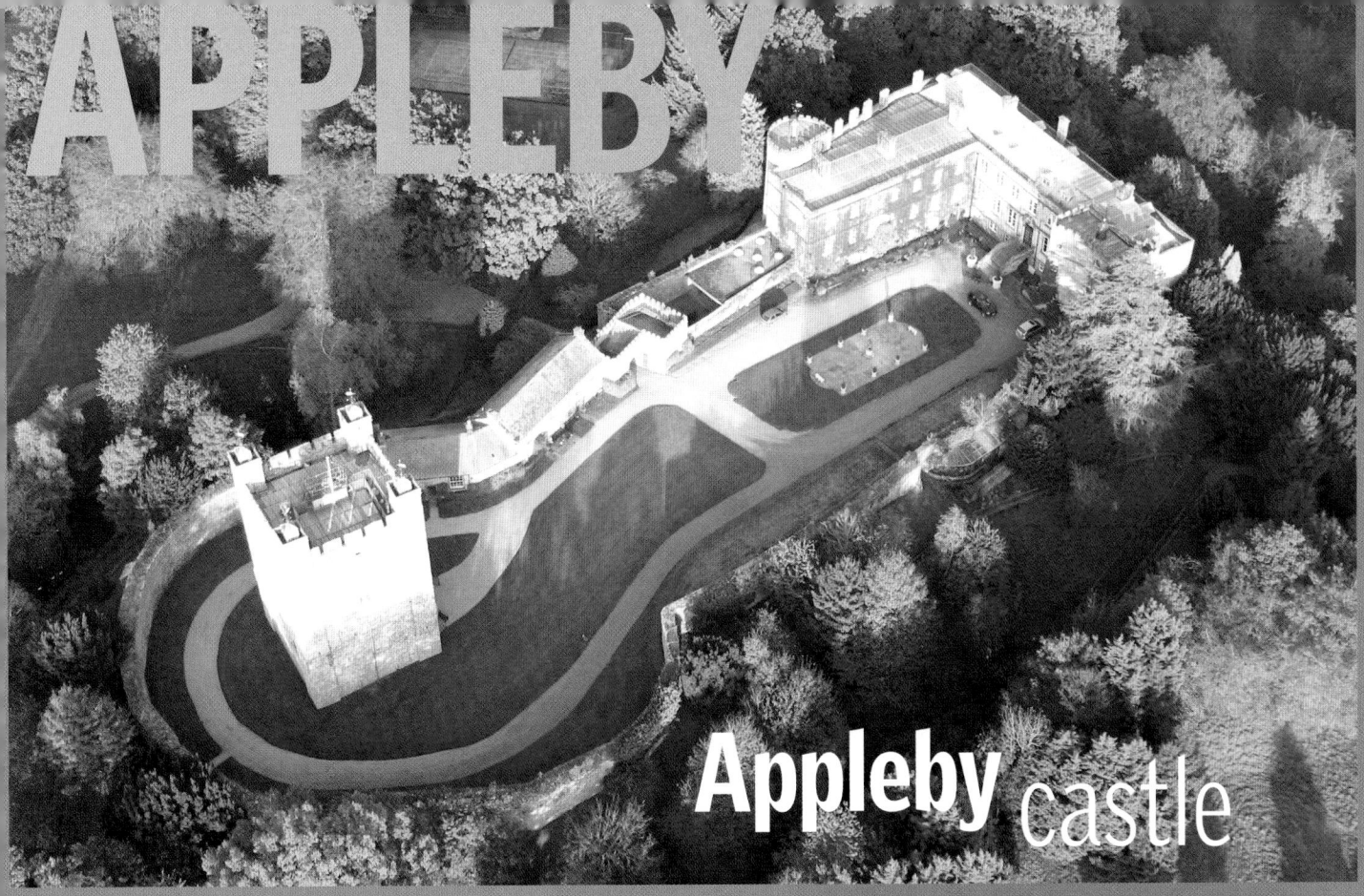

Appleby castle

☆☆ Home of Lady Anne Clifford with Norman keep

Boroughgate, Appleby; private house, exterior can be viewed

In 1649, the Royalist Lady Anne Clifford turned her back on Cromwell's Commonwealth and, at the age of sixty, went north to restore the name and property of the Cliffords, ancient lords of Westmorland. It was an extraordinary chapter in the history of the North.

Clifford's building frenzy was phenomenal, lasting over twenty-five years into her old age. She even seized and rebuilt deserted castles to which she had little or no claim, feeling all castles should be used. When Cromwell ordered her fortresses be destroyed, she promptly rebuilt them. Not just castles but houses, churches, hospitals and almshouses benefited from her largesse – and that of her heavily taxed tenantry.

Lady Anne had no truck with the Renaissance. All her restorations were medieval, so much so that dating them can be hard. She charged high rents and was a stern landlord, but she spent those rents locally. Travelling on a litter with an astonishing retinue of up to fifty carts, she stayed in her properties for months at a time. Her medieval clothes were, it was said at her funeral in 1676, 'not disliked by any, but imitated by none'.

Appleby Castle's keep and fortified house within a curtain wall are superbly sited on a bluff over the River Eden. The outer gate is reached from the town centre at the top of a fine avenue of 17th- and 18th-century houses. The inner bailey has a keep to the right and the old Jacobean house to the left. The latter was extensively improved after her death by Lady Anne's son-in-law, the Earl of Thanet. Although their family origins were in Kent, the Thanets remained devoted to Appleby until its sorry sale in 1962.

The Thanets' Great Hall was erected in stone taken from the swiftly decaying Brough and Brougham castles (see pages 24 and 25). The façade is in a robust Northern Baroque, of which Lady

Anne would not have approved. It has pilasters and dormers with both segmental and triangular pediments. Steps rise to the central door, which is crowned with a broken pediment.

Across the courtyard stands Appleby's Norman keep, called Caesar's Tower. It is in a colder, greyer stone and remains unaltered since the late 12th century, apart from a Georgianized top floor. The battlements offer a superb view of the Eden gorge below. The interior was partitioned for domestic use by Lady Anne. The walls have been left to the mercy of creeper, much to their benefit. The castle needs another Clifford with the imagination to seize it and reassert the supremacy of northern culture.

St Anne's hospital

☆ Almshouse in lee of Lady Anne's castle

Boroughgate, Appleby, private house, open all year

Lady Anne founded almshouses throughout her domain. Few are as charming as the 'hospital' she built under her own walls at Appleby. Begun in the early 1650s, the almshouses are as she left them and are still in use. They are among the most picturesque examples of this charming form of charity.

The building is formed of twelve houses round a rectangular, cobbled yard. It is of pink-grey Penrith stone, the only material to rival Somerset's Ham stone as a delight to the eye. Nowhere is it better displayed than on a warm afternoon in the inner court of St Anne's. The stone is crowned by blue-grey slates.

In one corner of the courtyard is a tiny chapel, in which services continue to be held. A fountain and small rock garden stand in the middle. Beyond is a paddock with a view of the Pennines. This is a sublime place. In matters of welfare, small is beautiful.

APPLEBY

St Anne's Hospital

Lady Anne Clifford
1590–1676

Lady Anne was born at Skipton Castle in 1590. When her father the Earl of Cumberland died in 1605 Anne, as his only surviving child, expected to inherit his estates. They went, however, to her uncle. She spent the next 38 years fighting this injustice in the courts and only won the right to her inheritance in 1643 when her uncle's line died out.

In 1609, Anne married Richard Sackville, Earl of Dorset. Her husband did not support her claim to her father's lands – he wanted her to settle for a cash payment – and their marriage was not particularly happy. He died in 1624 and she married again in 1630. Although her new husband, Philip Herbert, Earl of Pembroke, supported her claims their marriage was no happier and they lived apart. Lady Anne moved to the North in 1649, dying at Brougham Castle in 1676.

Blackwell

☆☆☆ Lakeland Arts-and-Crafts house by Baillie Scott

Near Bowness-on-Windermere, 3 miles S of Windermere; museum, open part year

The saving of Blackwell in 1999 was a conservation triumph. This masterpiece of the Arts and Crafts architect, M. H. Baillie Scott, had survived the 20th century mostly unaltered, as a school and offices. The building was then acquired and restored by the Lakeland Arts Trust, under the auspices of the Abbot Hall Gallery in Kendal.

The house was designed in 1898 as a holiday home for the Manchester brewer, Sir Edward Holt. Outside and inside, it held to the vernacular manorial style espoused by William Morris. There were bold gables, round Lakeland chimneys, stone mullioned windows and a central Great Hall. The interiors, like those of Norman Shaw, were a series of variations on a theme of the hearth. 'In the house the fire is a substitute for the sun,' wrote Baillie Scott. 'The cheerfulness we experience from

Above The peacock frieze in Blackwell's main hall came from the wallpaper manufacturer Shand Kydd. The door beneath leads into the dining room; its massive inglenook mirrors a similar fireplace in the hall. Pew-like bench seats are built into either side of the inglenook. Above the end of each seat, on either side of the fire, is a small window; both windows are glazed with Art Nouveau stained glass.

the fire is akin to the delight sunlight brings.' The result was rich and warm, refined Art Nouveau decoration co-existing with Holt's 17th- and 18th-century furniture.

The house and its decorative programme have been restored by the Modernist architects, Allies and Morrison. They have left it naked of any Victorian traces in their quest for 'pure Baillie Scott', which is based on early drawings for the house. The rooms seem bare. There are no curtains. The daylight is glaring and the fireplaces are reduced to mere decoration. The domestic rooms are reached through a reception area that is aggressively modern. House has surrendered to museum. Blackwell is what an Arts and Crafts house might have been like if only its architect had been Le Corbusier.

Enough carping. Blackwell sits bold on a bluff above Windermere. It contains three exquisite rooms, the dining room, hall and drawing room, representing the Indian summer of England's contribution to European Art Nouveau. It was the era of Charles Voysey, Charles Rennie Mackintosh and Baillie Scott.

The focal point of each room is the inglenook. In the dining room, this is formed by a sweeping stone arch, its benches lit by fine stained-glass windows. The fire grate is backed by Dutch tiles. Floor, ceiling, panelling and furniture are all of exposed wood. The liveliest

Above The White Drawing Room is home to another magnificent fireplace, which was where Baillie Scott felt 'that the interest of the room is focused'. This inglenook has built-in settles, just like the fireplaces in the hall and dining room, but here Baillie Scott included shelves for books and artefacts above each bench and, instead of a mantelpiece, a mullioned cupboard that jetties out above the fire.

feature is the hessian wall-hangings, of birds and flowers, 'full of still, quiet earnestness which seems to lull and soothe the spirit,' wrote Baillie Scott. Every corbel or boss or bench-end is turned into a depiction of nature, as a rowan berry, a daisy or an oak leaf. Manchester brewers on holiday were expected to celebrate nature.

The hall has heavy beams and Tudor half-timbering. Its glory is another frieze, this one depicting peacocks. More carvings fill the panels of the minstrels' gallery, a feature above the inglenook. The fire surround is a bold composition of pilasters with naturalistic capitals. The 'Manxman' piano – Scott lived for a while on the Isle of Man – is disguised as a cupboard. The room is as empty as a Shakespearean theatre without play or audience.

At the end of the downstairs passage is the White Drawing Room, with a spectacular view overlooking the lake. The decorative atmosphere shifts from warm oak to shimmering white. The chamber is serene, almost surreal. The ceiling and frieze are a forest of trees and flowers, but in white. Spindly columns round the inglenook branch out into birds and leaves. The fire-dogs become daisies and berries. An oriel window surmounts the stone fireplace with stained glass depicting swaying fronds and hidden birds. This must be one of the loveliest 20th-century rooms in England. I wish it looked as if someone lived in it.

Brantwood hall

Left John Ruskin (1819–1900) extended Brantwood during the 28 years that he lived there; his first addition was a turret, built on the south-west corner of the original house.

☆☆☆ Ruskin's house overlooking Coniston Water

Near Coniston, 5 miles SW of Ambleside; museum, open all year

After Wordsworth, the Lake District had no more influential sponsor than John Ruskin. Nowhere else in all England, he thought, could match Switzerland for scenic beauty. From here in his maturity he observed nature and the weather, honouring his dictum that 'to understand nature one must be able to see clearly what is really there'. There were, he said, hundreds who can talk for one who can think and thousands who can think for one who can see. 'To see clearly is poetry, prophecy and religion.' It was from Brantwood that he saw.

The house was Ruskin's home from 1872 until his death in 1900. He bought it sight unseen, in the sole knowledge that it faced 'five acres of rock and moor and streamlet' on the best water in Lakeland. He built a turret high on the corner of the house overlooking the lake, and this served as his study, bedroom and inspiration.

The house expanded considerably during his occupancy. It was here that he moved his art collection from Herne Hill in South London and here also that he invited his cousins, Arthur and Joan Severn, to join him. He left them his entire property, with disastrous results.

Ruskin told the Severns that he wanted the house and its collection retained as a museum, open to the public. The Severns disobeyed him and instead sold or destroyed the contents. Quantities of Ruskin papers simply disappeared, and many were later found floating on Coniston Water. Turner watercolours that famously covered the walls of the bedroom were sold, along with medieval manuscripts and paintings by Gainsborough and the Pre-Raphaelites. Not until 1932 was John Whitehouse, MP and fanatical admirer of Ruskin, able to buy back the property and reassemble some Ruskiniana. This is now admirably displayed under the aegis of Lancaster University. It is the best of Cumbria's artistic shrines, if only because it is a little off the most beaten tracks.

The interior is furnished in Victorian style with works that would have appealed to Ruskin. The drawing room has wallpaper designed by him and contains his drawing of St Mark's, Venice. The house also has a number of copies he made of Old Masters, including a 'Botticelli' and a 'Tintoretto'. Next door is the study from which there emitted a constant stream of correspondence, books and essays. Works by Luca della Robbia and Samuel Prout remain.

The dining room was designed to admit glimpses of Coniston Water through lancet windows, as if nature were itself a picture on the wall. Ruskin's Turret Bedroom has been restored, up a small staircase from the old house.

Next door is the Turret Room, from which Ruskin spent hours watching the lake's changing moods. In few places can man, nature and artistic inspiration be experienced in such harmony.

Below Ruskin occupied this small bedroom in the Turret at Brantwood from 1872 until he suffered a mental breakdown in 1878; he then moved his bedroom into an even smaller room next door. The room was once hung with paintings, including at least 18 watercolours by Turner. Today, prints of some of these pictures line the walls.

Brough castle

☆ Clifford castle with Norman keep and medieval range

At Brough, 4 miles NE of Kirkby Stephen; English Heritage, open all year

Forget the sun. See Brough if possible against storm clouds rolling down from the north like invading Scotsmen. Even ruined, it is imposing, its broken walls and staring windows bravely deterring all-comers. The castle was first built as a keep by the Normans to shut out the Scots. The location was that of an old Roman fort, whose pattern can still be made out in the surrounding fields.

The keep enclosure at Brough was fortified and given a Great Hall range by Robert Clifford at the turn of the 14th century, with the Clifford Tower as his private residence. These buildings were gutted by fire in 1521 but were restored and made habitable by Robert's indomitable descendant, Lady Anne Clifford (see pages 17 and 18), in 1663. The castle then resumed its story of decay until taken into public guardianship in 1919.

Today, Brough's appeal is mostly scenic. Clifford's Tower still stands, with the third-floor windows which Lady Anne inserted and behind which she stayed on her feudal tours. The remains of the kitchens and servants' quarters can still be seen, including the vaulted storerooms below the hall.

Most majestic is the keep, in rich red stone. Safety officials now stop people entering and climbing the steps to the upper parapet and viewing platform. When will this sort of nonsense end? A kindlier character was the pixie, Hobthrush, said to inhabit a latrine hole in the curtain wall near the keep. Each year, on receipt of nocturnal gifts, he helped gather the local harvest.

Brougham castle

☆ Norman Border castle and Clifford stronghold

1½ miles SE of Penrith; English Heritage, open part year

Brougham Castle is among the most romantic of Clifford residences. Here Wordsworth and his sister would be taken as part of their education in the Picturesque. Here they 'crept along a ridge of a fractured wall,/ Not without trembling, we in safety looked/ Forth, through some Gothic window's open space./ And gathered with one mind a rich reward/ From the far-stretching landscape.'

The castle endured the usual Border history. Founded by the Normans it was fortified by Vieuxponts (later Viponts) and then Cliffords during the 14th century. It changed hands during the Wars of the Roses but returned to the Cliffords. It was at Brougham that George Clifford, 3rd Earl of Cumberland, was born. It fell to ruin, was restored by his daughter, Lady Anne Clifford, and then fell to ruin again.

The castle remains impressive, beautifully sited on the banks of the River Eamont. The approach to the massive gatehouse, with the hall to the left and the great keep contiguous behind, is still impressive. Robert Clifford built the gatehouse at the end of the 13th century. It is, in reality, two gates divided by a court and must have challenged the most determined attacker.

The keep is in good condition. The exterior has grotesque corbel heads peering from its string courses and is covered in aubrietia. Inside stairs give access to the upper floors, including a small oratory. On the second floor is a Roman tombstone fragment built into the wall. The outer walls of the 14th-century hall and chapel remain to roof height across the courtyard.

Brougham hall

☆ Ruin of a great house, under restoration

1½ miles SE of Penrith; private house, open all year

The last battle on English soil was fought in the meadows below Brougham on 18th December 1745, the climax of the '45 Rebellion. Converted by the Brougham family in the 19th century, the Hall became known as the Windsor of the North.

In the 1960s, Brougham Hall saw another battle, to conserve what remained of the house after the neighbouring landowner, Major Carleton Cowper of Penrith, bought and demolished it in what appeared a fit of pique. He had bought it from an impoverished Clifford descendant, Lord Brougham, with whose family he had a feud. Brougham had inherited a vast estate in 1927 at the age of eighteen and had squandered every penny of it by 1934. Carleton Cowper acquired the house, stripped it of its Victorian furnishings and began demolishing the medieval pele tower and Clifford ranges. He had declared his wish to 'see an oak grow in the hall at Brougham'. Cumbrian vendettas have a savage longevity.

The building was thus left unroofed, and the site was occupied by the army during the Second World War. There followed four decades of further decay, with plans characteristic of post-war Britain to flatten the site for bungalows or a caravan park. In 1968 a businessman, Christopher Terry, came upon the ruin and determined to restore it. Terry battled builders, developers, planners, bankers and accountants through the courts for some thirty years. Since 1986, the site has been owned by Terry's charitable trust and has seen the start of a remarkable revival. This is not to 'conserve as found' but to reinstate the house's Victorian state.

The site retains the fortified walls of the original enclosure. Within the courtyard is a scatter of outbuildings surviving from Carleton Cowper's wreckers. These have been converted for small-scale commercial activity. The ruin of the entrance is a teashop. The old Lord Chancellor's Den, which belonged in the 1830s to the reformer, Lord Brougham, can still be seen as a ruin. It will be a massive task to re-create the old house but such a dedicated owner should be given his head by all in a position to help him.

Prior's tower

CARLISLE

☆ Former pele tower with prior's solar and 16th-century painted ceiling

Cathedral Close, Carlisle; private house, open by arrangement

The cathedral is surrounded by residential buildings, only one of which dates from its pre-Reformation days as a priory. The Prior's Tower has its origins in an ancient pele tower on the city ramparts, immediately adjacent to the cathedral itself. To this pele was added a hall to form a conventional Cumbrian residence. The hall has vanished but the tower remains, housing the prior's solar with a wide vaulted undercroft beneath it.

The solar is a gem, a small room with deep, recessed windows. Its most spectacular feature is its roof of painted oak beams. Every inch is covered in 16th-century patterns and motifs. These include popinjays, shells, heraldry and mottos. Bosses fixed to the beams depict a jester and a pelican 'in her piety'. The paintings were discovered and revealed in 1975, requiring only minimal restoration. Over the fireplace is a fragment of a carved choir screen, a maze of intricate ogival patterns.

The decoration is wonderfully colourful. It must have enlivened the droning hours of diocesan business beneath.

Below The walls of a small cell on the second floor of the castle are decorated with emblems and symbols, carved into the stone by prisoners held captive here by the future Richard III in the 1480s. Richard, then Duke of Gloucester, was engaged in a series of campaigns to defend the Border country from attack by James III of Scotland.

Carlisle castle

☆☆ Keep and gatehouse lodgings within a mighty Border fortress

Castle Way, Carlisle; English Heritage, open all year

The city of Carlisle was once the graceful capital of the North. Today, it is tormented by poor redevelopment and one of the worst traffic schemes in England. A dual carriageway separates the cathedral and old quarter from the celebrated castle, leaving it isolated in a desert of English Heritage lawn.

Carlisle and Newcastle were the two great forts protecting England against Scotland throughout the Middle Ages. They hosted English kings when they came north to do battle against the foe but Carlisle was not impregnable. The walls and keep were first built by Henry I but completed by the Scots king, David, during his brief occupation of the North in the 12th century. Carlisle was captured for England by Henry II in 1157 and held even after Edward II's defeat by the Scots at Bannockburn in 1314. No English castle has seen more blood shed in anger, or more treachery. It was in the hall at Carlisle in 1323 that the loyal Earl of Carlisle was murdered 'for disloyalty' in the king's name by his rival, Anthony de Lucy.

Under the Tudors, Carlisle was a crucial bastion against the Franco-Scots alliance. It was held for the King in the Civil War and seized by Bonnie Prince Charlie in 1745, by which time the castle was vulnerable to artillery and the defenders did not bother to resist. It later became a centre of military administration and is still used by the Territorial Army today.

Two residential interiors are accessible, the Steward's rooms over the gatehouse and the early royal quarters in the keep. The gatehouse is unusual in its confined space. The hall is small and behind it is a solar. These rooms have been furnished in what can be described as English Heritage's 'modern medieval' style.

The keep is reached through the Captain's Tower, past the site of the demolished Queen Mary's Tower, where Mary, Queen of Scots was imprisoned in 1568. The great keep was David's palace in the 12th century and retains the proportions of an early Norman fortress, square and with massively thick walls. The round-arched entrance to the old Great Hall looks as though excavated through solid rock, as do the spiral stairs to the rooms above. The lower and upper halls were later divided into two rooms but retain their deep-splayed windows. There are storerooms and dungeons below and private chambers above. A small oratory on the second floor has been closed by a modern glass door, as has a small cell with charming carvings on the walls made by prisoners, *c*1480. The roof offers a fine view of present-day Carlisle.

The guidebook states that the castle today 'has a well-used look'. It does not. Every blade of grass is the statutory inch long. Not a dandelion or trace of ivy is permitted. From outside, Carlisle Castle looks almost as if it had been built by the architect of the adjacent motorway.

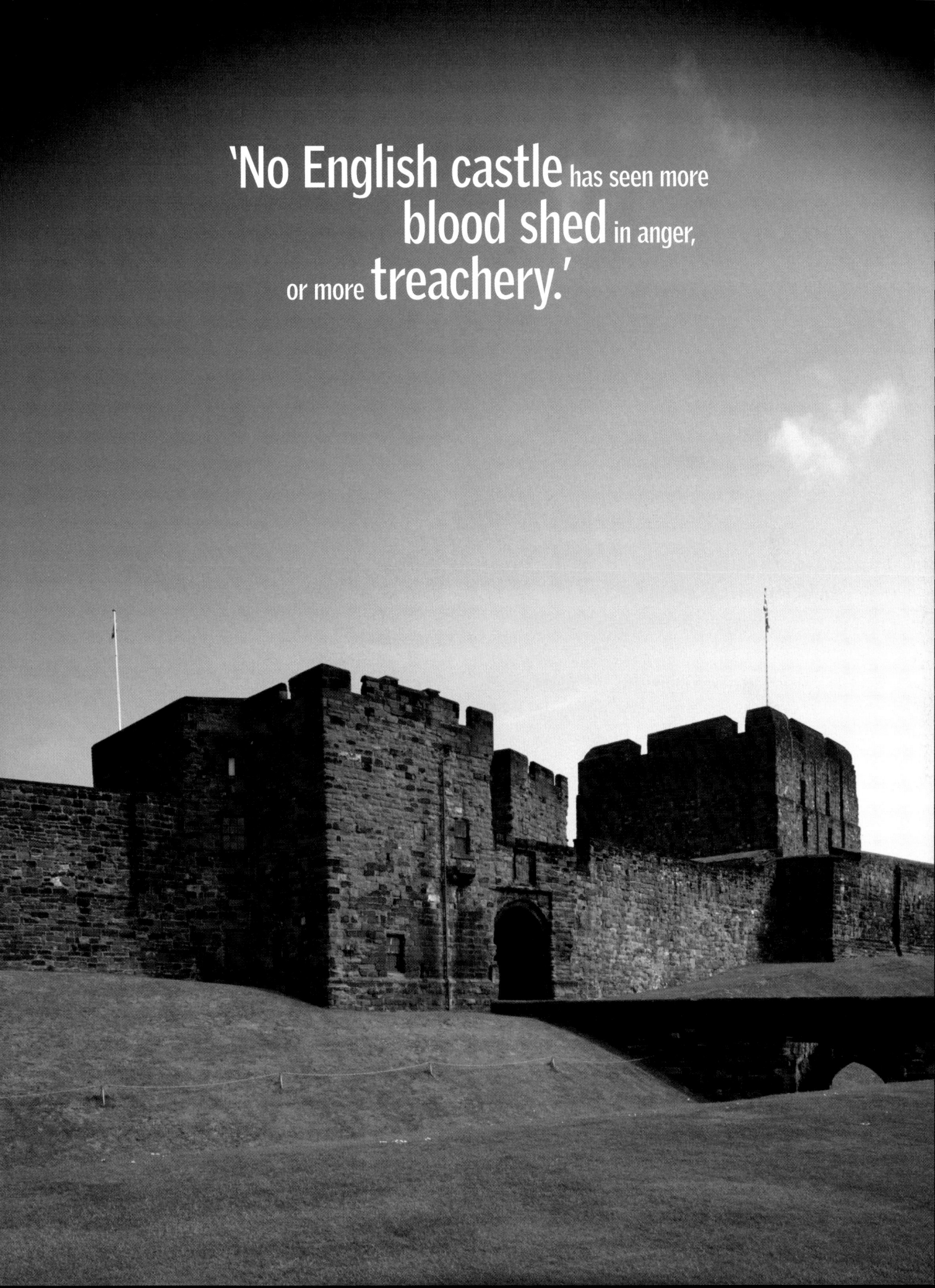
'No English castle has seen more
blood shed in anger,
or more treachery.'

Cockermouth: Wordsworth house

Right The best parlour of John and Ann Wordsworth's home in Cockermouth was comfortably furnished; Mrs Wordsworth had her spinning wheel and mahogany desk set in one corner, close to the fire.

☆☆ Georgian town house and Romantic poet's birthplace

Main Street, Cockermouth; National Trust, open part year

Wordsworth's father, John, was agent to the Cumbrian magnate, Sir James (later Lord) Lowther. A solid house on Cockermouth's main street came with the job. It had been built for the Sheriff of Cumberland in 1745 but passed into Lowther hands. Here the poet was born in 1770 and found his earliest inspiration on the banks of the River Derwent that flowed past the end of the garden. The Derwent was 'the playmate whom we dearly lov'd', Wordsworth wrote. It was to him 'the fairest of all rivers' as it 'blended with his nurse's song'.

The garden was where he established his bond with his sister, Dorothy, and learned with her a love of nature. All this survives, largely thanks to the efforts of Cockermouth people who saved the house from demolition in 1937. The terrace where the children played is still in place. The Derwent still flows between grassy banks. There is still a meadow on the far bank.

The house is run by the National Trust as a Wordsworth Museum, rivalling the shrines at Dove Cottage and Rydal Mount. Of the three, Cockermouth is at present the least evocative. It is a conventional Georgian town house with a distinguished façade to the street, declaring little more than the poet's comfortable origins. Its memorabilia collection is modest.

The interior is filled with Georgian furniture, much of it Chippendale and Hepplewhite. Parlour and dining room downstairs have good ceilings, with cabinets, clocks and displays of Staffordshire and Coalport china. Upstairs is a more remarkable room, the drawing room. This was presumably the sheriff's reception room. Scrolled pediments surmount the doorcases, one of which is an elaborate fake. Rococo console tables divide the windows. The chief interest in the house is its admirable collection of paintings, prints and drawings of the Lake District.

Conishead priory

☆☆ Extravagant Gothick mansion; now a Buddhist retreat

2 miles SE of Ulverston; private house, open part year, grounds open all year

There is no house in England like Conishead. The priory has long gone. What we see today is a fantasy originally created by Colonel Thomas Richmond-Gale-Braddyll to a Gothick design by the little-known Philip Wyatt in 1821. The house was an exercise in pure show, set in a splendid park on the Furness peninsula. Wyatt was a wastrel who soon went to prison for debt. What he began is largely a masterpiece by the cultivated and hardworking local architect, George Webster of Kendal. But the project bankrupted Braddyll. The house changed hands many times. In the 1880s it became a luxurious 'hydropathic hotel', with resident orchestra and thousand-volume library. In the 1920s it was converted into a miners' convalescent home. By the 1970s it faced demolition.

Salvation came in the unusual form of a Mahayana Buddhist community from Tibet, who bought the building in 1976. Recruiting local volunteers, the Manjushri Centre restored the shell of the house, giving it a not implausible oriental overlay. Saffron robes glide through the trees. Bright banners deck Gothick corridors. Shrines punctuate niches and Wyatt's colossal billiard hall is a Meditation Room, its walls lined with mandalas. A temple in the grounds contains the largest Buddha ever cast in the West. Conishead is a strange concordat between original priory, Braddyll's Gothick eccentricity, which included the hiring of a so-called 'house hermit', and the present use as a religious retreat.

The forecourt shows the building in all its eccentric glory. Wyatt designed, apparently at random, a chaotic series of gables, turrets and façades, some in brick, some in render. The entrance is between two octagonal turrets roughly based on King's College Chapel, Cambridge. The doorway leads directly into a large hall modelled on a medieval chapel, with tall stained glass windows. At right angles beyond is a corridor which is designed as a cloister, forming the spine of the building. The main reception rooms are gigantic, some of them 50 feet long.

The staircase fills an inner hall, rising and returning in two wings. The newel posts still carry the Richmond crest, which resembles a strangely upright badger. Little remains of the furnishings of the old house, but care has been taken to protect what does survive. Neo-Jacobean plasterwork has been reinstated in a number of rooms. A fine overmantel adorns the panelled Oak Room upstairs, with twisted columns and Mannerist motifs. Conishead appears to be in safe hands.

Dalemain

☆☆☆ Georgian façade enclosing medieval core

3½ miles SW of Penrith; private house, open part year

Sir Edward Hasell bought Dalemain in 1679. His descendants have lived there ever since. The photographs in the guidebook offer a gallery of Hasell ladies down the ages. Regency Dorothea Hasell is in a flurry of muslin and ribbons, inter-war Gertrude Hasell is in pearls and fur, and post-war Sylvia Hasell poses with dogs and cut flowers. Today, however, Jane Hasell-McCosh is pictured kneeling in the garden, hard at work in dungarees and with a trowel.

Their house sits proud on a slope overlooking the north end of Ullswater. Part pele tower, part Tudor and part Georgian, it is clearly in family use. The ostensibly severe exterior was built in 1744 to enclose the old house round a courtyard. Its soft pink ashlar with grey parapet looks across a fine garden to the water in the distance.

The approach from the main road sweeps round to the back of the house as though tourists were emphatically 'trade'. But the back forms an intriguing contrast to the elegant Georgian front. It displays the house as it has evolved from the Middle Ages. Three-storey barns surround a courtyard and the remains of the ancient settlement, as it would have sheltered in the shadow of the two pele towers. Here the back of the house is 16th century and earlier. The truncated towers and linking hall range are of roughcast stone.

Dalemain's interior has not been altered since the mid-18th century. The entrance hall contains a superb shallow staircase of rich local oak. The walls are of dark crimson hung with van Dycks. Deer trophies are from the estate. The adjacent dining room, known as the Chinese Room, is a brilliant chamber. Its chinoiserie wallpaper is in excellent repair, if odd in these most English of surroundings. Pheasants and foliage swirl upwards from the floor, with birds and insects added by hand when the

'The **approach** from the main road **sweeps round** to the back of the house as though **tourists** were **emphatically 'trade'**.'

Above The medieval origins of Dalemain as a group of buildings surrounding a pele tower are revealed in the courtyard to the rear of the house. **Below** The hand-painted wallpaper in the Chinese Room arrived in England as part of the ballast aboard an 18th-century tea clipper. Purchased in London in 1757, the paper has a background pattern of Chinese pheasants and trees. After the paper was hung, individual birds, butterflies and insects were added to balance the design.

paper was hung. The room also has an exquisite Rococo chimneypiece by Nathaniel Hedges in 'Chinese Chippendale' style, complete with fierce dragons. Portraits are by Zoffany and Devis.

The drawing room is oak panelled, its stern family portraits contrasting with jollier modern photographs. Beyond is a passage, devoted to relics of Cumbria's early railway age, leading to Dalemain's pele tower. This once belonged to John de Morville, whose brother Hugh was one of Becket's assassins. A room is a museum of the Westmorland and Cumberland Yeomanry, a troop of mounted infantry led traditionally by Hasells. It was 'a force of countrymen and horsemen bound together in a rare comradeship of neighbours and friends, all from the same district'. They were mounted on bicycles in the Great War and then disbanded.

Upstairs in the pele tower is a panelled chamber with geometrical ceiling, dating from the mid-16th century. Over the Tudor fireplace is a portrait of Lady Anne Clifford (see pages 17 and 18), looking every bit a match for Cromwell. Her secretary was a Hasell. Beyond, in the second pele tower, are nurseries and a Victorian housekeeper's room.

The Old Hall below contains a giant fireplace kept ablaze on a cold afternoon. It serves as a teashop and is an ideal refuge from the worst of the Lakeland weather.

William Wordsworth
1770–1850

William Wordsworth was born at Cockermouth (see page 30), the second of five children. He was sent to school at Hawkshead in 1779, after the death of his mother, and then left Cumbria for Cambridge in 1787. Wordsworth did not return to live in the Lake District until he moved into Dove Cottage in 1799 with his sister, Dorothy. In 1802, he married his childhood friend, Mary Hutchinson, with whom he had five children. In 1808, the family moved, first to Allan Bank, then in 1810 to the Old Rectory, both in Grasmere. They settled at their final home, Rydal Mount (see page 54) in 1813. Wordsworth died here thirty-seven years later at the age of eighty.

Grasmere: Dove cottage

☆☆☆ The simple cottage home of Wordsworth and his young family

Town End, Grasmere; museum, open part year

Visitors to Dove Cottage must expect to share it with the world. The Wordsworth Trust, like Stratford's Shakespeare Birthplace Trust, wrestles with the task of matching overwhelming demand to miniscule supply. The cottage in which the poet and his sister and wife lived for eight years from 1799 is Lilliputian. From spring through to autumn, the place is under siege. Wordsworth was surely thinking of more than daffodils when he wrote, 'A poet could not but be gay/ In such a jocund company!/ I gazed – and gazed – but little thought/ What wealth the show to me had brought.'

The cottage is in the hamlet of Town End, just outside Grasmere (not to be confused with the house of that name). It was formerly an inn, The Dove and Olive. Here, the twenty-nine-year-old Wordsworth moved with his sister, Dorothy, and a seemingly endless troop of friends, including Southey, Hazlitt, Lamb, Walter Scott and Coleridge. They passed the cottage to Thomas de Quincy in 1809. Wordsworth moved his growing family elsewhere in the village and, in 1813, to Rydal Mount (see page 54).

Dove Cottage has been restored as near as possible to its original appearance, although the crowds require it to be stripped of domestic clutter. The parlour, that of the old inn, has a blazing fire and rich Georgian wood panelling. A rag rug covers the flagstone floor. Another fire burns in the spotless kitchen, with its candle-making equipment. A spring flows under the larder floor.

The cottage was the scene of Wordsworth's most fertile inspiration. He paced its tiny garden, his 'domestic slip of mountain', and gazed out over the ruffled waters of Grasmere. Upstairs is the sitting room where Wordsworth would return from composing in the open air and write from memory. His sister wrote that he 'laboured in that one room, common to all the family, to all visitors and where the children frequently play beside him'. Its old oak floorboards are still polished by hand every day. Here are Wordsworth's skates, cuckoo clock, cameo portraits and other mementos.

Next door are the simple, and minute, bedrooms. Fire grates are still blackened, windows leaded and pots and pictures arranged. One room to the rear has been left wallpapered for warmth with yellowed copies of *The Times*. They are dated 1800, when the Budget Statement recorded the nation's total wealth as £54,566,206/9s/4d. Another sheet has an advertisement for Wordsworth's *Lyrical Ballads*.

Wordsworth wrote of a poet's home, 'This small abiding-place of many Men/ A termination and a last retreat,/ A centre, come from whereso'er you will,/ A Whole without dependence or defect,/ Made for itself and happy in itself,/ Perfect Contentment. Unity entire.'

The garden has been restocked with wild flowers and herbs. Climbers envelop the cottage walls. The library, shop and study centre are well concealed down the road. Dove Cottage is a homage fit to the man.

Left The parlour at Dove Cottage, also known as the houseplace, would probably have been the main room when the house was an inn. The Wordsworths took their meals here and did a little cooking and some domestic chores. Most of the cooking, washing and heavier housework, however, took place in the kitchen next door. The family ate three simple meals a day, 'two of which were porridge' according to Walter Scott.

☆☆ Beatrix Potter's farm and inspiration for her illustrations

At Near Sawrey, 3 miles SW of Windermere; National Trust, open part year

The house owned by Beatrix Potter during her most fruitful years is now a heavily visited shrine. This is no surprise. Potter reproduced every inch of the house, garden, lane and landscape in her book illustrations. The crossroads is *Pigling Bland*, the front path is *Tom Kitten*, the farmyard is *Jemima Puddleduck* and the gabled porch is almost everywhere.

Potter had visited the Lake District as a girl in the 1880s with her South Kensington parents (see Wray Castle, page 63). After the sudden death of her fiancé, Norman Warne, in 1905 she used the profits on her first books to buy Hill Top Farm. She left the farmer in residence, building a small extension for herself in which to write, paint and observe the animals and garden. She then used every penny she earned from her books to buy and protect property in the neighbourhood. She continued to live with her parents in London until, in 1913 at the age of forty-seven, she married the local lawyer, Willie Heelis, who had handled her purchases.

Although Potter never lived permanently at Hill Top and moved elsewhere when she married, she worked at the house, showed visitors round and fashioned it as a backdrop for her stories. Well before her death in 1943, she and Hill Top were internationally famous. She did not mind. Potter capitalized on every aspect of her celebrity, one of the first writers to market and franchise products generated by her characters. She patented 'Peter Rabbit' in 1903. The house is a museum created by Potter herself. She also became an expert Lakeland farmer and breeder of Herdwick sheep. A fierce conservationist, she bought and gave to the National Trust over 4,000 acres in the area.

The house is a curiosity rather than a beauty and visitors are ruthlessly bossed by the National Trust's warders. The familiar path through the front garden leads to a simple 17th-century farmhouse. The slate porch is covered by a rambling rose. The interior is small and fragile, furnished neither as a traditional farmhouse nor quite in keeping with the Adam-style fireplace, furniture and porcelain imported by Potter. Her taste is clearly that of a London lawyer's daughter.

Above Beatrix Potter painted this view of her staircase for *The Tale of Samuel Whiskers*. In the story, the rat Samuel is shown pushing a stolen rolling pin across the landing, 'like a brewer's man trundling a barrel', on his way to make Tom Kitten into a roly-poly pudding.

Downstairs are the kitchen and the parlour, kept implausibly immaculate for what was a farm. The chief pleasure lies in identifying objects with scenes in the books. The dresser is that of my favourite, *The Tailor of Gloucester*. The Georgian staircase is *Samuel Whiskers* and the bedroom *Two Bad Mice*. The most popular room is the Treasure Room, built by Potter to display her collection of Lakeland objects and of the merchandise inspired by her characters. Here too are some of her original paintings and photographs, skills at which she was proficient. Potter's books and drawings fuelled a worldwide popularity for 'English cottage' vernacular. But there is more of her spirit in the hills outside.

Hill Top

Below When Beatrix Potter died, she left Hill Top, 4,000 acres of land, 14 farms and 15 other Lakeland properties to the National Trust. When the Trust moved its headquarters to Swindon, it named the building 'Heelis' in her honour.

Holker hall

☆☆☆ Victorian mansion by Paley & Austin with lavish Crace interiors

Near Cark-in-Cartmel, 4½ miles W of Grange-over-Sands; private house, open part year

One night in March 1871, Lord Frederick Cavendish, son of the 7th Duke of Devonshire, was awoken by a crash and found his house on fire. Holker was gutted, its paintings and library destroyed. Only the neo-Jacobean wing remodelled in the 1830s by George Webster of Kendal survived. True to the spirit of the age, the family promptly rebuilt on an even grander scale. They commissioned the firm of Paley & Austin, doyens of late-Victorian architecture in the North-West. The result is sumptuous.

The property was owned by Cartmel Priory and passed by descent after the Dissolution to Prestons, Lowthers and then Cavendishes, who hold it still. The exterior offers a contrast in early and late Victorian between Webster's Jacobean and Paley & Austin's adjacent exuberance. The new building includes a massive tower, apparently modelled on a pele, and another with a copper cupola. With high chimneys, strong gables and stone-mullioned windows, the style is assertively Elizabethan. In sunlight, the sandstone walls radiate an Umbrian red-brown.

The interiors are to match. Holker (pronounced Hooker) is almost indigestibly rich. Warm panelling combines with stone, marble and heavy fabric, as if this were the ladies' wing of an Imperial club. For decoration, Paley & Austin employed the ubiquitous firm of J. G. Crace, without whom few Victorian houses were complete. The drawing room walls are hung with Macclesfield silk.

The billiard room is in the deepest green, described by Crace as 'hand-stencilled with eight layers of paint'. It is dominated by four huge scenes from nature by Jacques-Charles Oudry. No less

Above When Holker was rebuilt after the 1871 fire, the architects created an Elizabethan-style long gallery. The arches at the end are made from polished limestone that was quarried at Stainton, on the Holker estate. **Below** The billiard room is dominated by a locally-carved table of English oak. On the mantelpiece are some granite-ware carpet bowls; this was a popular game in the North in the late 19th century and would have been played in the long gallery.

confident is the red dining room, its overmantel flanked by four twisted columns carved from local oak and framing a self-portrait by van Dyck. The staircase, beyond an arch of polished local limestone, embodies Tudor solidity. It looks as if it were hacked from a block of solid oak.

The bedrooms are as richly furnished as the downstairs reception rooms. There are beds in Hepplewhite style, washstand sets by Minton and a dressing-room collection of blue-and-white Wedgwood. The Gloucester dressing room contains prints of Brighton Pavilion. Its chimneypiece is an exquisitely carved work brought by the 5th Duke from a German monastery, a common source of furnishings for Regency grandees.

Hutton-in-the-Forest

☆☆☆☆ Pele house with 17th-, 18th- and 19th-century additions

Near Unthank, 6 miles NW of Penrith; private house, open part year

How satisfying to find a 'forest' still in place. A clearing in the thick woodland north of Penrith reveals a shimmering palace of pink stone lying seductively across a meadow and waited on by ornamental trees. Hutton has remained in the Fletcher Vane family, now Lords Inglewood, with a hop, skip and change of name since 1605.

The original house was one pele linked to another by the customary northern device of a linking Great Hall. The house was bought in 1605 by a Jacobean knight, Sir Richard Fletcher, whose son built the Renaissance gallery and cloister that flanks the forecourt. His son, in turn, built the suave new front and entrance hall around 1685. The architect was Edward Addison. To this already remarkable building, the Fletcher Vanes in the late Georgian period had George Webster of Kendal add a great tower, pivotal in the composition of the two principal fronts. Anthony Salvin's 1860s revisions to Hutton are among his most successful essays in medieval revival.

Entry is under the old pele tower into the original barrel-vaulted Stone Hall. Grim as any dungeon, it is hung with a fearsome variety of weapons. This medieval hall adjoins the new hall erected by the Fletchers in the 1680s: the earlier hall retains its original panelling and large fireplace.

The most prominent feature of the new hall is the bottom of the magnificent Cupid Staircase. This dates from the 1680 remodelling and is gloriously vulgar. The putti do not merely adorn foliage or trophies in the baluster panels. They blow themselves up into grotesque nudes, completely filling the panels. I have seen nothing like them: they should have a parental guidance certificate. The staircase rises to a Mortlake tapestry and leads at right angles into the earlier Renaissance wing.

'I have seen **nothing** like them ...'

The voluptuously carved Cupid Staircase was probably constructed around 1680. It leads up to a landing, lined with tapestries. The tapestry opposite the top of the stairs is Flemish and dates from the 1670s; it depicts the *Banquet of the Gods*. On the adjacent wall is a Mortlake tapestry from around the same date, entitled *The Playing Boys*.

Above The gallery at Hutton-in-the-Forest dates from the reign of Charles I but is distinctly Elizabethan in style. Long galleries were rare in the North and Sir Henry Fletcher, who built this part of Hutton, may well have been influenced by the galleries of grand Elizabethan and Jacobean houses in the South. Today, the gallery houses several collections, including a range of spinning wheels and several Cumbrian court cupboards.

Although built in the 1640s, this gallery still has an Elizabethan air. A circular tower by the entrance looks out in contemplation over a walled garden, a wonderfully romantic spot. The south-facing windows survey the entrance court. Centuries of Fletchers gaze down from the walls. Shelves are filled with oriental porcelain. This is a superb room.

The Victorian library, created by Salvin over the hall, is lit by the five upper windows of the hall façade. It leads straight into the new wing, built by Webster and amended by Salvin at his most light-hearted. Still Regency rather than Victorian in atmosphere, it is filled with Gillow furniture and family portraits. The windows look out over the ornamental gardens and a most satisfying fall in contour. Salvin's rear staircase is lined with tapestries and a portrait of Sir Frederick Vane's huntsman, John Peel. He set a record in his profession, a single run of 70 miles in the 1830s, celebrated in the song, 'Do y'ken John Peel'.

The Cupid Room takes its name from the exquisite ceiling supplied to Henry Fletcher in the 1740s by Robert Adam's master stuccoist, Joseph Rose the Elder. Its central roundel depicts a cupid far more demure than his fellows on the old staircase. The room is a Georgian jewel, with fine doorcases and an overmantel framing a small Hogarth.

Lady Darlington's bedroom is an 18th-century room decorated with original William Morris paper and Arts and Crafts furniture. Morris wallpaper is also found in the dining room downstairs, graced with a modern chandelier in Art Nouveau style. The latter is decorated with cherries borrowed from the curtains and acanthus from the wallpaper.

Isel hall

★★ Medieval pele tower with Elizabethan range

4½ miles NE of Cockermouth; private house, open part year

On its eminence above a bend in the River Derwent, Isel from a distance looks more like a fortified town than a house. Even close to, the heavy pele tower and three-storey Elizabethan range is austere. This is the ancestral home of the Leigh and Lawson families, by devious inheritance from the 14th century to the death of Margaret Austen Leigh in 1986. The house is now occupied by the Cumbrian visionary, Mary Burkett, former director of Abbot Hall, Kendal (see page 44), which she elevated to Museum of the Year. Her reputation for scholarly eccentricity is shared with all those saints who devote their lives to the rescue of old houses.

The pele tower at Isel was rebuilt after a Scottish raid in 1388. It is oblong and unusually large, and has recently received a fierce pink covering in what is called lime-harling. It beams like a beacon down the valley. The main flank of the house is extraordinary. The original Great Hall, once detached from the pele, was extended in 1573 to form an extensive façade to the courtyard. It is a range of chambers just one room deep, unadorned in the rough northern style but with curious obelisks along the parapet.

The interior reflects a home much altered as succeeding generations wrestled to make an essential medieval plan conform to changing demands. The Hall, now a dining room, with its ceiling of *c*1520, has rich woodwork with fine linenfold panelling.

Beyond is an Oak Room with the ghostly outline of paintings on its panels. These appear mostly to represent the crests and arms of the first Lawson owner, presumably celebrating the acquisition of Isel by marriage in 1573. There are more such panels in the room above. Isel is filled with family memorabilia, warm, dark and eccentric.

Kendal: Abbot hall

☆ Georgian mansion, now an art gallery

Highgate, Kendal; museum, open part year

The mansion sits on the bank of the River Kent next to Kendal's sprawling parish church, forming rather an odd couple. The Gothic church has five wayward gables to the river, each of a different proportion. The house is Georgian and prim. Two canted bays separate three Venetian windows, all in soft ochre stone. In front is a demure lawn with municipal fencing.

The house was built for Colonel George Wilson, traditionally by Carr of York. Historians of inflation will note that it cost £8,000 to build in 1759, was sold in 1772 for £4,500, in 1788 for £2,650, in 1801 for £3,900 and in 1897 to the local council for £3,750, largely for its modest grounds. A century later that amount might buy a tenth of its garage.

The house was lucky to survive. It now houses the Abbot Hall Art Gallery which, since the 1960s, has acquired an excellent small collection of English paintings. Some effort has been made to render the downstairs rooms domestic, with the addition of furniture by Gillow of Lancaster. The main hall runs from front to back of the house, divided by handsome Doric columns. The old dining room has good plasterwork and doorcases.

These rooms contain works by William Larkin, Hogarth, Reynolds, Joseph Wright and a fine group by George Romney. The Green Room is dedicated to the memory of the 17th-century Lady Anne Clifford (see pages 17 and 18). Two side panels of Jan van Belcamp's picture of the lady show her at the ages of fifteen and fifty-six. The main central panel is too big to exhibit, so I am told. Any public gallery that cannot display its major work should give it to someone who can. (In 2003, the panel went on loan to Tate Britain in London, sadly far from Cumbria.)

Another downstairs room contains watercolours of the Lake District, by Turner, Ruskin, Girtin and others. The upstairs rooms are a modern museum.

Levens hall

☆☆☆☆ Elizabethan house in continuous family occupation with famous topiary garden

Near Levens, 5 miles S of Kendal; private house, open part year

Levens Hall speaks the comforts of the Elizabethan age better than any house in the north of England. The madcap guard of honour of yew trees, the medieval façade and rich Elizabethan interiors embody an architecture that has rarely been out of fashion. The house was a 13th-century pele tower and hall, converted by James Bellingham after 1580 into a gentleman's residence. Its acquisition by a member of the Howard dynasty, probably in settlement of a gambling debt, fixed Levens in time. The hearts depicted on the rainwater heads are said to refer to it being 'won on the turn of an ace of hearts'. Howards married Grahmes who in turn married Bagots. The house remains in that family today.

What Levens lacks in grandeur it has in intimacy. The informal, rendered front reflects the architecture of the rooms inside. A four-storey pele tower stands out to the right of the entrance, with

Above The walls of the Elizabethan Great Hall are panelled with local oak; above this runs a plasterwork frieze decorated with heraldic shields, each one containing the bugle motif from the Bellingham arms. A set of Charles II gilded brass candle sconces are mounted on the panelling. *The Holy Family*, painted in the 16th-century by Pieter Koeck van Aelst, hangs above a 17th-century oak refectory table that once stood in the servants' hall.

asymmetrical cross-wings on either side. The main reception rooms face the topiary garden, designed in the 1690s by Guillaume Beaumont. This is one of the oldest, oddest and most distinguished such gardens in England. Its strange, anthropomorphic shapes seem to fuse every corner of the house and people it with ghosts.

The front door opens directly onto the Great Hall, a rarity in a medieval house where entry was normally into a screens passage. The interiors at Levens seem at first overly modern. The Great Hall is carpeted, with sofas and a wood-burning stove in the fireplace. Many of the upstairs rooms were repanelled and furnished by the Howards in a neo-Jacobean style after 1818. These were depicted in the 1840s by the ubiquitous antiquarian artist, Joseph Nash, who wrote of Levens' 'genial warmth'. Yet Levens today is much as Nash saw it, the Elizabethan and neo-Elizabethan interiors barely distinguishable. This is an inhabited house, its rooms like its art adapted by families over generations. The hall fireplace is surmounted by an excellent coat of arms of Elizabeth I, with a lion and Welsh dragon rampant. The theme of James Bellingham's loyalty to his Queen is repeated almost tediously throughout the house. When she died, a distraught Bellingham rode over to Durham to greet the new Scottish monarch, James I, on the latter's slow and celebrated progress south. He then returned to Levens and never left it for his remaining thirty-eight years.

To the left of the hall is the old Great Chamber. The original panelling is lozenge patterned. Fluted pilasters mark the corners and flank the rich oak chimneypiece, heavy with coats of arms. A deep bay window looks out over the formal garden. Over one door, a statue of Bellingham appears to be holding a shield over his private parts. The walls are hung with Lelys and a fine portrait by Rubens of Anne of Hungary.

Equally fine is the adjacent Small Drawing Room, with its chimneypiece portraying the Four Seasons and Five Senses. They are accompanied by numerous American Indians, a sign of cosmopolitan sophistication in an Elizabethan house. The room contains a collection of Napoleonic

Below The library at Levens is lined with wood panelling, made in Warwick and installed in 1822. Elizabethan carvings – the figures representing Wisdom, Truth and Justice – were combined to create the overmantel. The library was originally used as the room to which ladies would 'withdraw' from the adjacent dining room. It may also have been used as a buttery, linked to the dining room by a connecting door.

Above When James Bellingham refurbished Levens Hall he created a separate dining room; his initials and the date 1586 are incorporated in the carved overmantel. The walls of the room are lined with intricately embossed Spanish leather and the dining table dates from the Elizabethan era. The set of chairs around the table are made from walnut and are believed to be the finest example of Charles II chairs in England.

memorabilia, a Bagot having married one of Wellington's favourite nieces. He gave her a number of Sèvres and Dresden depictions of the great man, and Napoleon's cloak clasp found in his carriage after Waterloo.

The upstairs bedrooms in this wing were mostly repanelled by the Howards, although one has fine antique leather wall-hangings. The ceilings are mostly neo-Jacobean. The Redman bedroom contains Gillow furniture, the Lancaster firm also supplying an early water closet.

In the dressing room is some of the oldest English patchwork, executed by the early 18th-century Grahme daughters at 32 stitches to the inch. I wonder how many 'daughters of the house' could today achieve that output of craftsmanship.

The house now returns downstairs to the library with an overmantel composed of Elizabethan fragments. Here is a rare portrait of a child by Aelbert Cuyp. The dining room, its walls covered in embossed and painted Cordoban leather, has a set of robust Charles II chairs.

Levens is alive with family history. Every wall seems devoted to old pictures of the house, to documents, miniatures, weapons, costumes and needlework. There are paintings grand and simple, china rare and ordinary. Objects seem to have no purpose, except that a Bellingham, Howard or Bagot at some point acquired them and hoped that posterity would find them interesting.

Lowther castle

☆ Dramatic façade of ruined Regency mansion by Robert Smirke

4 miles S of Penrith; private house, open by arrangement

Lowther Castle is open to the skies, if not as yet to the public. Its surroundings are so suborned by agribusiness as to drive any visitor west into the welcoming arms of the Lake District. At present, there are plans to restore and revive the old buildings. Ostentatiously built for show across the valley from the village of Askham, they can be admired from the road.

The original castle was begun by the 1st Viscount Lowther but burned down in 1720. It was eventually rebuilt by the young Robert Smirke in 1806, this being his first major commission on returning from a tour of classical antiquities in Italy and Greece. The drama of the setting demanded dramatic architecture, and got it. Smirke designed a medieval castle on a hillside across a sloping park, facing the old Lowther mausoleum on the edge of a ravine. He showed himself a true successor to Vanbrugh as architect of scenic theatre.

The house has a central keep, a curtain wall, turrets and angle pavilions. From a distance, the main front can be seen to rise in a series of battlemented tiers. The interior, which contained excellent plasterwork, was gutted and unroofed in 1957 and is now mostly a ruin. Even Pevsner was moved by the family's plight. While deploring its ruination, he added, 'Yet what pain must it be to the owners to live so near this memorial of past glories.' Other owners of great houses managed to keep their memorials in good repair and accessible. Lowther is now on its mettle.

Mirehouse

☆☆☆ Old Lakeland manor, refuge of Romantic poets

4 miles NW of Keswick; private house, open part year

At Mirehouse, the present fights the past in amiable combat. It overlooks Bassenthwaite, a magical lake. The massive flank of Skiddaw rises to the east, Grisedale Pike to the south-west. The house sits alone in its park, attended by a stand of Scots pines. Here, the ghosts of Wordsworth, Tennyson, Carlyle and their genial hosts, the Spedding brothers, fill the rooms and pace the grounds. Every corner is occupied by anecdote, to the point where the house is in danger of being a mausoleum of poetic inspiration.

Mirehouse's charm lies in its setting and the orchards and outbuildings restored by the Speddings, who still live at Mirehouse. This setting includes a herb garden, heather maze, lovers' lane and bee garden. Everywhere offers views over the lake and mountains.

The house itself is enjoyable rather than architecturally distinguished. The modest 17th-century manor was given a more substantial rear in the 19th century. As a result, the front and back ranges are startlingly different in scale.

Below Above the library mantelpiece at Mirehouse hangs a portrait of Tom Spedding (1800–70), painted by Samuel Laurence. Thomas Carlyle was one of Tom Spedding's closest friends and the library houses an important selection of his letters and manuscripts. Carlyle saw Mirehouse as something of a refuge and would often stop off there on his way to Ecclefechan (see page 142) in order to visit the friend he described as 'the Genius of the hills'.

The interior is essentially a memorial to the Spedding brothers, James and Tom, and their friends among the Romantics of the early 19th century. The house was inherited in 1802 by their father, John, who sent the boys to study in Bury St Edmunds and Cambridge. They felt no need to 'go up to London', being content with the society and stimulus of the North. James became a scholar of Bacon and turned down an offer of the Regius Professorship of History at Cambridge. Tom wrote a book on the reform of the Poor Laws and became High Sheriff of Cumberland. They entertained writers visiting the Lake District. After the death of his friend, Arthur Hallam, Tennyson sold a poetry medal for £15 to pay for the stagecoach fare to Mirehouse in 1835.

The front rooms are those of a cultured gentleman of the early 19th century. In the smoking room is a collection of Bacon memorabilia. The library ranges wide over the interests of the Speddings, with not just poetry but philosophy, science and the classics. The drawing room is chiefly dedicated to Tennyson, including photographs of him by Julia Margaret Cameron.

The study is devoted to Wordsworth and the Lakes, with stuffed ducks and Lakeland watercolours. Everywhere are ticking clocks, letters from celebrities, drawing desks and needlepoint stools. Mirehouse is more than the sum of its parts. It is the Lake District with hand on heart.

Muncaster castle

☆☆☆ Anthony Salvin's re-creation of an ancient castle

Near Ravenglass, 16 miles SE of Whitehaven; private house, open part year

Muncaster clings to the side of the Eskdale ravine at Ravenglass like a fantasy castle on the Upper Rhine. Its 77 acres of woodland walks and gardens in spring are ablaze with rhododendrons, azaleas, magnolias, maples and camellias. The Terrace Walk is the finest scenic promenade in Lakeland.

The gardens have long been eccentric and today embrace an Owl Centre and a 'Meadow Vole Maze'. Muncaster Castle, says its guidebook, 'lives entirely through the warmth and understanding which visitors bring during the summer months' – a handsome welcome which all houses might imitate.

The castle has been owned by Penningtons and their ancestors since 1208. The present owner glories in the name of Phyllida Gordon-Duff-Pennington. In 1464, Sir John Pennington sheltered the hapless Henry VI, who left his drinking bowl with a blessing that the family would prosper while it remained unbroken. Known as the Luck of Muncaster, it is wisely held in a vault, with a facsimile on display.

The present house is essentially of 1862 by Anthony Salvin, in his neo-medieval maturity. I like to think of old Salvin arriving at these northern castles and clapping his hands with delight at the opportunity they offered. His building incorporated an old pele tower in a rambling low-slung mansion of grey-pink stone.

The interior was completely rebuilt by Salvin. The Great Hall replicates the original and is filled with paintings, wood carving and heraldic windows. The guide apologizes for the family dogs lolling on chairs next to 'please do not touch' signs.

Above left Rare Elizabethan needlework panels hang along the passage. The scenes they depict include the tale of Lot's wife and the destruction of Sodom and Gomorrah. **Right** The fine octagonal library, with its galleried upper level, houses more than 6,000 books. Family portraits line the upper walls, including a Munnings of Sir William Pennington-Ramsden, aged nine. He later went on to take second place in the 1927 Grand National on a one-eyed horse named Bovril.

Pride of place at Muncaster goes to the library. It dates from 1780 but was relocated by Salvin on the site of the medieval kitchen. Octagonal in shape, it rises two storeys to a Gothic vault. The oak panelling seems designed to complement the bindings of the books. From the gallery above, Penningtons gaze down in approbation, including the last Lord Muncaster who was kidnapped by brigands in Greece in 1870. He looks more like one of his captors.

The dining room has walls coated in leather embossed with gold leaf, in poor condition but apparently impossible to restore. The pictures are mostly copies, including a remarkable 'Titian' by Thomas Gainsborough.

The main staircase is adorned with a great treasure, a set of marble reliefs by Canova of ladies dancing, apparently up to bed. The bedrooms contain much old woodwork and other antique fittings gathered from elsewhere by members of the family.

Rare Elizabethan tapestry panels hang in the passage, depicting couples cavorting in a castle landscape. Here too is a portrait of Tom Skelton, the 'last Fool of Muncaster'. He gave us the word tomfoolery and looks uncannily like Tony Blair.

In total contrast is Salvin's barrel-vaulted drawing room downstairs. It is in soft blue and white. The walls comprise a fine exhibition of family portraits by or after Lely, Kneller, Reynolds and Lawrence. The finest, and most swaggering, is a large de Laszlo of Lady Ramsden, the present owner's grandmother.

Rydal mount

Above The window of Wordsworth's attic study looks out over the gardens of Rydal Mount towards Lake Windermere beyond.

☆☆ The home of Wordsworth's mature years

At Rydal, 1½ miles N of Ambleside; museum, open all year

William and Mary Wordsworth and their three surviving children arrived at Rydal Mount with his sister, Dorothy, in 1813. They stayed until the poet's death thirty-seven years later.

Wordsworth had gained an appointment as local Distributor of Stamps. He was financially secure and on his way to becoming Poet Laureate. More remarkable, his political opinions were turning away from the youthful radicalism of Dove Cottage. He even opposed the 1832 Reform Bill, leading a new generation of poets to pour scorn on him. It was of Wordsworth that Browning wrote, 'Just for a handful of silver he left us, just for a ribbon to pin on his coat.'

I prefer to see Rydal as Wordsworth returning to the Cockermouth background of his childhood. It is certainly not the Bohemian residence of a poor poet but the comfortable home of a public official. The house sits on a steep slope north of Ambleside. A fine 4-acre garden slopes towards Rydal Water. The original building was a 16th-century cottage, surviving as the present dining room. It is heavily beamed and retains its spice cupboard. A print of Wordsworth's hero, Robert Burns, has pride of place over the mantelpiece.

Of the library, Wordsworth's servant said that it was 'where he keeps his books: his study is out of doors'. The portrait of the poet in his seventies by the American artist, Henry Inman, so delighted Mary that she insisted he paint a copy. The room has since been knocked through into the drawing room, and the old cottage extended into a substantial house. The result is a sitting room so conventional in appearance that we expect to see a television in a corner. The contrast with Dove Cottage could hardly be greater.

The bedrooms upstairs contain various Wordsworth memorabilia not already claimed by rivals at Dove Cottage or Cockermouth. There are vivid pictures of Wordsworth ladies, of the 'faultless' Mary, the devoted Dorothy and the adored daughter, Dora, whose death in 1847 from tuberculosis deeply affected the poet for the rest of his life.

At the top of the house is Wordsworth's study. Display cases detract from its atmosphere. This is sad because the little window in this room has the most evocative of all Wordsworth views. It looks out through a frame of wisteria to his 'study' beyond, the mountains and lakes of Cumberland.

Sizergh castle

☆☆☆☆ Massive pele tower with Elizabethan, Georgian and Victorian additions

3½ miles S of Kendal; National Trust, open part year

Sizergh is the ancient seat of the Stricklands, residents since the 13th century, now as tenants of the National Trust. Stricklands prospered during wars against the Scots and the French. They carried the banner of St George at Agincourt and sided with the Yorkists in the Wars of the Roses. Under the Tudors they married Parrs and Nevilles and prospered further. Only in the 17th century did Fortune turn her back on them. Catholic marriages, attendance on the exiled James II in France and a genetic propensity to gambling brought poverty if not ruin. This preserved Sizergh from demolition or substantial alteration. It stands with its neighbour, Levens Hall (see page 45), as twin glories of the Elizabethan North.

The core of the house is a Cumbrian familiar: a massive pele tower with medieval hall attached, and Elizabethan wings much embellished over time. The wings form two low flanks to a central courtyard, now privately occupied. The tower itself is visible on the right, with a Gothic coat of arms on its façade. The old hall in the middle is concealed behind a Georgian front. Its porch was altered by the Victorians to bring carriages under the house to shelter, a rare convenience in English country houses (found also at Raby Castle, see page 90).

Below A magnificent oak-panelled screen divides the entrance hall at Sizergh. It is topped by an ornately carved pediment that features an escutcheon of the Strickland family arms. **Right** The galleried banqueting hall rises through two storeys and is furnished with a Jacobean refectory table and Elizabethan benches.

This entrance hall, no longer for carriages, now contains a magnificent screen, probably from the original Elizabethan hall overhead. The latter had been built in the 1550s but destroyed in 1773 to create the present Georgian drawing room overhead. A flight of stone steps leads up to the first floor, on the landing of which is one of Sizergh's treasures, a scagliola table made in 1708 with birds and flowers surrounding the Strickland arms.

The medieval rooms to the left of the hall comprise two storeys of intimate chambers. The Stone Parlour has a Ferneley painting over the mantelpiece and the old dining room contains some outstanding marquetry furniture. Elizabethan bedrooms spill from one into another. The wood panelling, much of it moved here and there over time, is excellent, especially the swirling overmantel in the Boynton Room.

The Georgian drawing room comes as something of a shock amid Sizergh's heavy features and dark woodwork. It has sky-blue walls, a high ceiling and tall, effete wall niches. To make matters more fragile, it is filled with a collection of European and Oriental ceramics, including an exquisite pair of rustic boys in 'soft-paste' porcelain.

The old pele tower is on the right of the hall, its once-gaunt spaces now comfortable reception rooms. The old Great Chamber is now the dining room, its Serlian ceiling and carved chimneypiece similar to those at Levens, possibly the work of the same craftsmen. Stuart portraits line the walls

Below The Inlaid Chamber is one of Sizergh's finest rooms. The glowing panelling that lines the walls is made up of inlaid designs inspired by early Renaissance decoration; it was installed in the room between 1573 and 1582. The most dominant piece of furniture is the curtain-hung four-poster state bed, its canopy supported on heavily carved tapering columns.

and the shelves carry relics of the family's time in Jacobite exile in Paris after 1688. Lady Strickland was governess to the future 'James III', whose unfortunate portrait as a chubby boy hangs in this room. He was the Old Pretender and father of Bonnie Prince Charlie, whose bust is also displayed. This was a house of doomed loyalties.

The present banqueting hall was the medieval family solar, with deep-set windows and adze-hewn floorboards. A gallery surrounds its upper storey. Rich Elizabethan benches at the long table are decorated with carvings in strange imitation of hide.

Next door is Sizergh's showpiece, the Inlaid Chamber. The plaster ceiling drips with Elizabethan pendants. There is armorial glass in the windows and a domed internal porch. Most glorious is the panelling, considered the most elaborate of its Elizabethan date in any English house. Arched panels based on Italian Renaissance motifs are inlaid with poplar and bog-oak to give a glimmering sheen, as if the wood itself were impregnated with precious metal. In the 19th century, this sumptuous room was sold by a cash-strapped Strickland to the V&A Museum in London for £1,000, plus £400 for the bed. To the credit of that museum, the entire room has been loaned back and reinstalled.

Sizergh's garden falls away across lawns to a lake. To the north is a celebrated rock garden from which there are romantic glimpses of the house's gables and tower.

'On a bright day, the water's reflection shimmers over the grass and bounces off the stucco.'

Storrs hall

☆ Classical villa on the edge of Lake Windermere

Near Storrs, 3½ miles S of Windermere; now a hotel

Storrs recalls Windermere in its Victorian heyday, with picnics on the shore and candlelit barges on the lake. In 1825, Wordsworth, Southey and Walter Scott, crowned as 'bards of the Lakes', attended such an occasion. The host was John Bolton of Storrs Hall, Liverpool plutocrat and slave-trader. By then, this was already a disreputable business.

Today, Storrs is a luxury hotel. Standing at the end of a lakeside lawn, it is a bold, almost beefy, classical villa built onto an existing early Georgian house, fragments of which survive to the rear. The architect of the new building in 1808 was J. M. Gandy, assistant to Sir John Soane.

The house is covered in bright stucco. The entrance is behind a bold Doric porch inside which a small hall gives onto a grander one. This rises two storeys on stately Ionic columns. Its staircase has been well restored, with portraits and hunting trophies gazing down from the walls. Equally fine are the main reception rooms, still with their Regency plasterwork medallions and anthemion friezes. At the back, a conservatory looks out over Windermere. On a bright day, the water's reflection shimmers over the grass and bounces off the stucco.

Swarthmoor hall

☆☆ Elizabethan house and important Quaker centre

Near Ulverston, 7 miles NE of Barrow-in-Furness; private house, open part year

Swarthmoor was the northern home of the Quakers. Built in 1586, it later belonged to the Fell family, Judge Thomas Fell being Chancellor of the Duchy of Lancaster. One of Quakerism's founding fathers, George Fox, visited the house in 1652. Both Fell and his wife, Margaret, came under his charismatic influence. Fell continued to attend church, but when his wife held meetings in the house he sat quietly in his study, listening through an open door. Fell died in 1658 and Margaret married Fox, becoming leader of the movement in the North and serving four years in Lancaster prison for her beliefs.

The house later suffered from decay but in 1912 was bought and restored by Emma Clarke Abraham, a Fell descendant. It was sold to the Society of Friends in 1954 and is still dedicated to the 'sweet peace' of Quakerism.

The view of the front of the house from the garden is charming, with the Hall on the right and an eccentric single canted bay on the left, rising three storeys to the attic. It is all lop-sided. A balcony over the door is one from which Fox is said to have preached to a crowd outside – although preaching was not a Quaker practice. The entrance leads into a screens passage and the hall. The latter is panelled and furnished as the family eating room, with stools for chairs. Beyond is Fell's study, with its door through which he listened to meetings in the hall.

The staircase is most unusual. It rises round a so-called four-post newel, probably intended to support not just the stair but the roof. Fell's bedroom has been refurnished in Elizabethan style, with Renaissance fireplace surround, carved bed-head and magnificent chest. It retains its internal porch. The bed is original to the house.

Townend

☆☆☆ Ancient stone-and-slate Lakeland homestead

At Troutbeck, 3 miles N of Windermere; National Trust, open part year

The house appears to be that of an unaltered Lakeland farm. Whitewashed stone walls rise past small windows to a sloping roof and round Cumberland chimneys. Opposite is a fine 17th-century barn flanking the road. The ensemble, far from the Windermere crowds below, is a Lakeland timewarp.

Yet the house is not all it seems. It was home to the Brownes since the 16th century. Though always farmers, they became prosperous professionals, notably in the law. The Victorian owner was the antiquary, George Browne, who died in 1914. He preserved the house and amassed a library of 2,000 books. A master carver, he also both collected and created the ornamental woodwork with which the interior is embellished. What is old and what is his is near impossible to tell. His daughter died in 1943, after which the property passed to the National Trust.

This is a place of Cumbrian terminology. Entry is into the 'Down House' or kitchen, where a fire burns in a range festooned with hooks and pans. A grandfather clock ticks in the background. Steps lead up to a screens passage or 'Hallan' and into the main parlour with its big fireplace, known as the 'Fire House'.

Left The Fire House at Townend served as a communal living and dining room for centuries. Below The cooking was done in the kitchen or 'Down House'. In the early 18th century, this was the domain of Elizabeth Browne, who came to Townend on her marriage in 1702. She brought with her a hand-written book of recipes in which she had recorded the details of such local delicacies as spit-roast pike, mutton ham and clapcake. Her book has survived and has enabled food historians to re-create some of the typical Lakeland dishes served at Townend during the period.

The interiors are dark and oak rich. In the Fire House, the original fireplace has gone but one can still see where there used to be a projecting hood under which the family and servants would have sat for warmth, wearing hats to protect themselves from rain-filled soot coming down the chimney. It has been replaced with a Victorian stove. A huge 'board' or table occupies the space under the mullioned window. Here every member of the farm community would have eaten. The room is now full of spinning wheels, guns, pikes, rushlights and heavy Jacobean chairs. Many carry carvings by Browne, including his bizarre emblem and 'coat of arms': he chose a Hapsburg double-headed eagle.

Behind the Fire House is the library. The books are mostly on law, but also farming, topography and religion. It is the collection of a Lakeland yeoman, largely self-educated, well read and proud of his locality. The carpet is of Cumberland Herdwick wool, coloured with vegetable dyes. Browne bred his own upland sheep and had them painted, over and again, by the local artist, William Longmire.

The bedrooms upstairs are carefully divided between the family or 'posh' end of the house and the servants' end. The former displays Browne at his most effusive. The so-called state bedroom has panels, frames, bed-heads, chairs and cribs coated in carvings from the 17th to the 19th centuries. Browne's 'naïve' portrait is by the window.

This is the house of a comfortable Lake District family that had neither the inclination nor the money to rebuild, and who took satisfaction in the antiquity of their inheritance. Visited in solitude, Townend is the most evocative Lakeland house.

Workington hall

☆ Ruin of one of Cumbria's greatest mansions

Near Workington, 7 miles N of Whitehaven, private house, exterior viewed from public park

Few sights so embody the poverty of the North's heritage than Workington Hall. This was among the grandest houses of Cumbria. Home of the Curwens, rivals of the Cliffords and Lonsdales, it sits on a precipice above the River Derwent on the outskirts of Workington. It is still surrounded by its old park, yet the mostly ruined house, on which public money was spent in 1970, is closed and padlocked in the care of the local council.

It is still possible to walk round the walls of the house and see through the grille into its interior. On the precipice side is an old pele tower with a flanking 14th-century range. A medieval gatehouse guards the 'inland' side of a large surviving quadrangle. This is bounded by Elizabethan wings, which were extensively remodelled by Carr of York in the 18th century. The house was sold by the Curwens to the local council after the Second World War and then left to decay.

As a result, the later work was dismantled in 1972 on government advice in order to display the earlier structure more effectively. Yet all that is visible today is the ghost of Carr's internal façade. Rooms stand open to the sky. Stairs lead nowhere. Everything is a dangerous structure, awaiting stabilization and reopening to the public. Only the park retains the dignity of a great family, foolish enough to trust their inheritance to the public sector.

Wray castle

☆ Neo-Romantic baronial castle, set in landscaped grounds

3 miles W of Windermere; National Trust, some rooms open part year, grounds open all year

From a distance, the castle looks like a rich man's folly – and it was. Turrets rise across a magnificent landscaped park which stretched eastwards towards Windermere. Wray was built in 1840 for a Liverpool surgeon, James Dawson, at a cost of £60,000, in the most extravagant neo-Romantic style. The architect was H. P. Horner. It was one of the few new buildings admired by Wordsworth.

The estate has long been the property of the National Trust, which at one time thought to demolish the castle and retain only the park. The castle's most prominent feature is a gigantic *porte-cochère* with battlemented turrets, arrow slits and machicolations. The outside is bleak and wholly lacking in the picture windows which might have been inserted, considering the site overlooking Windermere. Inside, a grand staircase rises from the entrance up to the central hall, which itself rises the full height of the central tower. Horner's architectural medievalism was at least thorough.

The castle has passed through many hands, including recent use as a radar school. It is currently a training centre. The grounds are open to the public and access is permitted to some rooms. The castle's most implausible claim to fame was as inspiration for *Peter Rabbit*. The Potter family from South Kensington used to rent Wray Castle for holidays when their daughter, Beatrix, was a young girl. It was at Wray that she fell in love with the Lake District and its fauna.

Durham
Barnard Castle

Durham

Blagraves house

☆ Old town house with statues of musicians

The Bank, Barnard Castle; now a restaurant

Such façades would have filled the North in the 17th century. Their basements were for business and storage, with workmanlike alleys and courtyards behind. At the front entrance, steps led out of the mud to the main rooms which gasped for light and air by pushing their bay windows as far up and out over the street as money and gravity would allow. The front of Blagraves House is decorated with statues of four grotesque musicians. They were supposedly moved here, possibly from the side wall, when the house was a local museum in the 19th century. It is now used as a restaurant.

The property can be traced back to the Middle Ages, when it appears to have been an inn and alehouse. The stone cellar is vaulted and might have been a brewery. The house was known as the Boar's Head in Elizabethan times, the boar being the symbol of Richard III, a hero in these parts. Tudor windows flank the door. Oliver Cromwell is said to have stayed here in 1648, consuming mulled wine and shortcake and demanding the removal of all Royalist emblems before he would go to sleep. The prominent four-storey projecting bay is also 17th century – a room carries the date of 1672 – by when the house was owned by the Blagrave family.

The main dining room has an original plaster ceiling and fireplace. The staircase is 18th century. To the rear, across a courtyard adorned with a statue of a Stuart king, is what appears to be an ancient banqueting house, perhaps a relic of the inn, although the high windows might indicate use as a weaver's premises.

Bowes museum

★★ Fantastical facsimile of a French château and home to magnificent art collection

Westwick Road, Barnard Castle; museum, open all year

Bowes tries to look like a French château, and succeeds. To find such a structure on the outskirts of Barnard Castle is incongruous and gloriously inappropriate. An ocean liner might as well have been towed up the Tees and left forgotten by the bank.

Bowes was begun in 1869, intended to be part house, part museum, by John Bowes, the illegitimate son of the Scottish Earl of Strathmore and a local girl. He lived most of his life in Paris, his father having settled on him his extensive Durham estates. Bowes married his mistress, an actress named Joséphine Benoîte, buying her a Paris theatre and even a title, Countess Montalbo, to conceal her origins. Barnard Castle was near his old home and was to display their vast collection of pictures, sculpture and furniture. It was never used as a house (except for top-floor apartments) and did not open to the public until 1892, by which time both Bowes and his wife were dead. They left it as a gift to the people of Co. Durham.

The museum was designed appropriately by a Frenchman, Jules Pellechet, as an exaggerated facsimile of the new town hall erected in Le Havre in 1859. A drive curves up from the road past lawns to a grand entrance terrace. The two main storeys rise above a high basement, with a generous attic above. The mansard roof is richly punctuated by dormers and chimneys. The only comparable work in this style in

CASTLE

England at this time is Château Impney, (Worcestershire) designed the same year, and the slightly later Waddesdon (Buckinghamshire).

The building and collection suffered from lack of money for maintenance, passing to Durham County Council in 1952 and now to a trust. It should be the Victoria and Albert of the North but remains instead an exotic monument to the Bowes' taste. Flocks of reluctant schoolchildren wander past lofty cases of French china and Spanish glass, beneath lowering canvasses by little-known artists. The gods of education have replaced those of showmanship. They bring more grant.

Yet the Bowes is full of delights. It has a large collection of medieval altarpieces, works by Goya and other Spanish masters and two large Canalettos. Rooms are filled with furniture and porcelain, metalwork and needlework, armour and costumes. Other rooms have been rescued from demolished houses, including one from Chesterfield House in London. In the front hall is a huge mechanical swan which periodically comes to life. Although valiant efforts are being made to revitalize the place, the museum remains a treasure trove awaiting a locksmith.

Below A musical automaton in the form of a life-size silver swan is the most famous exhibit in the Bowes Museum. Probably made in the 18th century, the swan, when wound up, appears to catch and eat a silver fish, plucked from a shimmering stream of rotating glass rods.

The Castle

The castle is well sited on a bluff overlooking the River Tees. Walter Scott cried 'What prospects from his watchtower high,/ Glame gradual on the warder's eye.' It was built by Bernard, nephew of Guy de Baliol, in the 12th century and, despite subsequent ruin, still forms a magnificent pile when seen from below. The castle passed to the Beauchamp and Neville families and was held for the Crown against the 1569 anti-Reformation Rising of the

BARNARD

☆ Picturesque ruined remains of a 12th-century castle

Castle House, Barnard Castle; English Heritage, open all year

North. In the 17th century, the castle was owned by Sir Henry Vane of Raby, who used its stone for his own neighbouring castle. By the 18th century it was a ruin. Vane's descendant, Lord Barnard, put it in Crown guardianship in 1952.

The castle area is divided into three sections, an outer and an inner ward, and the castle itself surrounded by an internal moat. The wards are now gardens, manicured by English Heritage within a inch of their lives and sadly divorced from the main square of this handsome town. Architecture should find ways of linking such spaces together.

Of the original castle, the corner tower, Great Hall, Great Chamber and Round Tower survive, although much appears (from old prints) to have crumbled in the past two centuries. The Great Chamber's oriel window still looks out, forlorn, over the gorge. Given that so much money and effort has gone into building steps, ramps and health-and-safety contraptions, some effort could have gone into rebuilding walls and rooms.

The Round Tower was home in the 19th century to a recluse who dressed as a monk and showed visitors around the ruins. The tower retains its lower floors, which were used for storage. The ramparts offer a fine view over the valley and river below, with a picturesque bridge of 1772. Walter Scott's view must once have been spectacular. To Arthur Mee in 1953 it was still a 'glorious wooded gorge forming a lovely vista'. The castle now faces a housing estate and young offenders' prison, both designed with complete insensitivity to the landscape.

CASTLE

Beamish museum

At Beamish, 8½ miles NW of Durham; museum, open part year

Beamish Hall was the seat of the coal-rich 'Bobby' Shafto family and has now been converted into a luxury hotel. The estate is more ambitious. It is the most successful 'themed' re-creation of England's industrial past. The land originally comprised the home farm, manor house and various disused drift-mine workings. All are now restored and open to the public. A complete pit village adjacent to the mine and a reconstructed North Country town centre of the turn of the 20th century (there being almost none left *in situ*) have been added to them. A light railway and a tram serve these locations from the visitor centre and car park, offering a fine view of the valley from a distance. The danger at Beamish is now of gigantism. Large display sheds are starting to appear in place of what should be a gradual organic growth. But the presentation, with lit fires and costumed attendants, is immaculate.

Dentist's house ☆

originally at Ravensworth Terrace, Gateshead

The town high street is dated to 1913 and includes a sweet shop, solicitor's office, garage, bank, Co-op, newspaper office, inn and municipal park. All are refugees from various urban clearances in the North-East. At one end of the town is a row of houses built between 1830 and 1840 in Ravensworth Terrace in Gateshead. They were 'for aspiring professionals and tradesmen ... illustrating the growing sophistication of town life available to those who could afford it'. I wonder what horror has replaced them.

The Dentist's House is the most immediate draw. Two houses, just one room wide, have been combined to form a dentist's house and surgery next door. The profession was at the time still unregulated and profit went to the brave and the well equipped. Downstairs is a waiting room and upstairs the surgery, workshop and recovery room for those given laughing gas. The operation on offer is impressively free of fastidious hygiene. The 'dentist' on duty on my visit seemed only too ready to pull out my teeth for half a crown.

The domestic rooms show the move away from Victorian gloom and clutter towards a lighter 20th-century touch. They are lit by gas and electricity. The latest Shanks plumbing is in the bathroom with a shower and Doulton Patent Flushing Toilet. A fox stole adorns the bedroom, while downstairs are prints, William Morris wallpapers and display cabinets filled with china.

Music teacher's house ☆

originally at Ravensworth Terrace, Gateshead

The house, also from Ravensworth Terrace in Gateshead, is infused with the personality of its supposed occupant, Florence Smith, struggling to make a living from teaching music and elocution to Gateshead young ladies at 6d a lesson. Whereas the dentist was keen on 20th-century gadgetry, Miss Smith is firmly Victorian. The house is dark and heavy and so cluttered with *objets trouvés* as to leave no inch on which to put anything down. Lighting is still by oil lamp.

The main parlour has a large fireplace with the piano beside it and an old trumpet gramophone. Sheet music is littered everywhere. China dogs adorn the mantelpiece and ornaments are kept clean inside glass domes. The kitchen at the back is exceptionally simple, with an open range and stone floor. Upstairs windows contain stained glass. The bedroom furniture is heavy mahogany. Unlike the dentist's house, there is no bathroom, only washstands and chamber pots.

The Music Teacher's House is excellently done. I can remember in the 1970s when every London restaurant aspired to such richness of period taste and decorative clutter. The essence of these re-creations is to make us aware of our own taste changing over time. How soon the once familiar comes to seem antique.

BEAMISH

Pit cottages ✯

originally at Francis Street, Hetton-le-Hole

A lane leads from the drift-mine to a small colliery village of school, chapel and pit cottages. Each of the latter has a smallholding in front and an alley at the back, flanked by rabbit runs, chicken hutches and pigeon crees. They date from the 1860s and came from Francis Street in Hetton-le-Hole, once a terrace of twenty-seven such habitations. They are furnished as they would have been at the peak of the Durham coal boom in 1913.

Of the four cottages in the terrace, No. 1 is the colliery office, No. 2 housed an elderly Methodist couple, No. 3 an Irish Catholic family and No. 4 a miner's widow, the poorest of the row. Each of the cottages is single storey with parlour in the front, kitchen at the back and an attic bedroom. They are not spartan, the guide pointing out that miners' wages were not low and conditions considerably better than, for instance, those of farm labourers.

Thus the furnishings of No. 3 include a small pedal organ, dresser and oil-lit dining table with, in the kitchen, a grandfather clock and much decorative ornament. Furniture is solid and dignified. While the work was clearly hard and dangerous, it has none of the grimy overcrowding of the town tenements of the North. Fresh vegetables were available from the garden.

BEAMISH

Pockerley manor ✯

The manor house, still in its original position, stands in a copse of trees on the hillside overlooking the drift mine. Old labour looks down on new. The earliest part of the house dates from the 1440s, with a 'modern' farmhouse extension added in the 1720s. In front are a formal parterre, a kitchen garden and an orchard. The house is displayed as it would have been in 1825, a yeoman farmer's property of the sort common throughout England. This is the least 'Durham' of the properties at Beamish.

The house is small, with a kitchen and back kitchen to one side of the ground floor entrance and a parlour to the other. The former is well furnished with an open fire and oven, and oak farmhouse furniture. The long-case clock has an unusual face depicting a colliery scene. The parlour is more decorous, panelled in white-painted pine and with pictures of Durham cattle on the walls. Spode china is on the table and a handsome sideboard against the wall.

The upstairs rooms are more cottage than manor, with a patchwork quilt on the four-poster bed in the master bedroom. The furnishings have been carefully chosen. There is no sense here of any old junk having been amassed to fill a 'themed' room. Even the items of food in the pantry are to a purpose. The adjacent Old House is displayed as servants' quarters, dark, medieval and poky. A sign outside warns, 'all dogs shot'. We are not sure whether it is meant.

Bishop Auckland:

★★★ Bishop's palace restored in Gothick style by James Wyatt

Market Place, Bishop Auckland; private house, open part year

Auckland Castle is England's finest bishop's palace. It was seat of the one-time Prince Bishops of the Palatinate of Durham – once one of their fourteen residences. As protectors of the Border, they were granted secular as well as ecclesiastical authority under the Crown. This power was not formally rescinded until 1836, when Bishop van Mildert moved out of Durham Castle and made Auckland Castle his sole residence.

The castle lies at the edge of the town on a bluff overlooking the River Wear. The dramatic location gives it a superb park and woods. The entrance is Sir Thomas Robinson's Georgian Gothick gateway with clock-tower, built by the high-living Bishop Trevor in 1760. The drive then passes through a screen built by James Wyatt in 1796 for Bishop Shute Barrington. The medieval house was

Auckland castle

an episcopal manor with hall, domestic rooms and offices. This was gradually extended until Wyatt's arrival to impose an emphatic Gothick stamp on the palace in the 1790s. He rearranged the rooms and gave them the happily domestic touch that the late Georgians brought to so many ecclesiastical buildings. This has recently been enhanced with pastel shades and admirable red carpeting.

Above Zurbarán's paintings of Jacob and his Sons were sent to Mexico in the mid-1600s to promote Catholicism; it was believed at the time that the Aztecs were one of the lost tribes of Israel. While still at sea they were stolen by English pirates and found their way into the hands of the London merchant who sold them to Bishop Trevor.

Wyatt's entrance hall was the old 'Gentlemen's' or outer hall. It now opens from a pink lobby into a spreading double staircase which rises past a large picture window to a balcony with mural, a delightful sequence. The progress to the throne continues through an ante-room with its view of the Scotland wing, where the Bishops' Scots prisoners were once held. The main state or throne room lies through traceried doors and arches. It is not over-large, more a country ballroom in dimension, with the wooden throne surrounded by Gothick plasterwork, the coat of arms supported by a crook and a sword, indication of the bishops' monarchical dominion. Portraits of bishops line the walls. Wyatt's windows are tinted pink, 'to make the ladies appear less pale in sunlight'.

Beyond lies the Long Dining Room. The room was recast in 1760 by Bishop Trevor but given its oriel window by Wyatt. The walls are in a delicate turquoise. Here hangs Auckland's, indeed Durham's, pride and joy. Trevor's collection of thirteen Zurbaráns of Jacob and his Sons was bought for £124 in 1756 and brought

Above Wyatt's throne room at Auckland Castle is a fine example of his interpretation of Gothick architecture; unfortunately, his most famous buildings in this style – Fonthill Abbey and Lee Priory – have been destroyed. At either end of the room is a large Gothick arch, surrounded by plasterwork tracery and two smaller niches. At one end, the arch frames the Bishop's throne; at the other end, the arch is filled by a heavy wooden door.

to the Castle as part of his campaign to improve the status of Jews in English society. They stand 8 feet high and fill their canvases. *Benjamin* is an 18th-century copy, the original hanging in Grimsthorpe, in Lincolnshire. Each is dark and dramatic against a light sky, their costumes variously of 17th-century Spanish nobles, tradesmen and peasants. Painted in the 1640s, the sequence is a treasure of the North of England. This is one of the first rooms in England to be designed to house a specific group of paintings, which it does to perfection.

Beyond, we enter the bishop's suite of rooms. The King Charles Room, once the king's bedroom, is now a sitting room. It has bright pink walls and Rococo ceiling. The paintings are again from Bishop Trevor's collection. The Gothick music room is now a dining room, with delicate portraits of bishops' wives on the walls. The palace chapel was formerly the bishops' banqueting hall. Though rebuilt after the Civil War by Bishop Cosin, an enthusiast for elaborate church woodwork, it retains its Gothic arches. Cosin filled the ceiling with his heraldry and the west window with his glass. To one side is Nollekens' lavish memorial to Bishop Trevor, who nonetheless preferred to be buried at his beloved Glynde Place in East Sussex.

Chester-le-Street: Anker's house

☆ Rare surviving example of a medieval anchorage

Church Chare, Chester-le-Street; museum, open part year

No medieval practice is as obscure as that of the anchorite. An extreme form of hermit, the anchorite inhabited not a lonely cave but a walled-up sanctuary, a preliminary tomb, adjacent to a church. Special permission from a bishop was needed to become an anchorite, requiring both an endowment for sustenance and evidence of sufficient spirituality. He or she was, in effect, 'buried' to await eventual death in a twilight world of intense prayer. It was considered the most holy of vocations. Glory would attach to any church with a resident anchorite and shame would attach to any whose anchorite pleaded for release.

Conditions in such cells would have been near intolerable. The only apertures were a tiny view to the chancel itself and an opening for food and water to be passed through over a pit grave already dug outside. The Reformation banned anchorages as little short of witchcraft and almost all were obliterated. The Chester-le-Street anchorage, or anker's house, is a rare survivor. The chamber may have been preserved by being attached not to the chancel but to the tower where it gave directly onto the street, perhaps as an example to passing villagers. A squint enabled the anchorite to see the sacrament on the church altar. What appears to be the original anchorage window, carved from a single block of stone, is preserved just inside the church.

The cell was occupied from 1383 until the Dissolution and was then converted for occupation as a small almshouse. Two extra chambers were added and four poor widows took up residence. In 1626, a curate tried to evict the ladies to make the rooms his own, even obtaining a warrant from Durham to 'duck' them. The ladies employed three strong lads of the village to bar the door and force the curate to relent.

Croxdale hall

☆☆ Georgian house built on the site of a medieval manor

At Croxdale, 4 miles S of Durham, private house, open by arrangement

Croxdale is the seat of the Salvin family, on the old Great North Road between Darlington and Durham. Their name is derived from 'sylvan', reflecting their origins in Sherwood Forest. Croxdale was acquired by marriage in 1402 and the present family have held it through twenty generations, loyal throughout to Durham and to Catholicism. To Burke, the Salvins were 'one of those ancient houses established at the Conquest whose undeviating adhesion to the Roman Catholic faith consigned them to long and honourable retirement'. The great 19th-century architect, Anthony Salvin, was a scion of the family.

The house itself is not the prominent villa on the hill overlooking the road. That is Burn Hall, a Catholic seminary established by the Salvins on their land. Croxdale Hall lies hidden from sight, over a river and under a road and rail bridge. The drive passes through open parkland beneath thick woods. The house retains the old manorial proximity to farm and outhouses. When it was rebuilt in the mid-18th century it was on the old Jacobean and possibly Tudor plan, with two wings extending behind. The rear is, in effect, the estate farmyard and includes a row of ancient cottages. One of these is a medieval priest's house. Beyond is a magnificent 18th-century barn. The whole grouping is workmanlike.

The exterior is simple to the point of severity, with yellowing stone walls, Venetian windows and a plain pediment above the south façade. Carr of York is mentioned as a possible inspiration, although the house is probably by a local builder instructed, as the guide says, by 'an intelligent client'.

The rooms are those to be expected in such a house. Finest is the entrance hall and staircase. The latter rises and divides beneath two tall windows, the walls yellow and with gloomy Salvins gazing down on their descendants below. The Rococo ceiling is virtuoso plasterwork, possibly by Cortese, with elaborate cartouches and a central goddess.

The library's mahogany bookcases were designed for the room in the 1790s, outshining the books within. The drawing room has more good plasterwork and the dining room is decorated with fluted Tuscan pilasters, lit by a generous bow window. The north wing of the house contains the family's Gothick chapel, built in 1807. The altarpiece is by Maria Cosway in what Pevsner calls the 'swoony style' of pious Catholic art.

By the rear entrance is surely the most evocative boot-room in the county, crammed to the ceiling with old hunting gear, boots, hats, capes and dust-laden trophies. The smells are of leather and canvas, wood and field. The clutter is inimitable. Such places are as precious as any drawing room.

The house is magnificently sited above evidence of an important 18th-century garden sloping down towards the river. One of these is walled and large, guarded by a crinkle-crankle wall and overlooking a lake and wooded ravine.

Durham: Crook hall

☆☆ Medieval hall house overlooking the river

Sidegate, Durham; private house, open part year

The immediate environs of Durham are as grim as the city centre is charming. Ring roads and flyovers are flanked by concrete walls and overpowering office blocks. Tucked above one such wall is a medieval hall house with traces of 13th-century walling. It sits in a small garden across a field, and is now being restored by the Bell family. They were students at the university who loved Durham so much they decided to stay, much to Crook Hall's good fortune. The place is overgrown, creeper-clad and delightful.

The core of the house is a square 14th-century hall of roughcast stone walls, inside and outside. This hall has two trefoil Gothic windows and is open to the roof. It is extraordinarily primitive in appearance, unfurnished, candle-lit and ideal as an 'historic' wedding venue. The screens passage is of stone, supporting a tiny gallery reached from what would have been the domestic wing. The kitchen, with its large fireplace, later became the main parlour. There are traces of 17th-century paintings on its beams. A fire burns in the grate and a phantom staircase of quartered logs rises into the ceiling. A new stair turret was built at the rear in the 1980s.

Linked to the old manor is a fine Georgian house facing the lane. The history of the place is a jumble but it is known to have been inhabited in the 19th century by Dr James Raine, the historian of Durham, who claimed visits from the Wordsworths, John Ruskin and numerous ghosts. The grounds are being laid out as pleasantly wild gardens overlooking the river below.

Durham castle

☆☆☆ A Norman castle with medieval additions, now part of Durham University

Palace Green, Durham; private house, open all year

'... stupendous relics of the Norman Conquest.'

Durham Cathedral and Castle justly form a World Heritage site. They rise on their rocky peninsula over the River Wear, stupendous relics of the Norman Conquest. While the cathedral is imperious, the castle is intimate and eccentric. A gatehouse leads into a medieval courtyard overlooked by a high mound and keep. Ahead was once the Norman hall, later rebuilt as state rooms. In the 14th century a later, Gothic, hall was built to the left, the angle between them filled with a staircase tower. The Norman hall was turned into a residence. This remarkable enclave was the headquarters of the Prince Bishops of Durham until that function was discontinued in 1836 (see Auckland Castle, page 74) and the castle became the new Durham University. It has been part of the university ever since.

With true Victorian confidence, the university promptly rebuilt the ruined keep as a student residence. The remaining ranges contain interiors from all periods. On the left is the Great Hall, with a porch added in the 17th century by the flamboyant Bishop Cosin. The original screens passage survives, leading on the left to a black-and-white timbered buttery. Beyond are the original medieval kitchens with giant brick fireplaces and old utensils. They are still in use after 500 years, one of the longest serving kitchens in the country.

The Great Hall is a shortened version of what must have been a gigantic chamber. Its roof beams and windows are original. The walls are hung with Cromwellian armour. Portraits of bishops gaze down on the students dining beneath. Behind the dais end of the hall is Bishop Cosin's Black Staircase of the 1660s, leading to his domestic chambers. Its wide treads and robust openwork panels were once cantilevered from the

Above The Norman Gallery at Durham Castle was once the Constable's Hall, or armoury, and formed the upper storey of a building erected by Hugh de Puiset (also known as Bishop Pudsey), bishop of Durham from 1154 to 1198. As nephew of King Stephen and, reputedly, great-grandson of William the Conqueror, de Puiset was possibly the most deserving incumbent of the title 'Prince Bishop'.

walls. Cylindrical pillar supports have since been inserted, but this is still a majestic work of carpentry, with voluptuous baluster panels.

In the 16th century, a gallery was built along the exterior of what was the original Norman hall. Even the Tudors could not bring themselves to destroy its great doorway. This survives as one of England's finest Romanesque compositions.

In place of the older hall is now a suite of state rooms, once used as Judges' Lodgings and for university guests. (I once stayed here in great splendour.) The Senate Room has a fine Jacobean fireplace and is hung with tapestries. On the floor above is the original Norman Constable's Hall, now a gallery with deep-set 12th-century windows behind double arches. Half has been converted into small rooms, surely the oldest student quarters in Europe. Laptops and film posters nestle amid Norman dogtooth and zigzag.

At the far end of this gallery, an old spiral staircase leads underground to an early Norman chapel. It was long ignored and thought to be a storeroom. When excavated in the 1950s it was found to date from the earliest post-Conquest castle of about 1080. The eerie animals that adorn its capitals speak from an older age even than the cathedral itself.

Finchale priory

★ Monastic buildings on the banks of the River Wear

4 miles N of Durham; English Heritage, open by arrangement

This idyllic bend in the River Wear was a retreat for the Benedictine monks of Durham. It was founded by the flamboyant St Godric, a giant of English history. Born shortly before the Norman Conquest, Godric was an itinerant pedlar who went to Rome and graduated to Mediterranean sea captain and pirate. He visited Compostela, Jerusalem and Rome three times.

At the age of forty, Godric put all this behind him and became a hermit. He settled at Finchale and established a reputation for asceticism and sanctity until his death at the age of 105 in 1170. He wore a hair shirt and chainmail coat. His hermitage soon became a priory of Durham, founded in 1237. It was rebuilt with a 13th-century church and cloister. The full-time complement was four monks and a prior, with a further four as visitors 'on retreat'.

It must have seemed a sublime place. Although the county council has unbelievably permitted a large caravan site a hundred yards from the ruin, the slope to the river and the steep wooded bank opposite remain picturesque. Most remarkable is the survival of the refectory, undercroft and much of the prior's house. The refectory was presumably for visitors as the prior's accommodation must have been sufficient for most domestic purposes. It includes a hall and prior's chamber to the east. At the other end of the hall is a large surviving kitchen.

In the prior's study is a seat in an oriel window. It was said to be able to cure women of barrenness if they sat on it. This power was mysteriously lost after the departure of the monks at the Dissolution in 1538. It is a charmed spot indeed.

Harperley camp

☆☆ World War II POW camp, now rediscovered and restored

Near Firtree, 6 miles NW of Bishop Auckland; private house, open all year

Weardale is the most exotic of the Pennine dales and nowhere more so than above Bishop Auckland. Here, hidden on the steeply wooded slopes of the dale, is an intact German prisoner-of-war camp. Although occasionally visited by trespassing German veterans, it was left derelict in the woods for half a century, partly used for farm buildings. In 2002 it was 'discovered' and listed for preservation and is now being restored by a grant-aided local farmer for public display.

Designated Camp 93, Harperley is extensive. Its fifty huts housed 1,400 inmates in 1945. The structures are of brick, wood and breeze-block with corrugated iron roofs. They stand in rows, the windows and doors broken and falling out. One was converted into a theatre, with orchestra pit and even a prompt-box. German newspaper cuttings litter the walls. Everywhere are signs of the small comforts of prison, such as fake curtains made of hardboard and canteen wall paintings of scenes of the German countryside.

The prisoners worked on farms and building-sites. They enjoyed sport and gardening in the camp grounds and made small items of souvenirs for sale. While prison is prison, those inmates who have returned to Harperley expressed some affection for the place. One prisoner, Rudi Lux, who never returned to Germany and lived out the rest of his days in nearby Newton Aycliffe, was heavily involved in the rescue of the camp.

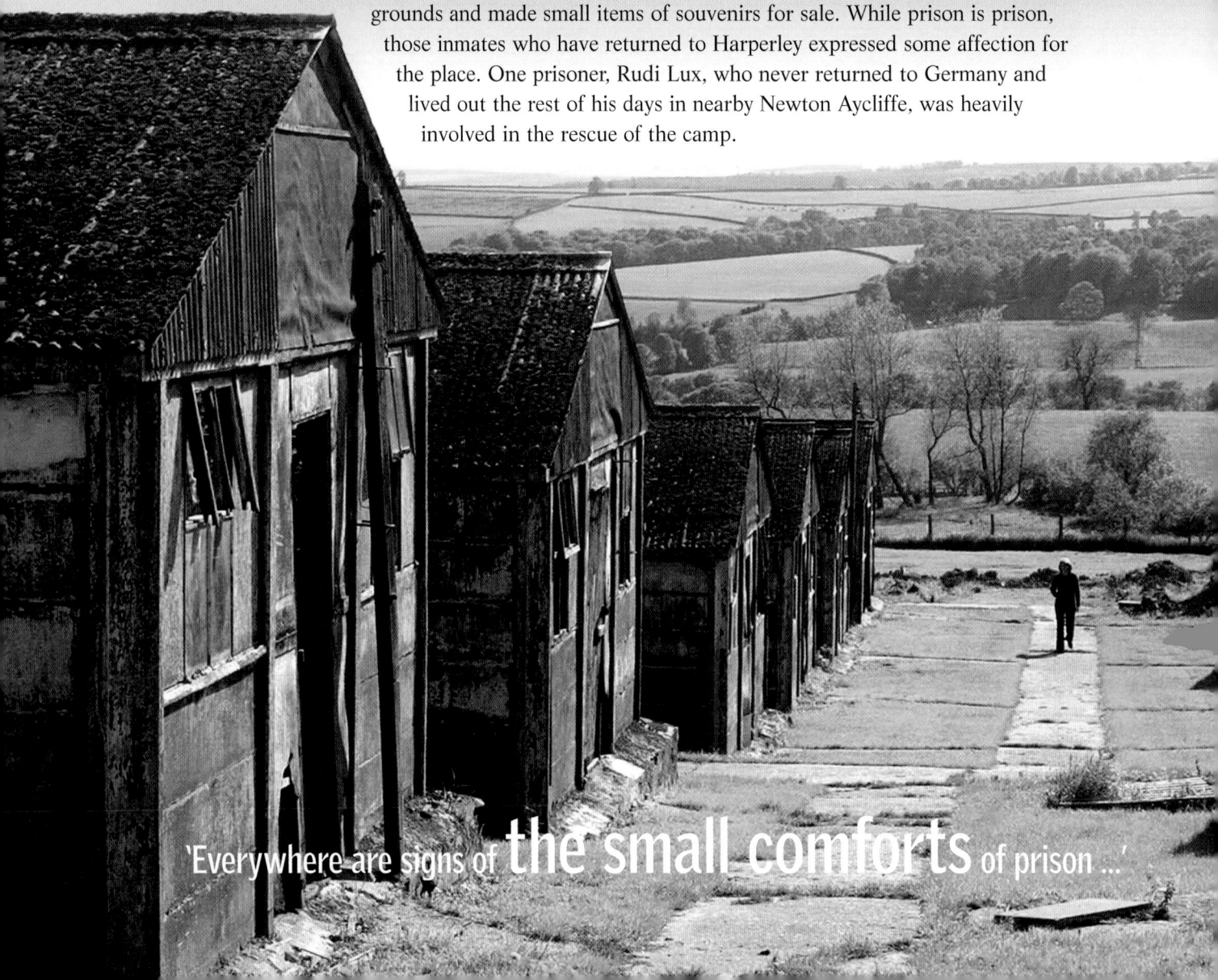

'Everywhere are signs of **the small comforts** of prison ...'

British POW camps in World War II

Harperley Camp was built in 1943 by its first inhabitants, a group of Italian prisoners, and was one of around 1,500 POW camps in Britain during World War II. In 1939 there had been only two; with invasion a real threat in the early years of the war, most German prisoners were transported to North America to stop them from providing Hitler with a ready-made army on British soil. But by 1942, after military success in North Africa, the war began to turn in Britain's favour and the number of Italian and German prisoners increased. More camps were needed and although most were created out of existing buildings, around 100, including Harperley, were purpose built. After Mussolini surrendered in 1943, Italian POWs were gradually repatriated and at Harperley their place was taken by a group of low-risk German prisoners who arrived in September 1944, a few months after D-Day. In less than a year the war was over. The camps, however, remained open; repatriation took several years and the last prisoners did not leave Harperley until 1948.

Right Although the prisoners at Harperley worked six days a week on local farms and other businesses, they did have some leisure time. One unknown prisoner, identified only by the initials 'MR', painted the walls of the camp canteen with rural scenes. A theatre, complete with tiered seating for the audience, was created in one of the huts and prisoners transformed the grounds around the camp into flower-filled gardens (see above).

Headlam hall

☆ Manor house with 17th-century front and Georgian rear

At Headlam, 8 miles NW of Darlington; now a hotel

Headlam has the loveliest of approaches. It lies off the main road through whitewashed farm buildings which appear to be sheltering it from prying eyes. The house itself is a much-altered manorial jumble.

The front of the house faces the garden with angular yew hedges stretching into the distance. It has five bays of sash windows. The entrance façade is manifestly 17th century, with stone mullions and an embarrassment of hipped roofs. The formal Georgian façade at the rear – which is strangely wider than the front – also has five bays of slender windows. These surround a doorway which is crowned by a single carved bracket.

The chief feature of the interior is the old hall, now a sitting room. This is graced with two bold Tuscan pillars. A Jacobean oak chimneypiece carries the coat of arms of the Birkbeck family, who built Headlam at the turn of the 17th century. The house is now a hotel owned by the Robinson family, 'who have farmed at Headlam for four generations'. They have found a new crop.

Hylton castle

☆ Fifteenth-century tower house with Victorian Gothic remodelling

3 miles W of Sunderland; private house, exterior can be viewed from public park

Hylton is for addicts of architectural heartbreak. The battered old castle is black and ruined, its windows cemented and its park lost to municipal grass, entirely surrounded by housing estates to the west of Sunderland. Nowhere is Durham's disrespect for its past so blatant as here. To add to the poignancy, Hylton gazes across the Wear valley at the great classical folly, the Penshaw Monument, on a distant hilltop. The latter was erected in memory of a Lord Durham in 1842, a Theseion in honour of this fantasy Athens of the North.

Hylton was a 15th-century tower house. It was given wings but these were later demolished. The building was acquired by William Briggs in 1869 and rigorously gothicized. This was Victorian not Georgian medievalism. The result is severe. Four towerlets rise sheer the full three storeys of the main front and continue into the sky with crenellated crowns. The roofline is battlemented all round.

Now without its roof or upper floors, the interior is hard to make out. It once included the normal arrangement of vaulted ground floor with Great Hall above and Great Chamber next to it. Ghosts of vaults, stairs and fireplaces can still be made out. With its outer walls intact, the place would be easily restorable, if anyone cared.

A few yards away is the ruin of an old chapel, apparently later converted for use as a banqueting hall. It is no less forlorn.

★★★ Medieval castle with Tudor additions and Vanbrugh alterations

Near Chester-le-Street, 4 miles N of Durham; now a hotel

Lumley castle

From the A1 heading north near Chester-le-Street, Lumley Castle rises splendid on a hill. The outward appearance is of the 14th century. Elizabethan adornments and alterations by Vanbrugh in the 18th century merely added to its majesty. Its conversion into a luxury hotel by the present Lumley, the 12th Earl of Scarborough, is firmly in the medievalist tradition of his Tudor ancestors. Everything from Vanbrugh's stylish dining room to the 'medieval' banquets in the Great Hall is done with ostentation. The bedrooms have well-stocked libraries and antique four-posters. The receptionists are in costume. Where some employ pastiche, Lumley Castle uses panache.

The castle was built by Sir Ralph Lumley in the 1390s on a 'modern' plan of four uniform walls and corner towers round an internal court. A gatehouse punctuates one side, the raised Great Hall fills the other. The ground floor is stone-vaulted. Lumley's Tudor descendant, the 7th Lord Lumley, added shields of great northern families to the wall outside the Great Hall and surrounded the mighty fireplace inside with similar heraldry. Lumley even crammed Chester-le-Street parish church with fake medieval effigies of his supposed ancestors.

Vanbrugh arrived at Lumley in 1722 at the invitation of the 1st Earl of Scarborough and proceeded to change everything. He reversed the hall, entering it not in medieval fashion from inside the courtyard but from a new platform on the outside, facing the valley. A medieval fort was thus made a spectacular Baroque folly.

Vanbrugh is most evident in the courtyard, on whose south side he inserted a new staircase with Venetian windows. This stair serves a new range of state rooms, forming the finest of the Lumley interiors, their ceilings stuccoed by Italians some years later. Considering the battering they must get as hotel reception rooms, they are superb. Adjacent to the Great Hall, the Garter Room has fine plasterwork, deeply coved and decorated with cherubs, arabesques and foliage. Over the fireplace is a remarkable composition of cherubs building a fire. This work dates from 1745, after Vanbrugh's time.

Beyond is the panelled dining room, with more restrained Palladian decoration. The saloon is decorated in the most effete Rococo, with a large central panel of cherubs kissing. The boudoir beyond is also Rococo. Nor was this all. Vanbrugh's masterpiece at Lumley is the old library built into the medieval undercroft. This is a Piranesian chamber of groin vaults divided by heavy rusticated columns, ancient Rome come to County Durham. It is now a dining room, and a superb one.

Otherwise, the present Earl's interior decorators have been at work. Vaulted passages are lined with busts. Sitting rooms are heavy with books and ornaments. Spiral staircases shoot upwards and alcoves dart off at odd angles. The restored castle is dark and mysterious and would have delighted the Elizabethan Lumleys.

Preston hall

☆ Victorian villa set in parkland overlooking the Tees

2 miles S of Stockton-on-Tees; museum, open all year

When David Burton Fowler built himself a villa by the River Tees in 1825, he little knew what was to hit him. Within a year 'Locomotive No. 1' of the Stockton to Darlington Railway destroyed his silence and deposited cinders on his plantation. Within three years, Fowler was dead. The house was sold to a succession of owners, the estate finally being allocated to housing in 1944. However, wartime shortage denied it building materials and, three years later, the house and park were bought by the council and saved.

The house is of brick with extensive Victorian additions in stone. These include a porch, ballroom and conservatory looking out over the park to the banks of the Tees. The interior retains its 19th-century plan and decoration, but has been woefully restored. Someone has picked out every plasterwork detail in primary colours, so that a leaf must be green, a grape purple and a cherry red. More successful is the Victorian 'street' re-created in the service wing to the rear of the building.

Panelling has been left in place in most of the main rooms. Although the furniture has gone, the house still hangs many of its donated pictures. Among these was a recently discovered masterpiece for which alone the house merits a visit, Georges de la Tour's *The Dice Players*. Congratulations to the council for not only not selling it but for displaying it in a room of its own.

Raby castle

☆☆☆☆ Medieval fortress guarded by its battlements and the famous nine towers

Near Staindrop, 6 miles NW of Bishop Auckland; private house, open part year

Raby Castle is the lion of the North, yet a lion that still sleeps. The estate is undeveloped and undisturbed. Countryside stretches to the horizon. The old castle lies along a fold in the moors, its forest of towers and battlements gaining full majesty close at hand. Legendary home of King Canute, it passed through descent and marriage to the Nevills, Earls of Westmorland, forebears of the Plantagenet line and thus of the Royal Family. The Nevills did not recover the inheritance when it was confiscated after the Rising of the North in 1569. In 1626, Raby was bought from the Crown by the Vanes, later Lords Barnard, who hold it to this day.

Although the medieval appearance of the castle was embellished by antiquarian Barnards in the 18th and 19th centuries, Raby remains as it was, essentially a true palace of the Middle Ages. From the outside, it is immensely forbidding. This is no picturesque folly or Gothick conceit but a fortress protected by nine towers, linked by a battlemented curtain wall. They were once protected by another outer wall, now reduced to no more than a parapet surrounding the terrace. The enemies of such places today may be bureaucrats and taxmen, but even they must give a shudder as they pass beneath Raby's great gate and enter its dark court.

The exterior towers are all different and of differing periods. Clifford's Tower is massive and domineering, followed clockwise by the Kitchen Tower, Mount Raskelf, the Chapel turrets and Bulmer's Tower, the last reputedly the keep of King Canute.

The Nevill Gateway leads to an inner courtyard. This has been much remodelled but retains its medieval atmosphere. The massive keep on the left guards the old Great Hall ahead.

A serious deficiency of Raby to the visitor is that neither the keep nor the adjacent state rooms are open to the public. What can be seen is the Great Hall and the suite of family rooms inserted by James Paine and Carr of York in the 18th century, together with later work by William Burn in the 1840s. They made habitable what must have been an intolerably inconvenient place. But they are only part of what could be as rewarding as Warwick Castle.

The entrance hall was remodelled by Carr in 1787 beneath the old Great Hall. Since the courtyard was too small for 'modern' carriages to turn round, he allowed them to drive into the lowered hall and set their passengers down under cover, before leaving on the far side. The effect on visitors was dazzling, alighting beneath a great rib-vaulted Gothick ceiling to find fires blazing and steps leading up to grand chambers on either side. The columns are of ox-blood scagliola.

The rooms open to the public are mostly those of a comfortable country house, with a fine private collection of pictures and furniture. The Small Drawing Room has an 18th-century ceiling depicting musical instruments, the walls hung with sporting paintings by Herring, Marshall, Wootton and Munnings. The library, formerly a dining room, is richly panelled with, as its climax, a voluptuous Lely of the Duchess of Portsmouth. She stands above a japanned chest flanked by Chinese porcelain pagodas. The adjacent Victorian ante-library contains pictures by de Hooch and Teniers and a tortoiseshell Flemish cabinet. On the floor appears to be the skin and head of one of the Lord Barnards' pet King Charles Spaniels splayed out in front of the fire like a tiger rug.

The ante-library leads into the virtuoso room of Burn's 1840s renovation, the eclectic Octagon Drawing Room. Yellow silk, white paint and Rococo gilding rise to a sumptuous frieze of neo-

'The effect on visitors was **dazzling,** alighting beneath a great **rib-vaulted Gothick** ceiling ...'

Left To celebrate the coming of age of his heir in 1787, the 2nd Earl of Darlington commissioned a new entrance hall at Raby that allowed carriages to be driven directly into the castle. The 10th Lord Barnard (1888–1964) and his family would mount their horses in the hall before riding out to join the local hunt. **Above** The Octagon Drawing Room was created by the Scottish architect William Burn in 1848 from an existing circular room. The decoration has remained in remarkably good condition; when the room was renovated in the 1990s, the paintwork and gilding of the plasterwork ceiling required only gentle cleaning.

Jacobean scrollwork. A giant pendant supports the chandelier. For good measure, the doors are of a neo-Jacobean style used by maharajahs in Indian palaces. A malachite and giltwood side table glows by the window.

The dining room, also by Burn, has rich red walls and carpet. Here are some of Raby's finest pictures, including a swirling Luca Giordano, portraits by Lely and Reynolds and an exquisite work by Cornelis de Vos, *A Gentleman and his Wife*. A few bedrooms are open upstairs, specifically the Blue Bedroom which contains a state bed; it is Regency Gothick in style with domed canopy and coronet. In contrast, a servant's bedroom is also on view.

The last room on show, the Barons' Hall, is essentially Burn's work, its floor having been raised to make space for the new entrance hall beneath. With red walls, dark beams and giant proportions, this is well suited to medieval functions. Nevills and Vanes gaze down from the walls. At one end, five sensational Meissen birds contort themselves into noble poses. It is said that 700 knights would gather here in fealty to the Nevills.

Here was plotted the disastrous rising of the northern earls against Elizabeth in 1569, which was to lose the Nevills Raby for ever. The Chapel has early 20th-century decoration, with painted walls and portraits of family figures in medieval costume. That on the right is of the 'Rose of Raby', mother of Edward IV and Richard III.

Although Burn destroyed much of 14th-century Raby, the castle retains most of its medieval servants' quarters. The kitchen dates from 1360 and is as built. It was still in use until the 1950s, the fumes rising to a huge lantern above. Next door is the medieval servants' hall with its long battered table and dresser filled with Minton plates. But more Raby, please.

Rokeby park

☆☆☆ Georgian mansion inspired by Palladian style

2 miles SE of Barnard Castle; private house, open part year

Rokeby, pronounced Rookby, will always be known for the Rokeby *Venus*, the Velasquez nude sold by the Morritt family to the National Gallery in 1906. It is sad that smaller English houses seem unable to keep hold of the greatest art. The *Venus* would make Rokeby a sensational attraction were it still there today. A good copy hangs in the saloon.

Rokeby deserves to be equally well known as an early manifestation in the North of the Palladian revival. It was built in 1725 by and for Burlington's associate, Sir Thomas Robinson, as a graceful Georgian box with recessed wings. To the rear is a more complex plan, of central bay with towers and projecting wings. It is a variation on a formal Palladian theme, the towers borrowed from Pliny's Tuscan villa and apparently unique in England. The exterior is virtually unaltered: the main block is of stone and the wings are painted a rich yellow ochre. In this rugged landscape, Rokeby is a dash of Italian refinement.

'Rokeby is a dash of Italian refinement.'

Left According to Robinson's original plans for Rokeby, what is now the saloon was intended to be the main hall. Set on the first floor, it was to be approached from the outside by a stone staircase. Although one is shown in an engraving of the south front, c1741, there is no staircase there today and in fact one may never have been built. In the 19th century, the Morritts reorganized Robinson's interiors and turned the hall into the saloon. But much of Robinson's original decoration remains; the frames for the circular paintings that run around the upper walls are part of his scheme and contain portraits of historic figures.

Robinson's house was bought by the Morritt family in 1769 and has been in the family ever since. Its most remarkable member was Anne Morritt, a Georgian needlewoman who specialized in re-creating paintings in embroidery. The house is full of her work, including, on the stairs, a needlework copy of a portrait of her by Benjamin West. Her work is of astonishing virtuosity.

The entrance under a porch is into a stone hall on the 'rustic' ground floor. This floor contains a complete suite of domestic rooms, an 18th-century mirror for the family of the state rooms on the *piano nobile* above. The print room is a survivor of the 18th-century custom of papering rooms with prints.

Bold Doric columns screen the stairs to the rear, with copies of Roman reliefs on the walls. Busts of the family line the passage to the stairs, the walls hung with twenty-three of Anne Morritt's needlework pictures. The first floor was at some stage reversed, so that the rear saloon is now the music room, with a ceiling later painted by J. G. Crace. This gives onto the main hall, now the saloon, which rises the full two storeys of the main front. It is curious in appearing Georgian at eye level – notably the superb door to the Music Room – above which is a Victorian ceiling, again by Crace. Over the fireplace is *Hope Nursing Love* by Reynolds and opposite hangs the ghost of the *Venus*.

The dining room fills one wing of the house and is now attributed to Carr of York. It has a Rococo plasterwork ceiling and a large apsidal alcove with small niches flanking the fireplace. Grand portraits of Hanoverian royalty adorn the walls. To one end is an unusual Venetian window – Carr, if not Palladio, at his most inventive.

Washington Old hall

☆☆ Putative home of George Washington's ancestors

At Washington Village, 4 miles W of Bishop Auckland; National Trust, open part year

Contest is fierce to be considered 'home' of America's first president. The rewards are great: Malden in Essex and Great Brington and Sulgrave in Northamptonshire all exploit their claims. Washington has the advantage of the name. All known Washingtons seem to have originated from a William de Washington, alias de Wessyngton, in the 12th century. A family of that name occupied the property until the 17th century.

The old house passed to the James family, descendants of a Bishop of Durham, and was mostly rebuilt in the 1620s. It then deteriorated until declared unfit for habitation in 1932. A committee was formed with vigorous American support and the house was saved in 1951, restored and given to the National Trust in 1956. The interior has been given back its 17th-century appearance, but with an American spin. A gift shop greets visitors immediately inside the front door and the upstairs is now a museum. George Washington's links with a building which is now submerged in Washington New Town sprawl seem tenuous.

The house is impressively simple. The symmetrical E-plan exterior of honey-coloured local sandstone faces south over a sloping garden. Over the old porch is a prominent Jacobean staircase tower, with the entrance on one side of it. Inside is a Great Hall, with solar/parlour wing to the right and kitchen to the left. Two medieval arches form openings to the latter. The rest of the building appears to be a 17th-century rebuild. The parlour is the smartest room, panelled and with an imported classical fireplace decorated with scrollwork.

The rooms are furnished in the Jacobean style, with much oak, pewter, Delftware and primitive pictures. The kitchen has National Trust wax food. The house's best feature is the oak staircase, a robust work of vernacular carving apparently donated from a building in Guildford, Surrey. One bedroom has been restored upstairs.

Witton castle

☆ Medieval revival castle in faded grand park

At Witton-le-Wear, 4 miles W of Bishop Auckland; private house, open as part of holiday complex

The guide to Witton admits that the place 'seems to have a curse upon it'. War, destruction, fire and bankruptcy have followed from one generation to the next. Nor is the present an exception. The castle is approached through a sea of caravans, uglier than any housing estate, followed by walls and gates festooned with signs ominously banning intruders and drunks. By the time I had reached the castle's outer walls, I wondered if this was a holiday camp for young offenders. Five mangy peacocks and a row of wrecked fruit machines in the yard did not restore confidence.

The Eure family built the castle in the early 1400s as a keep within an extensive curtain wall. It was partly demolished in the 17th century, rebuilt but gutted by fire in the late 18th. Eures gave way to the D'Arcys who gave way to Cuthberts who gave way to Chayters, each suffering misfortune or calamity in turn. The politician, Viscount Lambton, bought it in 1963 'for the creation of an important public amenity', apparently a euphemism for 'profit'. It is now ignominiously the clubhouse and entertainment centre for the caravan park.

Yet for all these indignities, Witton is a splendid sight. The exterior is Victorian out of Georgian romantic. A fine crenellated outer wall shields an entrance courtyard with bold *porte-cochère*. The rear façade looks out over the park to a lake. From all angles, the central block rises splendidly in a forest of turrets and towers in appropriately grim shades of grey. The gatehouse, surprisingly, is by the musician and amateur architect, Jools Holland.

Witton's interior is now institutional. A fine 18th-century Gothick ballroom can be detected on the first floor, with panelling and traceried windows. The lounge bar retains ancient panels to its window recesses, the walls here being hugely thick and presumably medieval. Of the rest I know nothing: nor did Pevsner who commented that 'The history of this building is not sufficiently known.' But what an opportunity!

Northum
Wallington

berland
Northumberland

Alnwick castle

☆☆☆☆ Medieval ducal fortress, restored by both Adam and Salvin

At Alnwick, 17 miles N of Morpeth; private house, open part year

Alnwick was and is the seat of the Percys, Dukes of Northumberland, 'a family nobler than kings'. The line traces its descent from a great-grandmother of Charlemagne. Through most of the Middle Ages, Percys were virtual rulers of Northumbria, from Durham to the Border. The castle came to Henry de Percy in 1309 and, except when ceded to the Crown for rebellion, has remained in the family ever since. Even rebellion had to be forgiven the Percys.

After its military importance declined, Alnwick became the headquarters of the vast Percy estate. It was comprehensively restored, first by Robert Adam and later during the Victorian medieval revival. Today, it is one of the leading tourist attractions of the North. The current Duchess's 12-acre garden round a grand cascade, still in the course of construction, is intended to turn the grounds into 'Britain's answer to Versailles'.

The castle now has the form of an outer bailey punctuated with gates, barbicans and posterns, enclosing a massive shell keep within. The latter is a cluster of towers round an inner courtyard and contains the main domestic rooms. Although the outward appearance and plan of the building has not altered much over time, that is not true of the interior. It was gothicized by Robert Adam in the 1760s and transformed by the 4th Duke during the 1850s and 60s. The state rooms had been in later buildings elsewhere in the outer bailey. The Duke now imported them into the keep. His architect in this medievalist venture was Anthony Salvin, with Italian craftsmen working on the interiors. It is their creation that is the glory of the castle today. Like its fellow ducal residence in the south at Arundel, in West Sussex, Alnwick is a monument to Victorian taste as much as aristocratic power.

The approach either from the town or from across the park is awe-inspiring. The castle sits above a steep slope landscaped by Capability Brown. Entry to the keep is Wagnerian, through two gates and across Salvin's rebuilt inner court. The first room inside, the lower guard chamber, is filled with the weaponry of the Percy Tenantry Volunteers. This semi-feudal territorial regiment survived until Waterloo.

A grand staircase now leads to the state rooms. Their character needs explanation. While Salvin was responsible for the architecture, for decoration the 4th Duke imported the Italian architect and archaeologist, Luigi Canina, and

Above The fireplace in the saloon was carved in 1857 in Giovanni Taccalozzi's workshop in Rome. Taccalozzi made gesso models of all the fireplaces he created for Alnwick and sent them to the Duke for approval before beginning work on carving them in Carrara marble. The sculptor Giuseppe Nucci was responsible for the figures of Dacian slaves that support the mantel on either side. **Right** Nucci also carved the figures of Justice and Britannia that occupy the alcoves on the east wall of the upper guard chamber. This room was one of the last to be redecorated by the 4th Duke's Italian architects. Montiroli, who had taken over supervision of the work at Alnwick on Luigi Canina's death in 1856, designed the Venetian-style mosaic floor himself; it was laid in 1864 by the Roman craftsman Luigi Malfatti.

his right-hand man, Giovanni Montiroli, from Rome. Italian craftsmen also came over but the brilliant Florentine carver, Anton Bulletti, was engaged to train twenty-seven men mostly from Glasgow and Newcastle.

This remarkable operation yielded what became known as the Alnwick School of craftsmanship. The state rooms are its memorial. The attention to detail, to cornices, picture frames, shelves and furniture was phenomenal. These are among the finest Victorian rooms in England, their quality compensating in part for the Duke's destruction of the earlier Adam interiors.

The upper guard chamber is chastely classical, with a Venetian marble floor. On the walls hang Canalettos, a van Dyck and a de Laszlo of the wife of the 8th Duke, painted in 1916. The small ante-library follows, with paintings by Titian, Palma Vecchio and Sebastiano del Piombo. Beyond is the library, a gallery with an upper balcony, its shelves of oak inlaid with sycamore. Busts of Bacon, Newton and Shakespeare are overlooked by emblems of arts and science.

The climax of the state rooms promenade is the saloon and drawing room, two rooms formed into one as they turn the corner and designed by Montiroli to complement each other. The fireplaces were imported from Italy, and are flanked by Dacian slaves in the saloon and caryatids in the drawing

room. The ceilings of the two rooms are of the most intricate geometry; that in the saloon turns the corner under one of the towers with a brilliant flourish of coffering.

Over the drawing room fireplace is a huge mirror, its frame an explosion of gilded foliage. On either side are two majestic Italian *pietra dura* cabinets. The paintings in these rooms include works by Reni, Dobson, Lely, van Dyck and Turner. Everything is of outstanding quality. My only quarrel is with the faux artfulness that leaves a glass of brandy and a cigar stub in an ashtray.

The last of the state rooms is the dining room, with portraits of the 1st Duke and Duchess gazing out over an Italian fireplace and beneath an Italian ceiling. In a cabinet is an extensive Meissen dinner service. Salvin's picture gallery beyond begins a sequence of museum rooms that detract from the studied domesticity of the state rooms. They contain the family's second division pictures and works of art.

Raphael's superb *Madonna of the Pinks* has been removed to the National Gallery in London, another sad case of great houses unable to retain the finest treasures, passing them to national or regional collections.

Aydon castle

☆☆☆ Early medieval hall house within a fortified enclosure

4½ miles NE of Hexham; English Heritage, open part year

Aydon claims to be the most complete 13th-century manor house in the North. It sits isolated in rolling hills above the ravine of the Cor Burn, between Corbridge and Hadrian's Wall. It seems gloriously lost in an antique world of its own.

The castle has, as its core, a fortified hall house, built largely in the late 13th century and fortified in 1305. The house was under constant threat from Scottish raiders although the owners, the de Reymes family of Suffolk, were able to do no more than build a wall and gatehouse round what was the old farmyard. The house was tenanted and refashioned in the 16th century. Kept in repair as a farm from the 18th century, the house remained unaltered for 400 years until entrusted to the government in 1966.

As a result, Aydon is spartan and unfurnished, yet it remains a remarkable survival. The outer courtyard, grassed by English Heritage like a municipal garden, leads to an inner yard with the old kitchen and byre to the right. The Great Hall is ahead and the solar wing to the left. The house rises two storeys, with ancient lancet windows and external stair to the hall. On the far side, where the house overlooks the ravine, can be seen Aydon's celebrated chimney flue, built out from the wall and rising to a conical cap.

The finest of the interiors is the Great Chamber. This has Gothic windows and a carved fireplace, possibly moved from elsewhere. More unusual is the even grander fireplace in the room beneath, a room normally occupied by servants, which is decorated with face masks. This must either have been intended also as a family room, or be a sign of an owner concerned for his servants' comfort.

Both solar chambers have rear latrine extensions of considerable size, possibly used as both garderobes and closets. (Garderobe smells were believed to keep cloth free of lice and moths, from which the word wardrobe is derived.) These rooms are like those at the similar Stokesay Castle, in Shropshire, desperately in need of a breath of life.

The solar wing at Aydon Castle, the private quarters of the de Reymes family, consists of two chambers; the Great Chamber on the first floor, the Lower Chamber (above) on the ground. This room was probably used as a servants' hall and as accommodation for the men-at-arms who defended the castle. Unlike the Great Chamber, which has large ornate windows, it was originally lit only by narrow slits. The room was heated by the huge and highly decorated fireplace.

Bamburgh castle

☆☆ Coastal fortress, heavily rebuilt in the late Victorian era

At Bamburgh, 15 miles SE of Berwick-upon-Tweed; private house, open part year

I wish at least some English castles could be left looking as they did in old prints, if only from the outside. Bamburgh is the definitive Northumbrian fort. It stands on a rocky outcrop, 150 feet above the beach, surrounded by marsh and sea and visible for miles around. From the land side, it looks as massive as Edinburgh or Windsor, intended to be rough, tough and awe-inspiring. Yet its stone is today neatly tooled. Its bollards are brightly painted and acres of lawn are trimmed and immaculate. All castles are modern 'interpretations', but Bamburgh has lost its age.

The castle was a royal base from Saxon times through most of the Middle Ages, being regarded as impregnable and too important to be left even to the Percys. Built by King Ida in 547, it finally fell to the Earl of Warwick's cannon when defended by the Lancastrians during the Wars of the Roses. It was thus the first English castle to fall to gunfire. Three great guns, named Newcastle, Dijon and London, blasted its walls in the summer of 1464 and, in doing so, signalled the end of medieval fortification.

In the 17th century the castle fell into ruin under the ownership of the Forster family, who had been appointed Constables of Bamburgh. The castle was later used as a school, charity home and military base before being sold in 1893 to the Tyneside arms magnate, Lord Armstrong. He intended it as a nursing home but it became his family's second seat. It is now held by a family trust and much of the castle is a museum of Lord Armstrong's life and work.

The public rooms are mostly late Victorian, by C. J. Ferguson of Carlisle, better known as an ecclesiastical architect. We might expect archaeological reconstruction, but so little survived that what we see is mostly Ferguson.

The King's Hall was rebuilt at least on the site of the medieval Great Hall. It has a magnificent false hammerbeam roof rising above stone walls and panelling. Display cases contain loans from the Royal Armouries as well as family memorabilia, notably gifts from grateful foreign potentates who bought Armstrong warships and weaponry. The Cross Hall has flamboyant blind tracery over the fireplace and beautifully mounted Flemish tapestries. The Faire Chamber contains a rustic scene by Jan Brueghel the Younger and a set of Dresden china.

The keep includes the old court room and various ghosts of the Norman interior, including a kitchen with giant fireplaces. So much has been altered, rebuilt and built afresh that it is impossible to know what is medieval and what new. Bamburgh is essentially a Victorian magnate's idea of how a medieval magnate might have lived on this magnificent seaside rock.

Above Hammerbeam roofs were the wooden equivalent of the stone vaulting used in late medieval cathedrals of the Perpendicular Gothic style. The false hammerbeam roof of the King's Hall was carved from teak by Thomas Worsnop of Rothbury. A massive arch at one end of the Hall opens into the Cross Hall. Above the Tudor-style fireplace hangs a copy of *The Card Players* by Theodore Rombouts (1597–1637).

Belford hall

☆ Palladian hillside villa by James Paine

At Belford, 14 miles SE of Berwick-upon-Tweed; private house, parts open by prior arrangement

In a land of pele towers and castles, Belford looks defenceless and effete. Until recently, it was near derelict, next to a scrap-yard. In 1988 *Country Life* wrote that 'one more winter, and the roof would have fallen in and it might never have been saved'. The roof was rotten, the hall ceiling had fallen and wet and dry rot were rampant. Almost all the plasterwork was unsalvageable.

The story of Belford is that of English upward mobility. Abraham Dixon was bequeathed the Belford estate in 1743 by his father, a Newcastle master mariner, in the hope that he would become a country gentleman. He fulfilled his father's ambition. The estate was a wretched place, 'the most miserable, beggarly sodden town', but Abraham tackled its restoration with gusto. He drained the land, planted vegetables, built a tannery and a mill, mined coal and established an inn. In 1756, on the adjacent hillside, he built a house designed by the first-rate neo-Palladian architect, James Paine. Three years later he was High Sheriff of Northumberland.

Dixon did not establish longevity. The house was sold to William Clark during the Regency and given a new rear entrance by the Newcastle architect, John Dobson, in 1817. By the mid-20th century it was abandoned. Its subsequent rescue by the Northern Heritage Trust was a triumph. The interior had to be rebuilt but the exterior was as designed by Paine and Dobson. The interior is now divided into apartments, but the hall and garden are open to the public.

Paine's Palladian villa looks serene on its hill looking out towards Bamburgh. The main building is of just five bays, the central three with a pediment and attached columns. It is, says Paine's biographer, 'a wonderfully complete and subtle essay in movement'. Bold steps lead up to the former entrance above a rusticated basement. The small entrance hall contains a discreet row of columns. Dobson's graceful staircase has been rebuilt and Paine's hall reinstated, with a frieze, fireplace and suitably Georgian doorcases.

Belsay castle

☆ Fifteenth-century pele tower and adjacent Jacobean hall

At Belsay, 9 miles SW of Morpeth; English Heritage, open all year

There are two Belsays. They are like sisters not on speaking terms who have vanished to opposite ends of the park. The castle is old-fashioned, the hall desperate to seem modern. The castle was the seat of the Middleton family from the 15th century. When Sir Charles Monck (formerly Middleton) built a new classical hall in the early 19th century, he clearly intended the old castle to remain as a ruin. This was a common device of the Picturesque movement, as at Old Wardour Castle, in Wiltshire, and Scotney Castle, in Kent.

The old castle is reached from Belsay Hall along a rhododendron walk, through a dell and a romantic quarry, all carefully contrived. Even in its ruined state, Belsay Castle is majestic. The original structure was a fortified pele, erected by the start of the 15th century and still standing today. This has an oblong hall on the first floor, with adjacent private closet. The hall is impressive, with Gothic windows and window seats and heavy corbels to support the solar above. Fragments of heraldic painting survive in the plasterwork. Spiral stairs lead onto the roof, from which the battlements and surrounding country can be viewed.

Adjacent to the old tower are the remains of a Jacobean house, from which the Middletons moved into the new Belsay Hall on Christmas Day 1817. Of these remains little survives beyond the outer walls but the Jacobean façade of 1614 has a handsome entrance bay with paired columns. It looks diminutive against the massive masonry of the medieval tower next door. A subsequent Georgian wing was reduced to the ground floor. It seems that only the Middle Ages were able to produce truly indestructible architecture.

Belsay hall

☆☆ Regency mansion built in strict Greek style

At Belsay, 9 miles SW of Morpeth; English Heritage, open all year

The eccentric Sir Charles Monck succeeded to Belsay Castle at the age of sixteen in 1795, changing his name from Middleton to succeed to an inheritance. He promptly extended his father's park, demolished the estate village and built a new village, to his own design, by the adjacent turnpike. He then proceeded with his great work, the erection of a hall at some distance from the castle. It was designed when he came back from his eighteen-month honeymoon tour of Berlin, Dresden, Prague, Vienna, Venice and Greece in 1804–6. Greece was plainly the enduring influence. He made some 300 architectural drawings for his new home. It took over ten years to build. Monck and his wife did not move into the still uncompleted house until 1817.

To say that Belsay Hall is 'severely' Greek is an understatement. It was modelled on the Theseion at Athens. Most houses at this time were still in the Roman style favoured by Soane and the Wyatt family. Greek was almost unknown, being employed in this archaeological purity only by William Wilkins at The Grange, in Hampshire, and Downing College, Cambridge. The exterior is two storeys of warm sandstone, with a shallow roof and two Doric columns on the entrance front. Belsay is the most refined classical work of the Regency period.

The interior is even more severe than the outside although, to be fair to Monck, this severity is partly the result of the rooms being stripped bare. English Heritage was required to leave them thus under the will of the last occupant, who insisted that no refurnishing take place. The central Pillar Hall is one of the purest Grecian rooms in England. Two storeys of columns round four sides of the hall rise to a lantern, flooding the space with light. The columns are fluted, Ionic on the ground floor and Doric above, creating a four-sided colonnade on both floors. Each individual column was said to have been carved by a different mason. It is like a temple ambulatory with reception rooms as shrines. The material is entirely stone. The only adornment is the ornamental brass balusters.

Belsay is now empty and used for special exhibitions. On my last visit, each room was filled with seats 'as modern sculpture'. The alien aesthetic seemed an abuse of the stately dignity of Monck's rooms, which one day must surely be refurnished. The upstairs rooms retain some wallpaper but otherwise the house is bleak.

The two-storey Pillar Hall at Belsay is surrounded by a colonnade at both levels. The supporting columns on the ground floor are Ionic, and those on the first floor Doric, a reversal of the conventional architectural order which calls for the simplest style of column to be placed at the lowest level.

Chillingham castle

☆☆☆☆ A medieval castle with Jacobean improvements

At Chillingham, 17 miles S of Berwick-upon-Tweed; private house, open part year

The castle stands four-square in the heart of Northumberland, a landscape so deserted and dramatic as to seem like Tolkien's Middle Earth. Chillingham has long been famous for its breed of white upland cattle, threatened by European legislation. It is equally notable for its obsessive restoration over twenty years. The castle was gifted in 1981 to Sir Humphry Wakefield, husband of Katherine, whose family, the Greys, were ancestral holders of the castle since the 13th century. The place was, he says in the Chillingham guidebook, 'a roofless, floorless wreck of a castle with *jungle* having taken over the gardens and grounds'.

The building is at the end of a long drive, a pile of grey walls battlemented and with narrow stone windows. The original pele tower stands to the left of the entrance, with the old hall and second tower running at right angles behind it. A Jacobean entrance was then sandwiched across the front, probably to welcome James VI of Scotland on his way south in 1603. This progress was a huge event in the social and architectural life of the North, signalling as it did the onset of (relative) peace along the Border.

Through the entrance is a tall and impressive medieval courtyard of hard grey stone. On the far side rises the new Great Hall built in 1588. It is fronted by a Jacobean arcade above what appears to be a cloister, again probably a Jacobean addition. The far side of this range facing the garden has 18th-century windows. With battlemented towers on all four corners, the castle is hugely imposing.

The Great Hall has been stripped of later plaster and is displayed inside in medieval roughcast stone, festooned with pikes, antlers and elephant armour. Wakefield's magpie

Above Built in the 16th century, the Great Hall links the two south towers of the castle and is filled with assorted artefacts. The fireplaces are props from the 1998 film, *Elizabeth*; above them hang an elephant's chain-mail armour and a 17th century painting of riders and hounds chasing the Chillingham wild cattle which still roam the park. The chandeliers are mounted with antlers collected from Chillingham Park, and the bull-terrier is a famous Chillingham resident.

acquisition of anything he can find to fill his castle is eccentric. It includes Antarctic sledges. Yet his rescue has been thorough, Wakefield fighting the purists of English Heritage from room to room like a Hollywood musketeer.

The castle divides into the medieval chambers and the Jacobean state rooms. The former include a room used by Edward I in 1298 on his northern campaign. An eating room and chapel have been restored in the pele tower. The original 'minstrels' hall', now the restaurant, is presided over by what is alleged to be the world's biggest elk head. Dungeons have re-emerged beneath turrets, their walls marked with prisoners' carvings. Secret chambers have been opened onto roofs. There are fragments of medieval carving and dead bats everywhere.

Above The original pendant plaster ceiling of the James I drawing room, with its gilded ribs and pendants, has been fully restored. James I stayed at Chillingham twice: on the way to his coronation in 1603, and again in 1617, and is remembered in many of the castle's rooms. The ceiling and the elaborate armorial frieze date from the 1590s. The silk wall hangings come from a roll specially woven for the Duke of Devonshire; elsewhere hang Sir Humphrey's Wakefield armorial tapestries.

The three rooms built for James I's visit have been admirably restored. The drawing-room ceiling has geometrical patterning with pendants in rich cream and gold. The library overmantel is a superb example of 17th-century strapwork, framing the Grey coat of arms. Rich antique and reproduction furnishings and tapestries combine with roughcast stone walls, an authentic effect. Wakefield's hang of pictures is pleasantly idiosyncratic, with large white cows jostling Augustus John nudes.

The grounds have been restored in part as formal Italian parterres, in part as wild English garden. Like the house, the presence of a guiding spirit is everywhere. Chillingham is a case of house rescue as personal statement. It is most encouraging.

Chipchase castle

☆☆ A Jacobean house with Georgian additions and intact pele tower

Near Wark, 10 miles NW of Hexham; private house, open part year

Chipchase was the ancient seat of the Herons, lords of Tyndale and the Middle Marches. A hot-blooded family, their ambivalent relationship with both the Crown and the Scots made them rightly mistrusted. Their pele tower garrisoned fifty horsemen in time of war. Herons feuded both with their neighbours and with the Scots and their alliances were unreliable, perhaps understandable given their Border location. They did not long survive the modern age. The last Heron died penniless in a Marylebone garret in 1749. The house passed to a merchant, John Reed, and in 1862 to the Taylor family, whose descendants, the Tordays, maintain it to this day.

Chipchase overlooks the North Tyne in wild country on the edge of Wark Forest. From the south, we see the L-shaped Jacobean mansion with porch built on the site of an earlier house by Cuthbert Heron in 1621. With the coming of peace the Herons, like the Greys of Chillingham, gave their house a pacific face. In 1784 the Reeds georgianized the exterior and interior, inserting sashes in the side range and even the pele tower. The building, all of soft grey stone, is thus a delightful puzzle, of different periods yet all of a piece.

The post-medieval interiors are those of a comfortable mansion. The hall is now a sitting room with a remarkable set of cupboards for fishing tackle. A fine plaster ceiling survives in the drawing room. Most remarkable is the billiard room. The ceiling is vaguely Rococo but the chief glory is an imported Flemish overmantel depicting the March of Time: a chariot drawn by winged horses carries the world forward, surrounded by continents and biblical scenes.

The pele tower is reached from outside. The roofline is unmistakably medieval, with heavy machicolations and corner turrets. Inside is the familiar tower arrangement, with vaulted ground floor and three storeys above, of increasing security and thus importance. A lower hall, above the basement, was for the servants and soldiers. An upper hall, much grander, was for the family. It has sleeping chambers and garderobes in the corners. An oratory was also created within the wall's thickness. The tower is a fine survival, with its roof of stone slabs intact and its fortifications still trumpeting defiance of the Scots.

Cragside

☆☆☆☆ Norman Shaw's romantic masterpiece, built for Lord Armstrong

Near Rothbury, 12 miles NW of Morpeth; National Trust, open part year

Cragside is the creation of arms and the man. The arms were those of the Tyneside manufacturer, William Armstrong. The man was his architect, Richard Norman Shaw. The house they built on the wooded slopes overlooking Coquetdale embodied the mid-Victorian romantic ideal. Here were Gothic, baronial, Tudor and Jacobean fused into one. The mixture was to become familiar from the heights of Simla to the suburbs of Melbourne.

Armstrong was a titan of Tyneside industry. A local man, he trained as a mechanic and a lawyer. Throughout his life he 'swung like an erratic pendulum between the law office and the lathe'. He made waterworks, cranes, engines, guns and finally warships. In his old age he bought Bamburgh Castle (see page 106) for a nursing home, although this never materialized and the castle passed to a distant cousin adopted as his heir, as did Cragside on Armstrong's death in 1900. Within a decade, his heir had succeeded in dissipating the £1.4 million Armstrong fortune and had to sell the most valuable works of art. The house passed to the National Trust in 1977. It is set in a magnificent 1,700 acres of forests, drives and glades. The Douglas firs in front of the house include the highest tree in England.

Cragside had been built modestly in 1863, as Armstrong's weekend retreat, in countryside that he had known as a boy. In 1869, he asked Norman Shaw to expand it from lodge to mansion. The job took fifteen years, with Armstrong always at Shaw's elbow. They made Cragside a citadel of domestic technology. It was the first house to have hydraulic electric power and, in 1880, the first to have installed electric filament lamps. As at other houses with such lamps, guests were given cushions at dinner with which to smother flash fires.

The original house was steeply gabled on a bare hillside. Shaw added wings, drawing rooms, towers as and when Armstrong decided. The walls are of creamy stone with Elizabethan mullioned windows. The upper floors are timbered and gabled. The result is a romantic woodland folly, as if Ludwig of Bavaria had opted for 'Tudorbethan' rather than German Gothic. Armstrong's customers were ferried up from Newcastle at weekends. Japanese, Persian, Siamese and German dignitaries paid court to the man who equipped their armies and built their navies. They left an astonishing assortment of gifts now shared with Bamburgh.

The plan of the house is simpler than the exterior suggests. It is of reception rooms on the ground floor with kitchens and services closely adjacent. Bedrooms and 'day rooms' are above. A later addition was the astonishing suite of rooms across the arch in the courtyard, containing surely the world's biggest inglenook. Rooms are richly Victorian, mostly with panelled walls and ceilings and heavily curtained. This makes the house dark, exaggerated by enveloping evergreens and by conservators keeping blinds drawn. Add in the Northumbrian weather and we have a citadel of gloom, not at all Shaw's intention.

The chief reception rooms on the ground floor are the library and dining room. The library has glorious views over the ravine and is strongly Pre-Raphaelite in character, with Burne-Jones and Ford Madox Brown windows, de Morgan tiles and paintings by Spencer-Stanhope. The onyx fire surround was acquired on a sales

'The house ... **embodied** the mid-Victorian **romantic ideal.**'

Above The library at Cragside was the first room in the world to have a permanent system of incandescent electric lighting, powered by hydro-electricity.
Left The Owl Suite was created for a visit to Cragside of the Prince and Princess of Wales in 1884. Among the furniture commissioned for the rooms are the black walnut beds, designed by Norman Shaw and decorated with the carved owls that give these rooms their name.
Above right The drawing room was completed in time for the royal visit and gave Cragside a much-needed large and more formal reception space. But when a fire was lit in the magnificent marble chimneypiece it was as much for show as for warmth since the room had its own boiler and heating system, hidden below.

An additional tower suite of bedrooms was added in the 1870s for special guests. The sumptuous Owl Rooms are an up-market garret, panelled in American black walnut with coved ceilings and Shaw's great owl beds. It was here that the then Prince and Princess of Wales stayed in 1884, a scene much recorded in the house.

The gallery forms a corridor to the later drawing room wing added by Shaw in 1883. It is sadly denuded of Armstrong's Victorian pictures, and now contains mostly lesser works. The drawing room, however, is sensational, top-lit with a coved ceiling of ornate neo-Jacobean plasterwork. The chimneypiece of the inglenook is grander than anything of its sort in England, although it compares with a smaller one also by Shaw at Flete, in Devon. It is a room within a room, made entirely of marble and encrusted with Elizabethan relief statuary, swirls and motifs. It is the work of Shaw's assistant, the Arts and Crafts designer, W. R. Lethaby. The interior is lined in marble and the fireplace was designed to burn peat, the smoke escaping underground.

On the walls hang surviving pictures from the Armstrong collection, most of them concerned with mortality. The theme seems fitting for a man whose works caused so much death and destruction.

trip to Egypt. The dining room contains a Gothic inglenook, with stained glass, deep settles and magnificent brass fire irons. Emmerson's portrait of Armstrong relaxing on one of these settles embodies modest Victorian plutocracy. He is in slippers and reading a paper, his dogs sitting content beneath Burne-Jones's ladies. 'East or West, Hame's Best' says the mantelpiece.

The National Trust has restored the Cragside kitchens and plunge baths, leaving us sorry that neither is in use. A narrow wooden staircase with heraldic beasts leads to an upstairs passage with the principal bedrooms and sitting rooms. These have been furnished in the Trust's most assiduous style, making Cragside a northern Lanhydrock (Cornwall). However, the celebrated view from the morning room over the ravine is not permitted for fear of fading the fabrics. Oh dear. The Bamboo Room has Morris's 'Willow' design throughout.

Langley castle

☆☆ Fortified hall keep, restored by Victorian antiquarian

Near Haydon Bridge, 6½ miles W of Hexham; now a hotel

The castle lies hidden in a forest like something from an Arthurian romance. Langley is a hall keep, fortified by the de Lucy family in 1365, burnt out in the 15th century but well restored by the Northumberland antiquarian, Cadwallader Bates, in 1882. He moved there in 1897.

Northumberland's Victorian historian, J. Hodgson, enthused that Langley Castle 'bids stern defiance to the attacks of time, as if determined once again to resume its roof and hang out over its battlements its blue flag and pillared canopy of morning smoke, as emblems of joy and high-minded hospitality'. Langley is now a luxury hotel.

The rectangular keep is massive yet consists of just one large chamber on each floor. The corner towers contain extensive stairs and chambers. The garderobes are considered the finest anywhere. The original entrance, designed for security, is in the wall facing the garden, through a small door leading to a spiral staircase. The present Victorian stair is in the garderobe tower, its windows formed from the old latrine cubicles. The battlements and most of the Gothic windows are 19th century.

The old basement is now a low-ceilinged dining room. The first floor hall, now the drawing room, has a massive fireplace and some medieval slit windows. The second floor has been divided into bedrooms and the third is a function room. When Bates restored the house, he burned fires in every medieval hearth, but still found the place cold and damp.

The view from the roof is over woods and fields to Hadrian's Wall. The south-east turret is believed to have contained a chapel. This was restored in Bates's memory by his widow.

Lindisfarne castle

★★★ Elizabethan fortress, refashioned by Lutyens

At Holy Island, 10 miles SE of Berwick-upon-Tweed; National Trust, open part year

Lindisfarne is a castle-lover's castle, albeit born of a 20th-century sense of the picturesque. The neighbouring priory, founded by St Aidan in 635, ranks among the most historic sites of Christianity. Its ruin lies adjacent to the village of Holy Island on a sandy spit off the Northumberland coast. The island is inaccessible at high tide.

The castle lies on the tip of the island, a mile beyond the priory. Here Elizabeth I built a fortress in 1570, whose ruin appealed to Edward Hudson, the founder of *Country Life*. In 1902, he took a lease from the Crown and commissioned his friend and protégé, Edwin Lutyens, to rebuild it. Like Castle Drogo, in Devon, Lindisfarne displays Lutyens' talent at turning medieval forms to the needs of Edwardian comfort. The castle was never more than a holiday home and Hudson sold it in 1921. It passed to the National Trust in 1944.

Even modernized, Lindisfarne was to be emphatically medieval. There was just one bathroom, open fires for heat and candles for light. There was none of Norman Shaw's Cragside (see page 116) mod cons. Yet, like Drogo, this remains a house. There are no battlements and the outline from most angles is stark, almost Modernist. Access is by a ramp from the seaward side.

The entrance hall is 'Norman', with thick-set arches and a wide fireplace. A large wind indicator is decorated by the Arts and Crafts artist, Macdonald Gill (brother of Eric), with scenes from the Armada. The dining room and Ship Room, the two principal rooms on the lower battery floor, retain the vaulting of the old castle. Thick stone walls turn into barrel vaults, stained, calcified and rugged. The Ship Room was once the old gunpowder store and contains a charming Dutch Rococo china cabinet. The stone-vaulted roof is almost claustrophobic.

Left The Dutch Rococo cabinet in the Ship Room is decorated with painted panels that show scenes of peasant life. The room takes its name from the model of a 19th-century Dutch ship – the *Henrietta* – that hangs from the barrel-vaulted ceiling. **Below left** The Long Gallery is one of only a few completely new rooms created by Lutyens at Lindisfarne. It linked the new bedrooms with the living rooms downstairs. Another piece of important Dutch furniture stands against one wall – an upright cupboard, known as an aumbry, that probably came from a church. It is fitted with a water container and a small basin where vessels used in worship could be washed.

The upper battery floor is now a Long Gallery, with bedrooms leading off it. These have been furnished with vernacular pieces and whitewashed, monastery style. Bold Lutyens arches divide up the spaces. Steps lead from the gallery to the upper gallery, together forming the main reception space of the castle. The floors are carpeted and fireplaces are everywhere. In the upper gallery, Hudson's friend, Mme Guilhermina Suggia, would play Bach on the cello, as dramatically depicted by Augustus John in his Tate Britain portrait of her.

The deep windows look out, most days, onto a bleak grey North Sea. Many visitors, including Lutyens' wife, found Lindisfarne a miserable, smoky place. Yet it is one of Lutyens' most successful small works, quirkily medieval. His friend, Gertrude Jekyll, paid a visit to Lindisfarne in 1906, accompanied by a raven and a bag of bull's-eyes, to suggest the planting of a Walled Garden. It was a brave project for such a site but her flowers survive to this day.

On the night of 18th November 1772, Bessie Surtees climbed out of one of the first-floor windows of her father's house and down a waiting ladder to elope with John Scott.

NEWCASTLE UPON TYNE

Bessie Surtees house

☆ Rare survival of a 17th-century town house

Sandhill, Newcastle upon Tyne; English Heritage, open all year

Given the devastation visited on much of Newcastle by Victorian and late 20th-century development, the survival of a group of houses on the quayside is remarkable. They are sandwiched between the Tyne Bridge, Swing Bridge and High Level Bridge, beneath the castle. Nos. 41–44 are owned by English Heritage and house its northern headquarters. The left-hand house has a Georgian brick front and 17th-century interior much rebuilt and redecorated. The other two houses retain their timbered façades. No. 41 is Bessie Surtees House.

It is named after the daughter of the owner in the 18th century, who eloped with a coal merchant's son, John Scott. The young man later rose to become the celebrated Lord Chancellor, Lord Eldon. All were later reconciled. The house rises through five storeys. Later shop-fronts form the ground floor. Above are three storeys of continuous fenestration. Fluted pilasters, forming a smart 'curtain wall' above the jutting ends of the floor joists, divide the window frames.

The three houses were vigorously restored by Lord Gort in the 1930s. His wife was a Surtees and he was eager to preserve a corner of old Newcastle in her name. Most of the interiors are now offices, but two superb 17th-century rooms survive. That on the first floor has fluted classical pilasters and ornate panelling over its fireplace, with an accomplished plasterwork ceiling. It was from this room that Bessie is said to have eloped, presumably via the window.

The Castle

☆☆ Substantial Norman castle keep

Castle Garth, Newcastle upon Tyne; museum, open all year

Newcastle keep is the principal relic of one of the finest Norman castles in England, comparable in its completeness with Dover, in Kent, and Hedingham, in Essex. It rises mighty and black in early pictures of the city. Today, it sits rather pathetically next to a railway bridge, surrounded by the detritus of the inner city. The keep is now split from its protective Black Gate but survives intact.

The 'new castle' was built on the foundations of the old Roman fort by William the Conqueror's son, Robert, in 1080. The rebuilding was begun by Henry II in 1168 and maintained throughout the Middle Ages. The keep was fortified in the Civil War and restored in the 19th century, when the battlements were added. Much masonry has been replaced, but the form of a royal palace-fort survives, with its forebuilding and steps up to the Great Hall.

At the bottom are the customary dungeons and storerooms. Beneath the entrance stairs is a chapel, with Norman dogtooth decoration on its vault ribs. Next door is a vaulted garrison room, surrounded by walls of massive thickness. Above are two storeys of residential chambers, the lower for the constable, the other the Great Hall. Both have private solars built into the thickness of their flanking walls, along with garderobes and window slits. The Great Hall has been spoilt with modern display cases, but the King's Chamber off it remains plain, with stone floor and walls and a dogtooth arch to its fireplace.

As at Dover, the Great Hall has a gallery cut into the wall above it, from which retainers and others could watch the proceedings below. A maze of stairs, some straight, some spiral, fill the wall spaces, and seems to have been hewn from within the walls. One rises to the roof, from which there is an excellent view of central Newcastle and its celebrated bridges.

NEWCASTLE UPON

Preston tower

☆ Medieval pele tower, reduced in the 17th century

At Preston, 7 miles N of Alnwick; private house, open part year

Preston is a curiosity. It was a sizeable fortified pele or hall keep, built in 1392. After the passing of the Scottish threat in 1603, the tower was vertically sliced in half and the materials used to build an abutting farmstead. In the 19th century this farm was removed and replaced by buttresses and a belltower. The result is half a keep and two of the original corner towers.

The tower is exhibited with panache by the owner of the adjacent manor. The ground floor has a guardroom and prison cell. A narrow ladder leads to a fragment of the old Hall, with two tower rooms off it. One has been re-created as a medieval bedroom, the other as a living room. They admirably re-create their medieval appearance. Above is a small exhibition of the Battle of Flodden Field of 1513.

There is a fine, wild view from the roof of the tower over the Northumbrian plain to Bamburgh on the coast – England still unspoilt.

What a sad place! Having crossed miles of outer Tyneside, the road reaches the coast and a vista of power stations and wind turbines. Unlike Preston Tower (see page 125) this is England raped by the 20th century. Yet it was not always so. Seaton Delaval was a mansion built for Admiral George Delaval in 1718. Members of the family were notorious for their beauty, debauchery and violence, all of which seem to have been genetic. Sacheverell Sitwell remarked that the women were all lovely, while 'the males of the family drank to excess and fell down dead, never in their beds'.

In honour of these traits, John Vanbrugh gave Delaval one of his most powerful and original designs. The house was gutted in 1822, when a jackdaws' nest in an uncleaned chimney caught fire. It was never restored. Though re-roofed, its blackened façade still gazes bleakly out towards the shore. Lord and Lady Hastings, Delaval's (thoroughly sober) descendants, inhabit one flanking wing. The other is occupied by Vanbrugh's magnificent stables, among the finest in the country. Each horse had its own stall, with a classical niche for its hay and its name above.

Seaton Delaval hall

☆☆ Magnificent remains of ruined Vanbrugh mansion

Near Seaton Delaval, 9 miles NE of Newcastle upon Tyne; private house, open part year

Left At first glance, Seaton Delaval's Great Hall appears to have lost none of its grandeur. A closer inspection, however, reveals heat-scorched walls and fire-damaged statuary. Seaton Delaval was Vanbrugh's last, and some say greatest, commission and was finished in 1728, two years after his death. Although fairly modest in size Seaton Delaval is as imposing as Vanbrugh's other masterpieces, Castle Howard and Bleinheim Palace. **Far left** Vanbrugh designed Seaton Delaval around a central block, or *corps de logis*, that contained the Great Hall and other reception rooms. The block is flanked by two stair towers that still house cantilevered staircases, rising up through three storeys.

The house can be appreciated from outside even on days when it is not formally open. The front and back façades are composed of thrusting and receding bays, breaking the normal classical façade into what appears an operatic stage set. Three pavilions crown the roof on either side. A wide flight of steps leads up to the entrance, flanked by two massive attached columns. The sight through the front door into the main hall is surreal, offering a clear view to the back door, daylight and a distant obelisk beyond.

This is an eerie place, as if the fire were only yesterday. The stone walls of the Great Hall are still scorched pink, the fireplaces empty and the decorative statues broken and ragged. To the rear is the saloon, with fluted pilasters and the ghosts of Delaval beauties gliding overhead. On each side, Vanbrugh's cantilevered staircases rise to balconies overlooking the Hall.

The vaulted basements are green, damp and mysterious. The upper floors are mostly derelict, though one room has been restored as a 'tapestry room' with wall-hangings and faded pictures. A 'mahogany room' on the ground floor displays old photographs of the house in happier times, and of the Hastings family's other seat at Melton Constable in Norfolk. Seaton Delaval is used for concerts, but surely merits restoration and a grander role in Northumberland's revival.

Wallington hall
☆☆☆☆ Georgian house with Victorian central hall and Pre-Raphaelite art
Near Cambo, 12 miles W of Morpeth; National Trust, open part year, garden open all year
'This is more than a historic house.
It is a place to inflame the imagination ...'

Below Four grinning griffins' heads stand in a row on Wallington's east lawn. They originally stood on Bishopsgate, in the City of London, and were rescued by Sir Walter Calverley Blackett (1707–77). He had them placed around Rothley Castle, a folly he built in the Wallington park, but they were moved to their current position by Mary, Lady Trevelyan (1881–1966).

Wallington is more than the sum of its parts. Ostensibly an 18th-century mansion with dignified Georgian rooms, it was for a century and a half the home of the liberal-minded Trevelyans. Before them, it belonged to the Newcastle tycoons, the Blacketts, and before them the Fenwicks, pugnacious grandees of Northumberland since the Middle Ages. Sir William Blackett, who bought Wallington from the last Fenwick in 1688, demolished it and built what amounted to a shooting box. Such was the scale of Blackett's entertainment that six servants were retained specifically to carry drunken guests upstairs to their chambers.

It was Blackett's grandson, Walter, who, with architect David Garrett, remodelled the old house in a Palladian style in the years following 1738 and imported 'a colony' of Italian plasterers to decorate the interior. Sir Walter epitomized the Georgian gentleman who 'kept many thousand hands in motion'. On his death, the estate passed to his nephew, one of the Cornwall Trevelyans, a family celebrated for the length of their noses and the breadth of their opinions.

Modern Wallington is essentially the house of the Trevelyans. The young Sir John Trevelyan was an early aesthete and enthusiast of the French Revolution. He and his clever wife, Maria, turned Wallington into a place of art and science. Their son, Walter, was a serious-minded polymath and ardent teetotaller. He ordered the Wallington cellars to be locked throughout his life. He bequeathed what was by then one of England's great wine collections to a local vicar, to be used 'for scientific purposes'. It included port laid down for a visit of the Duke of Cumberland in 1745. Walter's artistic wife, Pauline, was a friend of Ruskin, Millais and the Carlyles and a patron of the Pre-Raphaelites.

Above Pauline Trevelyan intended Thomas Woolner's sculpture *Civilization* to be the 'crown and centre' of the hall. Sculpted between 1856 and 1867, it shows a mother teaching her child the Lord's Prayer. The walls between the piers on the ground floor of the hall were decorated by William Bell Scott with 'the history and worthies of Northumbria'. Scott also painted the spandrels around the upper level with illustrations inspired by the Border ballad *Chevy Chase*.

Walter left Wallington not to his heir but to a cousin whose radical politics he favoured. A grandson of that cousin, the Socialist MP Sir Charles Trevelyan, inherited in 1928. Distinguished Labour figures flocked to the Trevelyan table. It became the custom for Party grandees such as Attlee, Cripps, Bevan and Gaitskell to stay at Wallington rather than at a Durham boarding-house during their ritual attendance at the annual Miners' Gala. Sir Charles became the first landed aristocrat to give his entire estate to the National Trust, in 1937. His family were appalled and enraged. He pointed out that they were more likely to keep hold of the place with an assured tenancy than if the house were dissipated like many others by death duties. They in turn charged that he was a hypocrite, making his donation active only after his own death. The family still have a flat in the building.

The house is infused with the aura of a great Victorian family, dominated by the great central hall master-minded by Pauline Trevelyan. This was the old open courtyard, created as a roofed Italian cortile on the suggestion of John Ruskin in 1853. It is by the Newcastle architect, John Dobson.

The walls are painted with murals of Northumbrian scenes by William Bell Scott, a pupil of Rossetti. These include the *Arrival of the Danes*, the *Heroism of Grace Darling* and the *Triumph of Iron and Coal*. The panels are interspersed with native flora, painted on the pillars by Pauline and her

Above The drawing room, or saloon as it was known in the 18th century, is dominated by Sir Joshua Reynold's portrait of Sir Walter Calverley Blackett. The room was created during his remodelling of the house; prior to the 1740s the space had formed the main entrance hall. When Sir Walter inherited Wallington from his mother's brother in 1728 it was on condition that he took the Blackett name – he was born a Calverley – and that he married his uncle's illegitimate daughter.

friends: Ruskin chose to paint cornflowers, yarrow, wild oats and wheat on his pillar. Two sculptures in the central hall, Thomas Woolner's *Civilization* and Alexander Munro's *Paolo and Francesca*, became Pre-Raphaelite icons.

After this, it is hard to adjust to the Blacketts' surrounding Rococo reception rooms, which the Trevelyans must have found intolerably old-fashioned. The dining room and saloon were decorated by Pietro Lafranchini, though the more recent colours are those of John Fowler. The rooms are filled with family portraits by Romney, Reynolds and Gainsborough, far distant in time and mood from the Trevelyans out in the Central Hall.

The library and study bring us back to the 19th century, with walls of heavy leather books and a National Trust 'random scatter' of newspapers and reading glasses. The remainder of the house is an engaging clutter: a corridor is lined with model soldiers, the nurseries upstairs are full of rocking horses, a needlework room is lined with examples of 18th-century embroidery in Rococo frames. A 'cabinet of curiosities' gathered by Maria Trevelyan's mother is just that, including a ferocious porcupine fish. This is more than a historic house. It is a place to inflame the imagination, a country house still with its *genius loci*.

Warkworth castle

★★ Grand medieval castle and ancient Percy seat

At Warkworth, 6 miles S of Alnwick; English Heritage, open all year

The castle, guarding a loop in the River Coquet, towers over its adjacent village. This is the angle from which it should be approached, since miserable housing estates picket the southern gate. Warkworth came to the Percys in 1332 and they turned it into one of the most sophisticated palace-keeps in England. Like other Percy properties, it was often confiscated but always returned. No king could rule the North without the Percys. It became derelict in the 16th century, when Shakespeare in *Henry IV* referred to the haunt of Harry Hotspur as 'this worm-eaten hold of ragged stone'.

The castle still formally belongs to the Duke of Northumberland. The 4th Duke had Anthony Salvin partly restore it in the 19th century. He re-roofed the keep and even furnished rooms in one of its towers, hoping to hold manorial courts in the keep hall. The plan came to nothing. Devoted to restoring Alnwick, the family has put Warkworth in English Heritage guardianship.

The castle has a curtain wall, gatehouse, separate Great Hall range and a keep shaped like a Maltese cross. This last rises magnificently over the town, complete to its roof and with its polygonal walls and unusual cruciform wings intact. The castle's outer bailey is entered through the gatehouse over a moat on its uphill side. On the left is the old Great Hall, a strangely gaunt ruin with a corner rising to a pinnacled tower. The ceremonial entrance survives, over which an eroded Percy lion stares defiant from its panel.

The keep is at the town end of the site. This was built for the 1st Earl of Northumberland on a single plan in the 1380s. It is of traditional keep form, with rooms stacked above each other on three floors. This plan is given the greatest elaboration. The central core has complex early plumbing. Tall ventilation shafts combine with a complex system of channels for collecting rainwater to clean floors and flush garderobes. Much of this survives, as does the suite of rooms restored by Salvin.

The ground floor is a warren of vaulted stone passages, cellars and service rooms, all carefully labelled. The main staircase is grand for a castle, indicating Warkworth's role as a palace. It rises past a delightful lobby, with stone seats and views over the town, to its internal hall. This has an oriel window and fireplace, with a large kitchen and buttery to one side. Next door is a chapel and the Great Chamber, with private chambers leading from it. Above is the solar with its own garderobe. The medieval corridors, tunnels and chambers of Warkworth, bare and ruined though they are, well recapture the proportions of a medieval interior.

Warkworth hermitage

☆ Rare surviving medieval hermitage, carved from the rock

At Warkworth, 6 miles S of Alnwick; English Heritage, open part year

This house, if so it can be called, lies embedded in the bank of the River Coquet outside the village of Warkworth, half a mile along the river. The site is reached from the castle by footpath and then boat, apparently inaccessible any other way. With its rocky foundation and canopy of trees, it might be located in an oriental jungle.

The structure consists of the remains of a hall with small fireplace, kitchen and latrine. There is another chamber above and a substantial chapel and sacristy, all apparently carved from the rockface. The chapel is a most remarkable survival, with ribbed vaulting and eroded Gothic windows. It has an altar and squint from the sacristy, suggesting that the chapel was not solely for the hermit's use. A carved depiction of the Nativity is just discernible in the window frame, and dates from the 14th century.

The earliest Warkworth hermits are not recorded, but one was well established by the 15th century, with a yearly stipend from the Percys of 66 shillings. A century later, the hermit was doubling as the Percys' Warkworth agent, with a salary of £13 and grazing rights in neighbouring fields. The hermitage was clearly a form of 'tied cottage'. The post did not survive the Reformation.

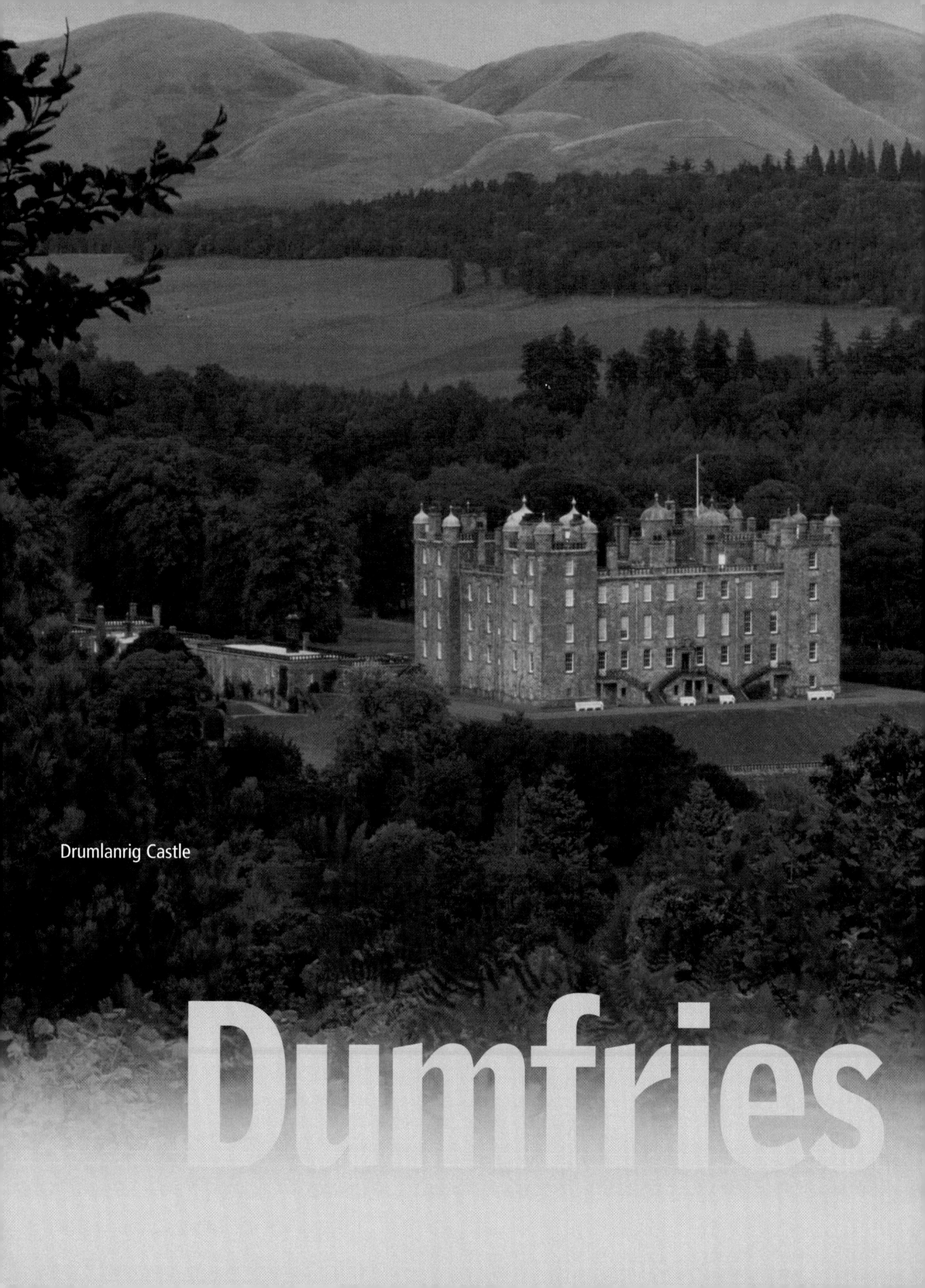

Drumlanrig Castle

Dumfries

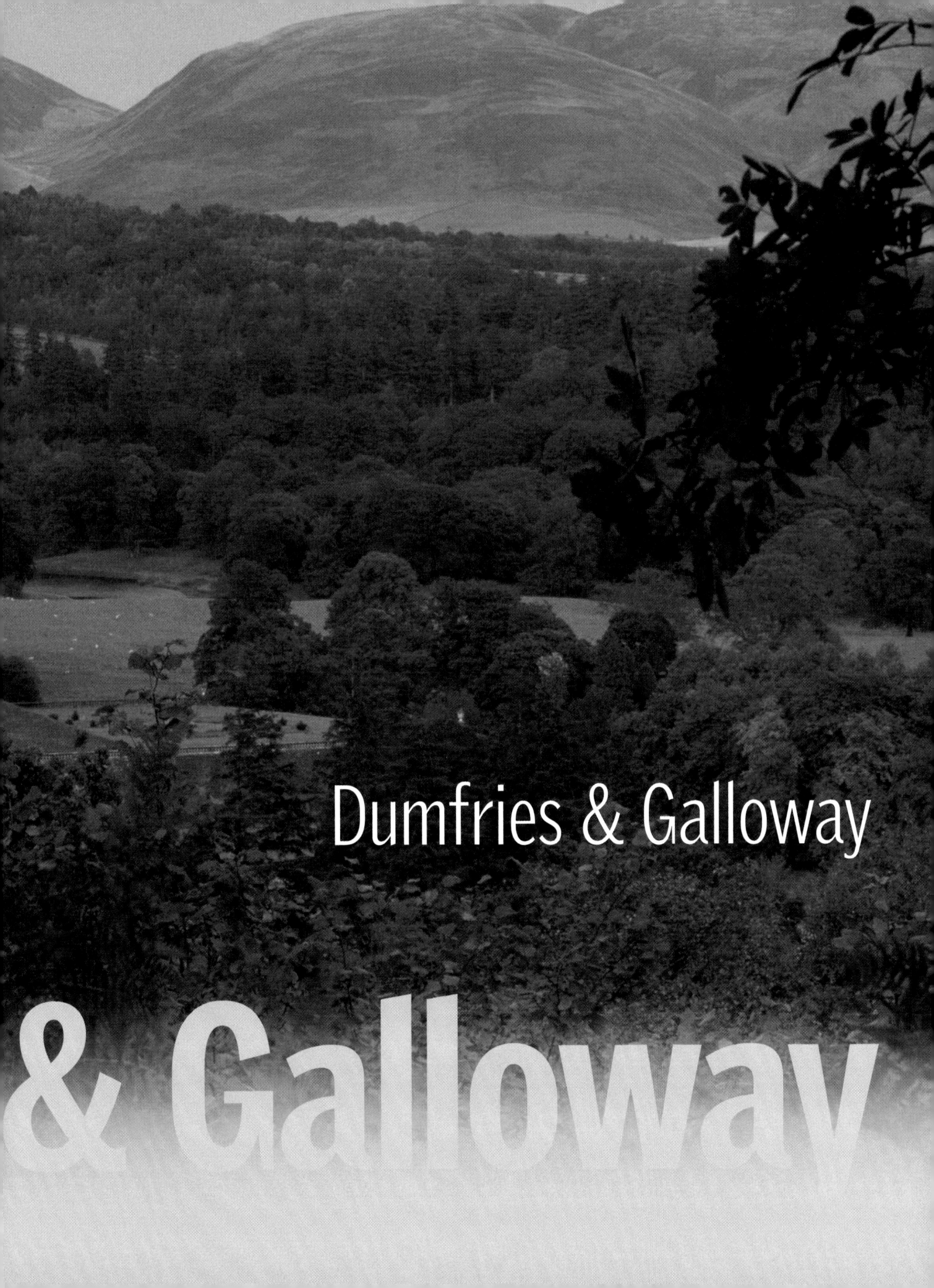
Dumfries & Galloway
& Galloway

Caerlaverock castle

★★★ Romantic ruined fortress with Renaissance architectural details

7 miles SE of Dumfries; Historic Scotland, open all year

Caerlaverock is one of the loveliest of ruined castles. Dating from the 1270s, it was one of several great 'castles of enclosure' built in Scotland in the 13th century. It was the chief stronghold of the Maxwells, a powerful family who, some 50 years before, had been granted estates in Galloway by Alexander II. The triangular ground-plan, which one medieval poet likened to a shield, is unique in Scottish architecture and is the castle's most distinctive feature. The approach is guarded by a massive gatehouse, flanked by a pair of drum towers, which originally contained the Maxwells' family apartment and a large vaulted hall. The other buildings that a household of this scale required were grouped around the three-sided court beyond.

Little of this original lay-out remains, for the castle was greatly altered in later years as the Maxwells responded to outbreaks of war and interludes of peace. Like many nobles of southwest Scotland, they played a fickle role in the Wars of Independence. In 1300 Caerlaverock was besieged and taken by Edward I, who nevertheless appointed Sir Eustace Maxwell as its constable. By 1312 Sir Eustace had come out in support of Robert Bruce and agreed to slight Caerlaverock's defences to deprive the English of its use. In time the castle was rebuilt, then partially demolished again in 1356

'... its tall, crenellated towers reflecting in the still waters of the moat.'

following another switch in loyalties. Despite such vicissitudes, the Maxwells managed to hold onto their lands and in the relatively peaceful 15th century they added a two-storey range along the west side of the courtyard; the gatehouse was strengthened and aesthetically improved. Renewed conflicts in the 16th century brought further damage and rebuilding, with the castle twice falling to the English.

The venerable fortress underwent its greatest transformation in the 1630s when Robert Maxwell, 1st Earl of Nithsdale, turned it into a magnificent Renaissance home. He rebuilt the south and east sides of the courtyard as a backdrop of ornate architecture symbolising lineage and power. Heraldic carvings and gloriously free-and-easy classical details hint at how Caerlaverock must have appeared in its few, final golden years when the Maxwells were at the zenith of their fortunes. It did not last long. In 1640 the castle suffered its final siege when the Catholic earl, with 200 soldiers, held out for 13 weeks against a Presbyterian Covenanting army. Once surrendered it was half demolished, its contents plundered and the Maxwells driven into exile. Ever since, it has remained a roofless shell, its tall, crenellated towers reflecting in the still waters of the moat.

Nearby, deep within the woods, the footings of an older stronghold have been excavated and conserved. Built in the early 13th century by John Maxwell, Chamberlain of Scotland, it was one of Scotland's first stone castles.

Drumlanrig castle

☆☆☆☆ Renaissance-style ducal palace and ancestral stronghold

18 miles NW of Dumfries; private house, open part year

The castle is first glimpsed from half a mile away, framed by a long straight avenue of trees. As the visitor advances the building swells almost imperceptibly, its towers and turrets shifting in perspective and proportion to perform a stately minuet against the sky. The great courtyard opens with a fanfare, its stairs curving up to a portico enriched with a chorus of columns, swags and crests. There is the final crescendo of the ducal coronet, raised high above the clock tower. Drumlanrig is an oratorio in stone celebrating lineage, power and tradition, a last spectacular flowering of Scottish Baroque before the Age of Reason demanded architectural restraint.

Drumlanrig is the seat of one of Scotland's oldest and proudest families. Sir James Douglas was knighted by Robert Bruce on the field of Bannockburn, and in 1330 he fulfilled his monarch's dying wish by carrying the Bruce's embalmed heart on crusade against the Moors in Spain. The Douglas motto 'Forward' and their crest of a winged heart – an omnipresent motif at Drumlanrig – stem from the legend that in one attack Sir James hurled the 'brave heart' forward into the thick of battle.

Ever loyal to Bruce and his descendants, the Douglas family were rewarded with titles and estates, and when the 2nd Earl died fighting at Otterburn in 1388, Drumlanrig was hived off from the Earldom to become the portion of a younger son, William. The Lords of Drumlanrig then steered their own course, rising through politics and marriage while other branches of the family declined. In 1675 another William Douglas, then 3rd Earl of Queensberry, began to rebuild the castle. By the time the work was finished some 15 years later, William was the 1st Duke and Drumlanrig stood much as it does today, a towering pink sandstone palace.

The 2nd Duke was Queen Anne's High Commissioner in Scotland who saw through the treaty of Union in 1707, but this success as a statesman brought more notoriety than respect among fellow Scots. Worse was to come. His demented eldest son infamously broke out of locked quarters in Queensberry House in Edinburgh to spit-roast and half-eat a kitchen-boy. Later in the century the 4th Duke, 'Old Q', financed his long life of excess by cutting down and selling ancient woods, provoking William Wordsworth to write a sonnet in complaint.

It seems there was bad blood in the male Douglas line, so it may have been fortunate that on Old Q's death in 1810 the Queensberry dukedom and Drumlanrig passed to a distant cousin, the 3rd Duke of Buccleuch, owner of Bowhill (see page 158). The present Duke – 9th of Buccleuch and 11th of Queensberry – remains Britain's largest individual landowner, with some 270,000 acres to his name. The woods devastated by Old Q have long been replanted and the Duke, a leading spokesman on country matters, takes great pride in their care.

The flamboyant family history is reflected in Drumlanrig. There have been three castles on the site in the past 600 years. Of the first no trace remains, for it was demolished in the mid-16th century to make way for a new 'house and pallice'. This, in turn, largely disappeared in the

'Drumlanrig is an oratorio in stone

celebrating lineage, power and tradition, ...'

Right In 1745 Prince Charles Edward Stuart and his force of Highlanders were in retreat. On 22nd December, the Young Pretender arrived at Drumlanrig and invited himself to stay. The room he occupied, known now as Bonnie Prince Charlie's bedroom, contains some of his personal effects, including his camp kettle and money box. Some of his accompanying supporters also left their mark on the castle. They vented their frustration on an equestrian portrait of William III by Sir Godfrey Kneller hanging in the staircase hall; traces of the damage done can still be seen.

1st Duke's rebuilding, although fragments survive: some basement vaults are plainly 16th century, for example, and on the east front blocked-in gun-loops can be seen. The old castle's sturdy iron yetts, or grilles, were retained to protect the entrances.

The castle's overall design has more than a hint of the ancestral stronghold, with corner towers and ranges enclosing a courtyard. There is also a similarity to Heriot's Hospital in Edinburgh, a Baroque masterpiece designed by William Wallace in 1628. But for sheer extravagance and nerve, Drumlanrig is altogether more extreme. The architect was probably James Smith, now remembered largely for the disciplined classicism of his later years. Here, however, he was perhaps recalling Renaissance palaces he had seen as a young man in Rome, where he briefly studied to be a priest.

In the 19th century, the old state apartments were re-arranged as less formal reception rooms and bedrooms, but the house remains palatial, with vast panelled rooms furnished with the heirlooms of three dukedoms. Leonardo da Vinci's *Madonna with the Yarnwinder*, once the pride of the art collection, no longer hangs in the staircase hall, having been stolen in a daylight robbery in 2003; valued at £30 million, it has vanished without trace. A Rembrandt and a Holbein are among the treasures that can still be seen. In contrast to this showy splendour, the morning room in the southeast tower is used by the present Duke when he comes to stay. Cluttered and comfy, with an open fire, framed photographs and tasselled lampshades, it is an authentic example of modern country-house style.

Far left Full-length portraits of James I and his Queen, Anne of Denmark, hang at one end of the drawing room, between them a Lely of Charles II. A large French cabinet stands beneath the smaller portrait; a slightly smaller but very similar piece stands at the opposite end of the room. Both were made for Versailles, *c*1675, and were believed to have been presented to Charles II by Louis XIV of France. **Left** An unusual portrait of the present Duchess hangs above the fireplace in the morning room. Painted by John Merton in 1957, the Duchess, then Countess of Dalkeith, is framed by a *trompe-l'oeil* arch. It has the distinction of being the only picture to receive an 'A' award from the Royal Academy during the 20th century.

Ecclefechan: Carlyle's birthplace

☆ The modest birthplace of a renowned Victorian writer

High Street, Ecclefechan; National Trust for Scotland, open part year

The writings of Thomas Carlyle are now so profoundly out of fashion that it is hard to appreciate his former influence and fame. As an historian and essayist he tapped into the self-improving mind-set of Victorian Britain and by the time of his death, in 1881, he was a national institution. His London home in Cheyne Row, Chelsea, was at once turned into a shrine. Carlyle's birthplace in the village of Ecclefechan has also been preserved and, some would say, it is more entertaining to visit than his books are to read.

The tiny cottage is one of a pair built by Carlyle's father and uncle, both master-masons who built many such dwellings in the area, of which this is a rare unaltered survivor. Consisting of a downstairs kitchen with an upstairs bedroom and a closet, it has remained structurally unchanged since the time of the writer's birth in 1795. It is a typical home of those families such as the Carlyles, hard-working products of the kirk and village school, who formed the backbone of rural Scotland in the early 19th century.

The house's contents are an odd but interesting mix of mementoes from the era of Carlyle's fame. There are books and manuscripts from Cheyne Row, along with rustic items more in keeping with the house, such as the giant oatmeal chest that has pride of place in the kitchen. Although the family (which eventually included nine children) moved to a slightly larger house when Carlyle was three years old, he never lost touch with his Ecclefechan roots and was buried in the village churchyard, having instructed his executors to refuse a tomb in Westminster Abbey.

Ellisland farm

The home of poet Robert Burns when he returned to life as a farmer

At Auldgirth, 6 miles N of Dumfries; museum, open all year

The three years that Robert Burns spent at Ellisland were among the happiest of his life and he wrote some of his best-remembered works here, including 'Auld Lang Syne' and 'Tam O'Shanter'. He was 29 when he took a lease on the farm in 1788. His first poems had been published two years earlier and caused a literary sensation that saw him lionized by Edinburgh society. Celebrity did not ensure an income, however, so to subsidize his literary career and support his marriage to childhood sweetheart, Jean Armour, he reverted to his old persona as a farmer, with help from one of his growing band of patrons.

Burns himself described Ellisland as 'a plain and simple domicile for humility and contentment', but it was not exactly an ordinary farm by the time he had completed its rebuilding. The farmhouse was architect-designed (by Thomas Boyd of Dumfries), with a parlour overlooking wooded banks above the River Nith rather than the farmyard. Burns proved as hopeless at farming as at holding onto any money that he earned, and in 1789 he took a post as local excise officer paying £50 a year. Two years later the promise of a better salary drew him to Dumfries, where he died, famous but penniless, in 1796.

The farm was altered in the 1820s and passed through several owners before it was given to the nation by John Williamson of Edinburgh in 1928. It is hard to know what remains from Burns' sojourn. Manuscripts and mementoes are displayed in the parlour and the kitchen range is supposedly the one on which he would have dried his socks. There is a 'Tam O'Shanter Walk' along a picturesque path above the river where it is said that he composed the poem. Yet even if the farm in its present form dates largely from the 19th century, only a cynic could complain. As in any shrine it is the aura that counts, and Ellisland conveys the sense that Burns once occupied this space and enjoyed these views.

KIRKCUDBRIGHT

Broughton house

☆ Artist's home with spectacular gallery

High Street, Kirkcudbright; National Trust for Scotland, open part year

Above At the rear of Broughton House is the garden, leading down to the Dee estuary. Many of its features were designed by E.A. Hornel himself and the influence of his visits to Japan can be seen in some of the planting schemes. **Right** The gallery that Hornel added to his house is hung with examples of his work. On his death, Hornel left his house and contents to the town as a gallery and library 'for the benefit of the people of the Stewartry and visitors thereto'. As well as his paintings, this included a collection of about 25,000 books and manuscripts, mostly of local interest.

In the late 19th century a group of artists known as the Glasgow Boys earned themselves a reputation as Scotland's avant garde. Their style was colourful and naturalistic, and as well as painting Glasgow they were attracted by scenes of rural life, which led them to the quiet town of Kirkcudbright. E. A. Hornel, one of their leading lights, came from a family long connected with the town, and in 1901 he purchased Broughton House, where he lived until his death in 1933.

At first sight Broughton appears to be a little-changed mid-18th-century town house with cosy, cluttered rooms. Such provincial modesty is utterly contradicted by the extension that Hornel had built at the rear. His studio here is as fine a working space as any artist could desire, while the salon – an enormous top-lit gallery by Glasgow architect John Keppie – is a room of breathtaking ostentation. Here, Hornel entertained smart Edinburgh society at private exhibitions of his work. A giant frieze, copied from the Elgin Marbles, runs around the mahogany panelled walls. The marble fireplace is so monumentally ornate it might be mistaken for a papal tomb. The paintings on display today are mostly from the artist's sentimental later years when success had dulled his youthful verve.

Broughton was taken over by the National Trust for Scotland in 1997. Since then more than £1 million has been spent on conservation, including the reinstatement of original decorative schemes. Almost better than the house itself is the lushly planted garden which appears in many of Hornel's works, disguised as wild countryside.

MacLellan's castle

☆ Ruins of an notable 16th-century town-centre mansion house

Castle Street, Kirkcudbright; Historic Scotland, open part year

In the eyes of the 19th-century Romantics, any Scottish ruin more than two storeys high had to be a castle, and with its rough stone walls and roofless towers MacLellan's appears to fit the bill. But this so-called castle was in fact a large, luxurious town-house. When newly built in the 1570s, it would have looked very different indeed, its walls encased in harling and painted a rich cream or saffron yellow. Corbelled turrets and ornamented windows added a picturesque touch; a few ill-positioned gun-loops were its only concession to defence. The apartments were stacked one above another over vaulted cellars and kitchen, in traditional Scots manner, but the broad staircase would have been a most impressive innovation for the time.

The house was built by Sir Thomas MacLellan, Provost of the burgh of Kirkcudbright, Collector of Customs and the richest man for miles around. Sir Thomas was the scion of a well-connected local family noted for their bravery in battle, but he himself was a man of less heroic talents that enabled him to thrive in an opportunistic age. A hint of the methods he used can be found on the first-floor landing, where a small chamber is equipped with a 'laird's lug' – a listening device that allowed him to eavesdrop on visitors in the Great Hall next door. Following his death, in 1597, his fortune was squandered by his son. By 1742 the house was a roofless shell. The last of Sir Thomas's descendants, though bearing the title Lord Kirkcudbright, was reduced to selling gloves in Edinburgh.

Rammerscales

☆ Georgian family hillside home, overlooking Anandale

7 miles E of Dumfries; private house, open part year

From its perch on the crest of a high wooded ridge, Rammerscales looks down over the fields and villages of Anandale as though delivering a lecture on the moral principles of classical design. Austerely rectilinear and restrained, it rejects Scottish architecture's old flamboyance in favour of a truly British uniformity. It is just the kind of medium-sized country seat that a sophisticated gentleman required in the mid 18th century, when even Edinburgh was being reinvented in a new modern style.

The architect was probably a local master-builder, although the quality of stonework and modernity of design suggest an unusual talent. Slightly more is known about the man for whom the house was built. Dr James Mounsey rose to the rank of privy councillor in the Russian Imperial court, becoming personal physician to the Tsarina. More dangerously, following her death he served her nephew, the wildly unpopular Tsar Peter III. In the autumn of 1762, when Catherine the Great staged a *coup d'etat* and deposed – by some accounts murdered – her husband, the good doctor returned hurriedly to his native land, where he had already bought a small estate in readiness for his retirement. The story goes that Rammerscales acquired its hidden spiral stair and several exits to each room because Mounsey had such a morbid fear of assassination at the hands of secret agents.

Following Mounsey's eventual death from natural causes, the house was sold in 1797 to James Bell, a Glasgow sugar baron, whose descendants live there still. It is elegantly furnished, with the layers of character and domesticity that come from long habitation by a family that holds onto mementoes of the past. The best room is the library, which runs the full length of the top floor. It was built to house the 6,000 books that belonged to William Bell Macdonald, a Victorian polymath who was fluent in more than a dozen languages, including Sanskrit, Coptic and Cree. The vast, dusty room recalls an age when the pursuit of knowledge was a gentlemanly pastime.

Shambellie house

Baronial-style Victorian home and museum of costume

7 miles S of Dumfries; museum, open part year

When newly built in the 1850s, Shambellie was the height of fashion. Its Scots-baronial architecture celebrated a romantic vision of the past, but it was a house designed for modern life with all the benefits of up-to-date technology, including lavatories, a hot-water boiler and a purpose-built bathroom. In an age of rigid hierarchies and divisions, just as every member of the household had a place, each room had its own specific purpose, with the Master in his business-room, the children in their nursery and servants in the basement underneath.

The house was built for William Stewart, whose family had been local lairds as far back as the 15th century. The total cost was just under £3,000 but the project proved a nightmare. Stewart was a careful man but his architect, David Bryce, was contemptuous of budgetary restraints. At the top of his profession, Bryce had expected his client to commission a much grander home.

The last of William Stewart's descendants to live at Shambellie was his great-grandson Charles, a fanatical collector of costumes and accessories who described his obsession as a form of 'holy greed'. In 1977 he donated his home and vast collection to the National Museums of Scotland. The rooms, which have been little altered since first built, are arranged as tableaux of country-house life from different periods between the 1880s and the 1950s, with figures in appropriate clothing. In any conventional museum, such set-pieces would look contrived. Here, in a house caught in a fully furnished time-warp, they are both informative and strangely convincing.

Threave house

Victorian shooting lodge with 1930s interiors

Near Castle Douglas; 16 miles SW of Dumfries; National Trust for Scotland, open part year

Houses cared for by the National Trust can sometimes give a false impression of the past, preserving only the exceptional and rare. Not so Threave, which feels typical of 1930s life, the white emulsion and restrained decor reflecting British taste in the age of Art Deco and Modernist design. It is not a style that gets the pulse racing, and nor is it intended to – it is a look that has survived shifts of fashion for more than 70 years. For many visitors, it is how a perfect home should be.

The house is a relatively modest exercise in Scots-baronial style, designed in 1871 by Edinburgh architects Peddie & Kinnear as a shooting lodge for William Gordon, a Scots-born businessman from Liverpool. The original, darkly panelled High Victorian interiors have largely gone, and the rooms have been refurbished to their arrangement between the two world wars, when Gordon's widow Kitty and her two unmarried sons entertained guests from London in fashionable style. The bedrooms are spartan. Excessive comfort would have been considered vulgar and guests were not encouraged to stay for longer than a weekend, with wildfowling on the river the main attraction of the visit. Although a re-creation of the past, the house would still pass muster as a country hotel.

In 1957, when the National Trust for Scotland acquired Threave House as part of the Threave Estate, Victorian architecture was so despised that its demolition was seriously proposed. Reprieved, it became a residential school for training the Trust's gardeners, until 2002 when it was at last restored and opened to the public. The luxuriant, elaborately planted gardens did not exist in earlier times – they were created by the gardeners who trained at the house.

Threave castle

☆☆ Picturesque island stronghold in the middle of the River Dee

Near Castle Douglas, 16 miles SW of Dumfries; National Trust for Scotland, open part year

Archibald 'The Grim', 3rd Earl of Douglas, built stern Threave Castle in 1369 when he was appointed Lord of Galloway by David II, son of Robert Bruce. Galloway was dangerously hostile territory for a supporter of the Bruce claim to Scotland's throne, and so he built his fortress on an island in the broad-flowing River Dee. Water was its first and best line of defence, since the castle can only be approached by boat to a tiny harbour in the shadow of the walls, or across a tricky dog-legged ford. The whole island was effectively the stronghold's outer bailey. Excavations in the 1970s revealed a great hall, a guest house and chapel, along with workshops, brewhouses and stables. The earl's household, including armed retainers, would have been at least a hundred strong and the most significant community for miles around.

'... a peaceful spot still reached only by ferry.'

The tower is massive, five storeys high, and was originally entered via a drawbridge at first-floor level, where a lobby and kitchens stood above storage cellars and a prison. A narrow turnpike stair rises to the hall above, where the earl would have held court. The next floor consisted of two bedrooms, whilst the attic, lacking any comforts such as fires or latrines, was devoted to defence, giving access to the battlements and fighting platforms cantilevered from the walls.

The low outer wall is later than the castle, dating from the 1450s when the Douglases were fighting what amounted to a private war with Scotland's James II. Hastily erected as the king's force advanced with heavy guns towards Galloway, it was the first purpose-built artillery defence in the British Isles. And it proved effective, for Threave held out for two months before its master-gunner gave in to a bribe. Thereafter the castle was a crown possession, with the Maxwells of Caerlaverock acting as keepers. In 1640, like Caerlaverock itself, it was sacked by a Covenanting army. Aside from a brief stint as a POW camp in the Napoleonic Wars it has remained ruined and deserted ever since, a peaceful spot still reached only by ferry.

Smailholm Tower
Scottish

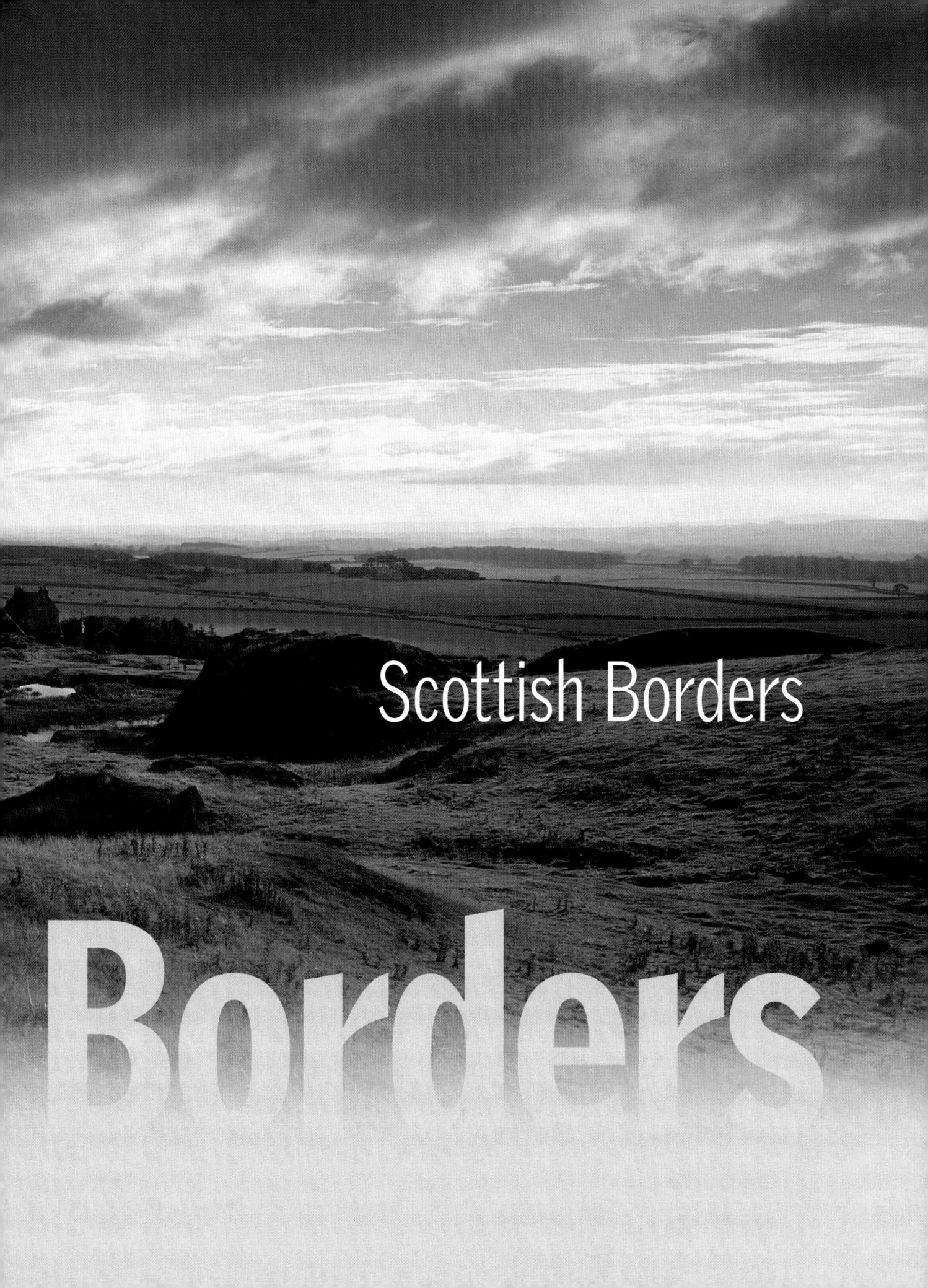
Scottish Borders
Borders

Abbotsford

☆☆☆☆ Romantic creation of eminent author

2 miles SE of Galashiels; private house, open part year

As a novelist, Sir Walter Scott played fast and loose with history to spin romantic tales, and he took the same approach when it came to designing his home. With its turrets, towers and crow-stepped gables, Abbotsford is an architectural romance intended to appeal both to the mind and the emotions. The English architect William Atkinson can take some credit as co-author, but the theme undoubtedly belongs to Scott.

Abbotsford sprawls in size yet is neither heavy-handed nor pretentious, rather it is higgledy-piggledy and charming, revealing witty flourishes at practically every turn. The house is not as old as it pretends. In 1811 Scott paid 4,000 guineas for a small farmhouse called Cartleyhole set in 110 acres of rough grazing land on the south bank of the River Tweed. He gave it the new name of Abbotsford, suggesting an entirely spurious association with the historic abbey of Melrose nearby.

Sir Walter Scott
1771–1832

Now known by name but little read, Sir Walter Scott was the most celebrated and successful British writer of the early 19th century. Although born in Edinburgh, he was the scion of an old Borders family and passed much of his childhood on his grandfather's farm where he absorbed a love of history, legend and landscape. Trained in the law, a profession he practised throughout his life, he first became famous as a poet in the early 1800s, reworking ancient ballads in a romantic style. He went on to write more than 20 novels, including *Rob Roy* and *Ivanhoe*, and a stream of other works that earned him wealth and fame. His business dealings were, however, catastrophic and following a financial crisis in 1825 his last years were overshadowed by debt, over-work and ill-health.

Right Sir Francis Chantrey's 1820 marble bust of Sir Walter Scott has long been considered the best likeness of the author. It was placed in its niche in the library by Scott's son on the day of his father's funeral. During Sir Walter's lifetime, a bust of Shakespeare occupied the same spot.

By 1817, the author's increasing professional success enabled him to set about enlarging the house to provide a dining room, a study and a smoking-room-cum-armoury in which to display his growing collection of curiosities and weapons. Five years later, what remained of the old farmhouse was demolished to make way for a new northeast wing with a medieval-style entrance hall, drawing room, library and a much larger study. It is these two sections of the house, containing Scott's apartments, that are open to public view. More than 20 years after his death, in 1853, a further wing was added to allow the family some privacy from the thousands of visitors who flocked to Abbotsford to pay their respects at what was by then a world-famous literary shrine. Queen Victoria herself visited in 1867.

The rooms in which Scott lived have been preserved virtually unchanged since his death in 1832. The gas lights – startling novelties when installed – were wired for electricity in 1962 and some objects have been moved around, but almost nothing has been added, altered or removed. The decor and furnishings date back to the 1820s. The books that Scott bought and read, and the bizarre collections he acquired, remain as they were in his lifetime.

The entrance hall sets the tone in terms of spectacle and eccentricity. It is of relatively modest size but truly baronial design; what appear to be heavy timber ceiling beams are, in fact, plaster painted to resemble wood. The ancient panelling above eye-level is equally false but the lower panels are genuinely old, having been salvaged from Dunfermline Abbey and eked out with pieces reputedly from Holyrood Palace in Edinburgh. The three plaster saints above the doors are copies of originals from ruined Melrose Abbey. Objects on view include suits of armour, swords from Culloden and Waterloo, the keys to Edinburgh's old Tolbooth, skulls of a walrus and a prehistoric elk, and a bust of William Wordsworth by Chantrey. The collection in the armoury is equally eclectic, ranging from Rob Roy's dirk and sporran to thumbscrews and chopsticks.

Left Scottish ecclesiastical architecture proved a valuable source of both inspiration and materials for the entrance hall at Abbotsford. Oak panelling and carvings that line the walls were taken from the Auld Kirk at Dunfermline, while the statues of Saints Andrew, Peter and Paul that stand above the doors were copied from originals in Melrose Abbey. The design of the stone fireplace was derived from one of the stalls in the cloisters at Melrose.

The carved ceiling in the library is based on designs from the Rosslyn Chapel, made famous as a climactic location in *The Da Vinci Code*. Some 7,000 books line the shelves revealing the breadth of its owner's interests – heraldry and warfare rub shoulders with travel and witchcraft. A further 2,000 volumes line the study, the inner sanctum where Scott's spirit properly resides. A battered leather chair stands pushed back from the desk, as though in readiness for his return.

The ever-sociable Scott passed his final days in the dining room. In September 1832, knowing he was about to die, he had his bed moved to this elegant reception room so he could bid farewell to friends with proper hospitality and style.

Scott occasionally referred to Abbotsford as 'Conundrum Castle', acknowledging the historical riddles and red herrings it contains. The fancy-dress medievalism of the place may look a touch absurd to modern eyes, but it can still be enjoyed as the architectural equivalent of a 'damn good read'. As in many of Scott's novels, a sense of fun underlies the melodrama.

Left Today, the dining room at Abbotsford is dominated by a table made for Scott by George Bullock of London out of oak trees from Drumlanrig Castle estate (see page 138). In September 1832 the room held Scott's bed, moved here as his death approached. He died on 21st September and was buried next to his wife, Charlotte, at Dryburgh Abbey (see page 160).

Ayton castle

☆☆ A Scots-baronial mansion with fine Victorian decor

At Ayton, 7 miles NW of Berwick-upon-Tweed; private house, open part year by arrangement

Scots baronial is a style that works only when done with passion and panache to proclaim the home of a magnate as powerful as a medieval baron. There must be a massive tower, suggesting the house has origins in some ancient castle. There must be battlements and turrets, parapets and crow-stepped gables. None of these archaic embellishments need serve the slightest purpose, nor add up to a balanced, unified design. Far better to mix in wild profusion with not a care for dull old rules of symmetry and order. Ayton scores on all counts.

The old castle at Ayton burnt down in 1834 and the estate was subsequently bought by William Mitchell-Innes, a director of the Royal Bank of Scotland, who commissioned James Gillespie Graham to design a new castle in keeping with his dignity and wealth, yet incorporating the conveniences of modern life. Though aged 79, Gillespie Graham took to the task with vigour, pulling out a performance of baronial extravagance that far surpassed the martial splendour of any genuine medieval tower. The house was further enlarged in 1860 by David Bryce, the maestro of High Gothic responsible for Fettes College in Edinburgh, and again in 1865 by James Wardrop.

Inside, the reception rooms are suitably palatial, with deep coffered ceilings, oak panelling and heavy furniture to match, and yet Ayton is a surprisingly homely house. Much of the original decor is intact, dating from a time when house-painting was a craft full of arcane lore and expertise. In the hall, the compartmented ceiling displays exquisite heraldic designs and the walls are painted to resemble damask using a technique of stencilling on varnish that is no longer fully understood. The effect, created by the Edinburgh firm of Bonnar & Carfrae in 1873, harks back to the 16th century via the Romanticism of Sir Walter Scott.

Elsewhere some effects have gone, painted over in the 1930s to brighten up the unfashionable gloom, but the present owner, David Liddell-Grainger, is patiently removing the whitewash to reveal the marbling beneath. He inherited Ayton as a child in 1935 and has been devoted to its preservation ever since.

Bowhill

★★★ Ducal seat with magnificent art collection

At Bowhill, 6½ miles SW of Galashiels; private house, open part year

Bowhill is the seat of the Dukes of Buccleuch, who began acquiring paintings in the 17th century. Since then, through inheritance, purchase and commission, they have built up one of the finest private collections in the land and much of it is on display in Bowhill. There is a stunning Canaletto of Whitehall, a roomful of Guardis depicting Venice, portraits by Gainsborough, Reynolds and Raeburn, dream landscapes by Claude Lorrain and a collection of miniatures second only to the Queen's. Sadly, with security tightened since the theft of a Leonardo from another Buccleuch home, Drumlanrig Castle (see page 138), visitors are now conducted round on guided tours – a frustrating way to view paintings, but worth it to see art of such quality.

The splendours of the art collection far outshine the attractions of the house. Constructed of grey, brick-sized stones and lacking in architectural detail, Bowhill looks respectable but dull. Perhaps this was the image that its owners wished to convey when they became one of Britain's wealthiest and grandest families in the early 19th century. But the Scotts of Buccleuch did not get to the top by being either respectable or dull. Originally from Galloway, they spread eastwards through the Borders from the 13th century, acquiring lands, building towers and playing an enthusiastic role in feuds, raids and wars against the English. A Sir Walter Scott fought at Flodden in 1513, and his son was at Ancram and Pinkie. In 1596 another Walter, known as 'Bold Buccleuch', rescued a fellow Borderer from Carlisle Castle in a raid that outraged Queen Elizabeth I.

By 1619 the family had an Earldom, but the climb up the social ladder still came close to disaster. In 1663 Anne, Countess of Buccleuch, married the Duke of Monmouth, Charles II's illegitimate son, who became the 1st Duke of Buccleuch. This union with royal blood must

Above The drawing room at Bowhill was formed in the 1830s by merging two rooms. One of these had been the front hall when Bowhill was approached from the south but in 1831 the architect William Burn moved the main entrance to the north side of the house. The newly created drawing room was decorated with crimson silk wall hangings and curtains which survive to this day, now faded in places to shades of pink.

have seemed the high point of Scott fortunes, until the Duke rebelled against James II and was executed in 1685. His widow was allowed to retain her estates, however, and the dukedom eventually passed to her grandson. The Scotts now went from strength to strength. The 3rd Duke married an English heiress, Lady Elizabeth Montagu of Boughton, in Northamptonshire, and in 1810, on the death of his distant cousin the Duke of Queensberry, he inherited Drumlanrig and a second dukedom. In some 20 generations, the family of cattle thieves had become the greatest landowners in Britain.

Bowhill is a product of this 19th-century surge in fortunes. In 1812 the 4th Duke turned his attentions to a modest villa which enjoyed an attractive setting on his vast estate, near the meeting of two tributaries of the Tweed. First a new front was added, then a pair of wings. The 5th Duke shifted the entrance to the north, built a new staircase and went on adding rooms as his whims dictated well into the 1870s. Almost inevitably, the end result of this piecemeal development has little coherence. But what the Dukes lacked as patrons of architecture, they more than made up with their phenomenal good taste as collectors of fine art.

The art collection is Bowhill's chief attraction, but it is also intriguing as a lived-in country seat. It is the present Duke's private home and even those rooms that open to the public are used at other times for family occasions. There is a mellow grandeur to the drawing room's gilt-edged plasterwork and walls of faded silk, while the enormous dining room is properly equipped for ducal entertaining.

Dryburgh abbey

☆☆ Atmospheric monastic ruins with well-preserved cloisters

Near St Boswells, 6 miles SE of Galashiels; Historic Scotland, open all year

The remains of the old abbey of Dryburgh sit picturesque and secluded on a bend of the River Tweed. We owe the park-like beauty of the setting to David Erskine, 11th Earl of Buchan, an eccentric antiquarian who bought the Dryburgh estate in 1786. Under his care, the abbey ruins were preserved as part of a vast conceptual landscape he designed around his home, Dryburgh House. A carved obelisk in the abbey grounds, a statue of William Wallace and a Temple of the Muses in nearby fields still stand witness to the scheme. Erskine himself lies buried in the sacristy, quite near the resting place of a far more celebrated son of the Romantic age, Sir Walter Scott.

The abbey's founder was Hugh de Morville, an Anglo-Norman knight in the court of David I (1124–53), while the canons of the Premonstratensian community came from Alnwick in Northumberland. The king hoped to reinvent Scotland as a modern feudal kingdom, perhaps even incorporating Northumberland, and in some respects Dryburgh's splendid architecture was propaganda for this new culture that was to sweep away the Celtic past. Such dreams were not be.

Like other abbeys in the Borders, Dryburgh suffered from centuries of English raids. It was attacked by Edward II in 1322, and torched again in 1385. Heat-cracked stones are still visible on a wall of the dormitory. The last assault was inflicted by the Earl of Hertford in 1545, but the *coup de grace* came with the Reformation. A few of the canons lingered on within the ruins, eking out a living from the land, but the last of them was dead by 1600 and sheep moved into the cloisters.

The East Range is the most complete, although its first floor dormitory is roofless and, confusingly, incorporates the ruins of a later house occupied by the Commendator, a secular controller appointed by the Crown in the 16th century. Beneath this, however, the chapter house is substantially intact. Entered from the cloister through a richly carved doorway, it is a spacious barrel-vaulted room, impressive but austere, lit by lancet windows. A stone bench runs around the walls, with elaborate arcading at the eastern end defining the seats of the abbot and senior canons. The arcade around the seating for lesser canons was simply painted on the walls and faint traces of this still remain.

Ferniehirst castle

☆ A 16th-century stronghold, restored as a family home

2 miles S of Jedburgh; private house, open part year

There is a raw, convincing quality to Ferniehirst Castle. It has the feel of a home that has belonged for centuries to a family of Border lairds. The Kerrs had a stronghold here from the middle of the 15th century. It was destroyed on no less than three occasions – twice by English raids and lastly on the orders of James VI as punishment for Sir Andrew Kerr's support of the rebellious Earl of Bothwell in 1593. Five years later, with Sir Andrew back in favour, the present house was constructed from the ruins of the old.

Ferniehirst is built to be defensible with a sturdy tower and thick rubble walls, but its design looks forward, albeit with caution, to a new age of prosperity and peace. So whilst the windows were originally barred, they are generously sized, and the gun loops have decorative carved surrounds. Heraldic plaques above the entrance and window jambs of curious design suggest a crude, inventive energy at play. This is a house designed by local craftsmen without advice from any architect in thrall to rules of style and taste.

Following years of neglect, Ferniehirst was restored by the 12th Marquess of Lothian in 1987, with conservation architects Simpson & Brown. It is now once again a Kerr family home, with a splendid reception room based on the original Great Hall. What was a buttery or ante-chamber has become a Hall of History, with a mural telling the story of the castle and the Kerrs. In the vaulted cellar, a survival from the early stronghold, there is a small and eccentric family museum. As in all Kerr houses the staircase rises anti-clockwise, designed to be defended with a sword held in the left hand; the Kerr family traditionally fought this way.

Floors castle

★★★ An Adam mansion transformed by Playfair into a Renaissance-style palace

Near Kelso, 9 miles NE of Jedburgh; private house, open part year

In their search for classical simplicity, early Georgian architects could be plain dull. That, at least, was the opinion of the 6th Duke of Roxburgh when he commissioned William Playfair to remodel Floors in 1837. The house had been designed more than a century before, when strict Palladianism was in vogue. In 1721 the 1st Duke was a Unionist politician in need of an impressive modern country seat and his chosen architect was William Adam, then just starting to establish his career. Adam gave his client what he wanted: a huge mansion – Floors is reputedly the largest house in Britain, with 154 rooms and 365 windows – rectilinear in outline with corner turrets and pavilion wings, in the plainest contemporary style.

By 1837 tastes had changed. The 6th Duke was a young Romantic who wanted a suitably fabulous home. Playfair was an ideal choice for such a job. When he received the Floors commission he was helping to restore Heriot's Hospital in Edinburgh, a prodigious Renaissance masterpiece crowned with turrets, chimneys and domes. This was the inspiration for his work at Floors, where he transformed Adam's rather dour design into a fairy-tale palace with a roofscape so fantastical it can scarcely be believed. Turrets (there must be 70 at least) stand in silhouette against the sky, with ogee caps resembling the tents of a medieval army. Ornate chimneys soar from battlemented walls. Water-spouts of every form protrude from the eaves. This is architecture as spectacle on a stupendous scale.

Above When William Playfair refashioned Floors between 1837 and 1847 he designed the ballroom with two walls of bay windows to take advantage of dramatic views over the River Tweed. In the 1930s Duchess May had the ballroom refitted with oak panelling, covering Playfair's ornate decoration and the bay window on the end wall, in order to create the ideal hanging space for a set of large late 17th-century Gobelins tapestries.

The interior, by contrast, is rather tame. Playfair reworked Adam's state apartments to provide comfortable reception rooms, that were in turn renovated in 1930 in an extravagant but bland mock-Adam style. The contents are very fine, however, as in 1903 the 8th Duke took the wise step of marrying an immensely wealthy American heiress, May Goelet. May was a passionate collector, as were her parents, whose art collections eventually found their way from the Goelet Chateau on Rhode Island to Floors, adding to their daughter's own acquisitions. The Duchess had what collectors call an 'eye' and she tirelessly trawled house auctions at a time when many stately homes less financially robust than Floors were selling off their contents to survive. With Gobelins tapestries, paintings by Matisse and Bonnard, oriental ceramics and French and English furniture, Floors is a treasure house in which every room contains something of rarity or beauty.

There is one room where the spirit of the 6th Duke lingers. A small study, tucked away behind the billiard room, houses his collection of some 400 stuffed birds, including eagles and a giant bustard, along with a cabinet of fossils, coins and minerals. This stuffy retreat comes as something of a relief from the ubiquitous good taste of Duchess May.

Hermitage castle

☆☆☆ A bleak medieval castle in a lonely moorland site

Near Hermitage, 12½ miles S of Hawick; Historic Scotland, open part year

Even on a sunny afternoon, uncompromising Hermitage sends a shiver down the spine. It is the best-preserved and most intimidating of the private fortresses that once controlled these lawless lands. Here are no picturesque niceties, just brutal geometry of square-cut towers and soaring arches that, like gateways in a nightmare, lead to blank walls. Pared-down and functional, this unique architectural machine was built in response to a dangerous, unstable world.

The site of the castle controls Liddlesdale, a strategic cross-border route. There was a timber motte-and-bailey castle here as early as the mid-13th century. With the outbreak of the Wars of Independence in 1296 it was hotly disputed by both sides and changed hands several times, whether by direct attack, treachery or marriage. In the 1350s it was held by an Englishman, Sir Hugh Dacre, who replaced the timber structure with a stone-built house arranged around a courtyard. Judging from the well-cut masonry and delicate arched doorways that remain, this was a sophisticated building for such a wild place.

Twenty years later Hermitage was back in Scottish hands and the Earls of Douglas had begun its transformation into an impregnable fortress. The courtyard was covered in to become an internal room within a central tower, entombing the whole of the existing house. Towers were added at each corner to provide the accommodation that a feudal baron and his retinue required – living apartments, kitchens and a prison. On the east and west external walls, the gaps between the towers were bridged with the flying arches that remain the most distinctive feature of Hermitage. They were built to simplify and strengthen the castle's high-level defence, which included a timber fighting platform projecting from the walls. The window-like apertures below the battlements are the doors that gave access to this covered walk.

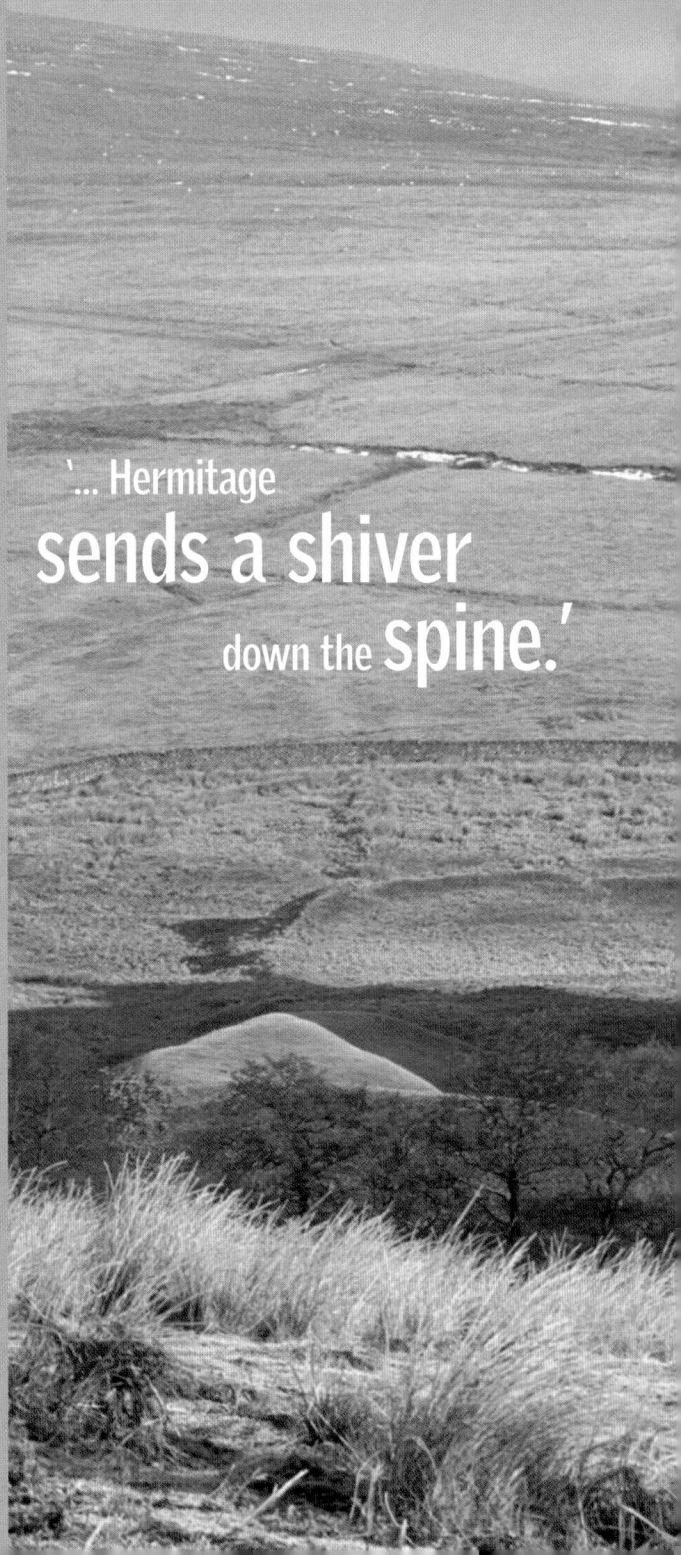

The Douglases proved more troublesome to Scotland's kings than they were to the English, and in 1492, on the orders of James IV, Hermitage was handed over to the Earls of Bothwell, who behaved even worse. In October 1566 Mary, Queen of Scots, paid a flying visit to the 4th Earl, her lover, riding the 25 miles from Jedburgh and back on the same day. Following the 5th Earl's exile in 1594, Hermitage once again reverted to the Crown and was passed on to the Scotts of Buccleuch.

With the Union of the Crowns in 1603, when James VI of Scotland became James I of England, the castle lost its purpose. It soon became a lonely ruin haunted, it was said, by the shrieks of tortured souls. Rescue came in the 1820s, when the 5th Duke of Buccleuch was inspired by Sir Walter Scott to undertake extensive restoration. Today, the interior is ruinous, the cobbled courtyard of the Dacre house once again roofless and exposed. The prison tower still displays accommodation designed with social class in mind. An upper cell, with a window and latrine, was for prisoners of gentle birth, who could look down through an iron grille into the dank and filthy pit where those from less privileged backgrounds were thrown.

Jedburgh Castle jail

☆☆ A Georgian model prison built on the site of a former castle

Castlegate, Jedburgh; museum, open part year

Turreted and curtain-walled, the toy-town castle that stands guard over Jedburgh is in fact a Georgian prison built in 1823. The fashionable castellated style of Archibald Elliot's design hinted at the town's history, recalling the medieval castle that once occupied the site. Inside, the design was radical, with cell-blocks radiating from a central jailor's house and segregated yards for outdoor exercise. Jedburgh's new prison was one of the most progressive of its age, modelled on ideas set down by John Howard in the late 18th century. It was a purpose-built institution, with well-ventilated individual cells, quite unlike the squalid, ill-regulated jails that were then the norm.

The cell blocks have scarcely altered since the last inmates left in 1886. The west block contained accommodation for debtors and female criminals. Debtors had a relatively easy time, with access to a day-room and outside yard. Work was voluntary, friends could bring in food and moderate drinking was allowed. Life was harder for other criminals. Cells were bare and unheated and men spent their days turning a crank, a deliberately useless form of labour, or unpicking rope for oakum. The workload for women was only slightly lighter.

As a visitor attraction, the jail is mercifully free of mock-ups, sound effects and interactive presentations. The frail remnants of a hammock or a hard wooden bed is quite enough to trigger the imagination. By the standards of the 19th century, the prison was well-designed and humane: with proper sanitation and a dull but adequate diet, many inmates would have known far worse outside. But this is an oppressive place of sunless corridors that reek of hopeless lives. The picturesque façade hid misery within.

'The picturesque façade hid misery within.'

JEDBURGH

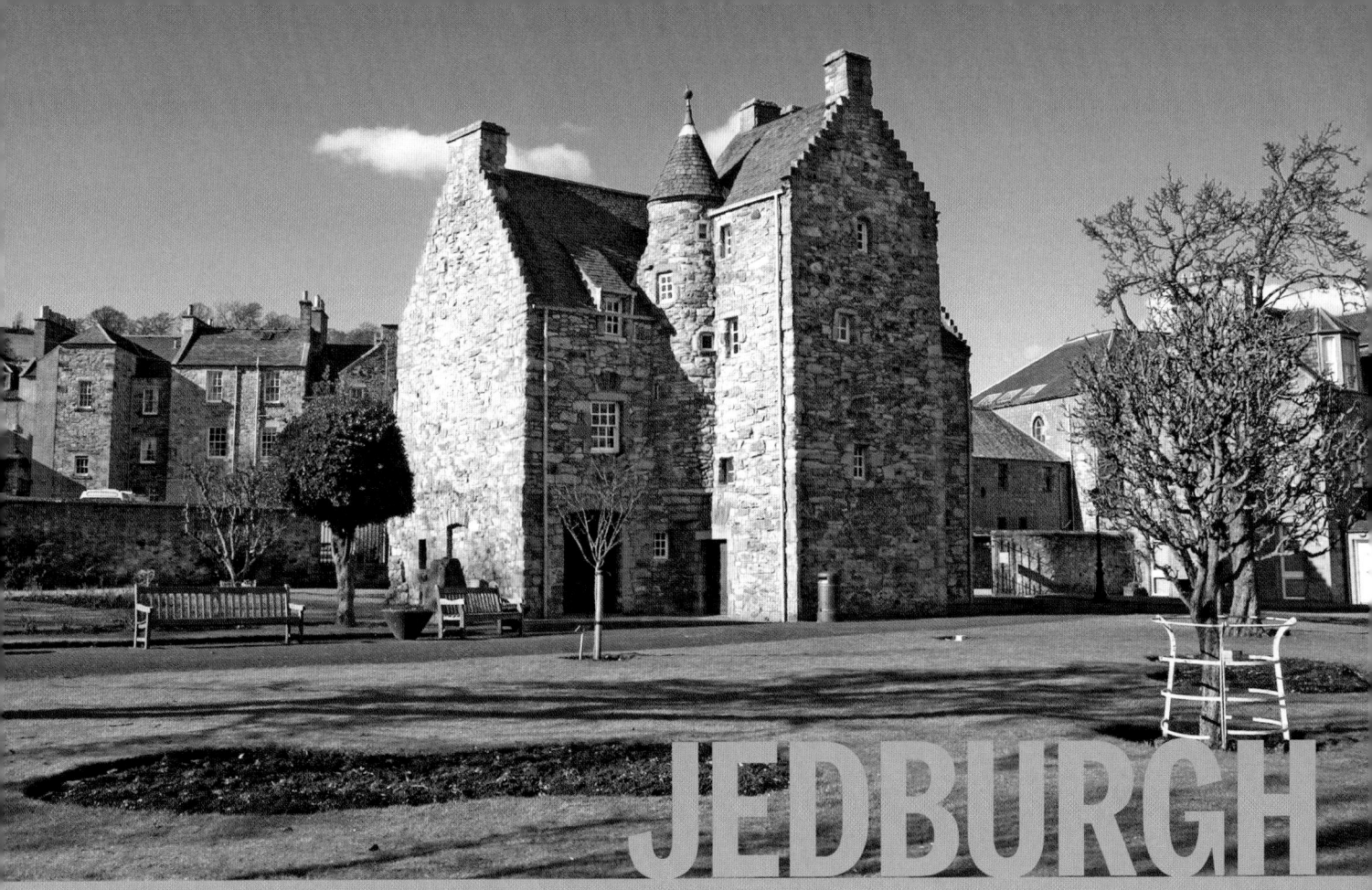

Mary, Queen of Scots' house

☆ A 16th-century town house, once the lodging of the ill-fated Queen

Queen Street, Jedburgh; museum, open part year

Tradition has it that Mary stayed in this town house during a month-long visit to Jedburgh in 1566. Even if the claim is not strictly true, the story has probably saved this fine old building from destruction. It is essentially a T-shaped tower house – a common design in 16th-century Scottish architecture – consisting of a main block with staircase wing behind. Two vaulted chambers, one a kitchen, occupy the ground floor, and a broad staircase winds up the tower to a spacious hall and private chamber above. From here a smaller stair spirals up to attic rooms (perhaps originally for servants) and two further chambers, one above the other, in the tower.

In 1929 the building was purchased by the town and restored as a museum. There is no attempt to re-create the original appearance of the rooms, and although the building has been well-preserved, its character has largely been excised by the heavy hand of museum-style presentation. But Mary's catastrophic life makes an enthralling tale. A tour of the building tells the story of her route from cradle to scaffold with a strange assortment of weaponry, documents, jewellery and personal possessions that have been accrued over the years. Pride of place goes to an exquisite pocket watch, lost by the Queen whilst riding through a bog and unearthed two and a half centuries later by a mole – a coincidence so bizarre it has to be true.

Manderston

★★★★ A Georgian-style Edwardian mansion, the epitome of luxurious country-house style

Near Duns, 12 miles W of Berwick-upon-Tweed; private house, open part year

Built in the style of a Georgian stately home and furnished with an opulence bordering on vulgarity, Manderston was one of the last and most grandiloquent country houses to be built before the First World War. Its Edwardian decor is virtually intact, and with an almost equally original 'downstairs' world of servants quarters, it is the architectural expression of a vanished way of life.

The house was built by Sir James Miller, who was a lucky man. In 1887, at the age of 25, he inherited the Manderston estate along with a fortune that his father had acquired from trading hemp and herring with Russia. He was a successful racehorse owner, winning his first Derby in 1890 with a horse that he had bought only two days before. In 1893, as one of the country's richest commoners, he married the Hon. Eveline Curzon, scion of the immensely aristocratic Curzons of Kedleston Hall in Derbyshire. The fact that his wife was raised in one of England's grandest houses may well have influenced his decision to rebuild his own home, a modest Georgian mansion that his father had enlarged in a rather heavy-handed manner in the 1860s. He began, however, with some smaller, less disruptive projects.

By way of a wedding gift, he gave his wife a pretty little boathouse, designed to resemble a Swiss chalet. Then in 1895 he gave his horses new stables, with teak stalls and posts of polished brass. Next he rebuilt the Home Farm as an utterly bizarre confection that includes a Scots Renaissance house, a monastic cloister and a dairy in the finest marble with a Tudor panelled tea-room in the tower above. The architect for all these weird and wonderful extravagances was John Kinross, a brilliant re-creator of the past who was also working at the time on Falkland Palace in Fife for the 3rd Marquess of Bute.

On returning from the Boer War in 1901, Miller finally turned his attention to the house itself, once again calling on Kinross. When the architect enquired about the budget, Miller was dismissive: 'It really doesn't matter', he replied.

The result, completed in 1905 at a final cost of £221,000, is spectacularly grand. Harking back to the 18th century, Kinross borrows elements from Robert Adam to give the house a patina of age. In the hall, both the fireplace and marble floor are copied from Kedleston, Lady Miller's childhood home, whilst ceilings are reminiscent of Syon House in London or Mellerstain (see page 172). Despite such period details, Manderston is utterly Edwardian in design. The vestibule, with a cloakroom half-concealed behind silver grilles, is reminiscent of the lobby of some luxury hotel.

It's all terribly pretentious, of course, but that was the whole idea. In the dining room, portraits pretending to be Miller ancestors gaze down grandly from the walls, but only the most naïve of guests would have been fooled. Miller was a parvenu, a man whose wealth derived recently from trade, so to gain acceptance from smart society he put on a show. And in dramatic terms, the house is a spectacular success. The silver-plated staircase may look ostentatious and absurd with a line of tourists tramping up its marble treads, but it would have been quite magical in the house's heyday, glittering with light as guests in evening finery descended to the sound of stirring music from the

Below The drawing room is a survivor from Georgian Manderston. It was extended during John Kinross's remodelling of the house and completely redecorated with sumptuous Louis XVI-style furnishings and Adam-inspired architectural details. A set of wide double doors allowed the drawing room to interconnect with the equally opulent ballroom and thus combine to form a grand and glittering reception space.

'... it would have been quite magical ...'

Left Once the Silver Staircase was completed it regularly took three men three weeks to thoroughly polish the silver-plated balustrade and brass hand rail. After the First World War, it remained uncleaned until 1980 when volunteers restored the staircase; an unpolished panel remains at the top of the stairs so visitors can appreciate the amount of work involved. **Above** The stables that Kinross built were undeniably grand; Sir James paid some £20,000 in 1895, when building costs were relatively cheap. Marble panels above the teak stalls bear the names of the horses that once lived there, names that all began with an 'M' – such as Monarch and Mystery – for Miller and Manderston.

organ in the hall. The ballroom and the drawing room display the same hedonistic opulence. With walls of silk brocade and curtains woven with gold thread, they were designed to match the glitz and glamour of the parties that Miller hoped to throw. There is no room for restrained good taste in this miniature Edwardian Versailles.

Behind the scenes, the Millers' world of glamour relied on a support system that operated with the smooth efficiency of a machine. In the basement an enormous white-tiled corridor runs the entire length of the house, connecting kitchen quarters as carefully designed as any of the rooms above. For Manderston's indoor staff of twenty-two, this world of bells and orderly activity must have seemed impervious to change, but now, just a century later, its workings are all so unfamiliar they need to be explained, like the rituals of a prehistoric tribe.

Luck eventually ran out for Sir James, who did not enjoy his house for long. On 7th November 1905 he and Lady Miller hosted a suitably extravagant ball in their newly finished mansion. The following January he defied a chill to go out hunting and subsequently died of pneumonia. His great-great nephew, Lord Palmer, now lives in the house. The so-called 'bachelor wing' that Sir James created as accommodation for his male chums is now the family home.

Mellerstain

☆☆☆☆ An Adam mansion with exquisite interiors

9 miles E of Galashiels; private house, open part year

The initial impression of Mellerstain is disappointing for an Adam house. Externally, it lacks the fluidity of line for which Robert Adam was renowned. Inside, however, it is superb, with some of the most splendid Adam rooms ever designed. The Baillie family, Mellerstain's creators and now Earls of Haddington, still use these grand reception rooms to entertain – rooms that have scarcely changed since the 1770s. New portraits may appear with every generation, the furniture may be moved around, but no Earl or Countess has ever dared to tamper with the colour schemes chosen by Robert Adam over 200 years ago.

Mellerstain belongs firmly to the 18th century, but its origins lie in the national conflicts of a century before. In 1643, as Scotland's Presbyterians squared up to Charles I, the estate was bought by George Baillie, son of an Edinburgh merchant. His son, Robert, was a Covenanter who was executed for high treason after the Restoration. The family estates were forfeited and his heir, another George, fled to Holland. The wheel of fortune turned, however, and in 1688 George took ship for England in the triumphant entourage of William of Orange. His estates were restored and in 1691 he married Grisell Hume, daughter of a fellow exile.

Like many Scottish gentry of the age, the couple had more dignity than money. Their home, at the heart of the estate, was a ruinous old tower, five storeys high with just one room on each floor. In 1725 they could finally afford to commission William Adam to design a house

Above The crowning glory of the library at Mellerstain is its plasterwork ceiling, still decorated in Robert Adam's green-and-white colour scheme and incorporating three painted medallions by Antonio Zucchi. Adam also designed the fireplace and the cupboards between the windows, each one mounted with a circular mirror. Stucco relief panels above the bookcases show scenes from ancient Greek history and legend.

more in keeping with their status. Two side pavilions were completed, one of which became the Baillies' home, but the central block was never built. Instead, the ancient tower remained, looming over the pavilions. The project was revived in 1770 by yet another George, their grandson, who engaged as his architect the most talented of William Adam's sons.

Robert Adam's work is easy to distinguish by his use of finely cut, polished stone in place of his father's old-fashioned rubble walls. There remains a heavy-handedness in the design, but the architecture is really just a package for the rooms inside. Adam's designs have been copied so often, and so thoughtlessly, that the strength of the originals comes as a surprise, and this was one of the rare occasions when he was given a blank canvas. His rooms form a stately enfilade with doorways perfectly aligned. Aside from a corridor, entrance halls and staircase, they occupy the entire ground floor – Mellerstain looks immense, but its central block is only one room deep.

The best room is the library, counted by many to be among Adam's finest works. The scale is almost intimate, not in any way pretentious, particularly in its present guise furnished with a homely mix of fine antiques and comfy modern chairs. Nor is it excessive: every detail is essential to the overall effect. Carving, painting, plasterwork and joinery combine in perfect harmony, in a composition based on Adam's notion of neo-classical ideals. The books are the most important element and were far from being just for show, for George Baillie was a highly educated man. Knowledge, especially knowledge of classical antiquity, is the unifying theme.

In comparison, other rooms appear relatively modest. All are exquisitely refined, with ceilings and carved fireplaces displaying Adam's lightness of touch. Shrugging off Palladian rectitude, he offered a new take on classicism that was frivolous and fun, but aside from the apsidal-ended front hall, which forms a stylish entrance to the house, there is little evidence of his usual skill in creating intricate geometric shapes to entertain the eye. The top-floor gallery is a magnificent surprise, with a barrel-vaulted ceiling and ionic columns at each end, and its wonderfully original design may have been a collaborative effort between architect and client. In a reversal of the usual roles, the richly ornamented ceiling that George Baillie had in mind was vetoed by Adam on the grounds that plain white plaster would be both elegant and economical. Judging from a drawing that survives, the ceiling would have been magnificent. Perhaps Baillie, like his descendants since, lacked the nerve to question Robert Adam's taste.

In the basement, the so-called 'Adam Bathroom' is a minor mystery. The delightful spouting dolphins that decorate the entrance to this small, vaulted room look too crude and playful to be Adam's work. Yet he was intrigued by Roman baths and that is what this is, albeit on a tiny scale. It is far from clear quite how it worked, but there may have been a plunge-pool, now concealed beneath the tiled floor.

Below Robert Adam's restraint is evident in the decoration of the inner hall; he designed the graceful gilt mirrors hanging on either side of a simple stucco motif. A Chinese *famille verte* bowl and pair of vases stand on an Adam table; above this hangs a portrait, *The 7th Earl Haddington and his Brothers*, by A. Nasmyth (1758–1840). The two mahogany hall chairs were probably made locally, especially for the house.

Neidpath castle

☆ An evocative tower-house, still ruined in parts

Near Peebles, 16 miles W of Galashiels; private house, open part year

Clinging to a rocky crag above the River Tweed, Neidpath is a stirring sight. For years the castle has lain poised between dereliction and rebirth, and it remains an atmospheric remnant of medieval Borders life. Dating from the 14th century, the castle was built by Sir William Hay, Lord of Tweedale. It was a typical L-shaped tower, its walls 11 feet thick, with three high-vaulted chambers piled one above another in the main block and additional accommodation in the wing. It was never Hay's main residence – a constable would have lived here, taking rents and handing out justice in his name. According to records in Edinburgh, the pit prison, which is still there, was last in use in 1594 when a Brown of Frosthill appealed to the Privy Council for release.

In the 17th century a grand staircase was installed, the vaults were subdivided to add extra floors and the roof was rebuilt in timber. Shortly after this make-over the castle saw its first and last military action when it was bombarded by Cromwellian artillery in 1650.

Far more lasting damage was inflicted by neglect after the sale of the estate to the Duke of Queensberry in 1686. A century later, with the 4th Duke, the notorious 'Old Q' of Drumlanrig (see page 138) in charge, the castle was in terminal decay.

The ruin was partially consolidated for use as accommodation for estate workers, then in the 1960s the 12th Earl of Wemyss began ambitious restoration. The fact that this work was not completed only adds to the castle's charm. The entrance hall promises a habitable house, and there is indeed a large first-floor hall that is now a stylish venue for weddings, but elsewhere is only emptiness and ghosts, with rooms of faded panelling and bare plaster walls. The two topmost floors are a shell, with stone dust underfoot and faint traces of medieval painting visible on ceiling joists.

Left The 17th-century ceiling at Old Gala House is covered with decoration; the panels between the joists are painted with designs that incorporate the initials 'IP', for Jean Pringle, and 'HS', for Hugh Scott.

Old Gala house

☆ A 16th-century bastle, now historic town house

At Galashiels, 12 miles N of Hawick; museum, open part year

The dignified country mansion looks out of place in a street of 19th-century suburban villas, but Old Gala House has survived by adapting to the winds of change. Its core, the northeast wing, dates from 1583 when Andrew Pringle, Laird of Gala, built a small bastle, a fortified farmhouse, at the heart of his feudal estate. A generation later this was enlarged into a comfortable and stylish house by his son, Sir James Pringle, one of a new breed of Border lairds who benefited from peace with England. Sir James's extravagance eventually forced him to retire to his family's grim stronghold at Smailholm (see page 179), leaving Gala to his son-in-law, Hugh Scott.

As the leading family of Galashiels, the Scotts enlarged the house in 1760 and again in 1830, only to abandon it in 1876 as mills and suburban housing encroached across their views. For a century the mansion's future was in doubt until it was acquired by Borders Council and refurbished in the 1980s as an arts centre and museum. Few internal details survived the transformation, aside from two impressive ceilings. One, dating from 1635, celebrates the union of Hugh Scott and Jean Pringle in colourful, naïve designs painted onto joists and boards. The other, in what was once a Georgian drawing room, portrays the *Four Ages of Woman* in delicately moulded plaster. Unlike these ageing ladies, the house has been reborn and despite the loss of character, it still serves a purpose in the modern world.

Paxton house

Perfect Palladian country villa, above the River Tweed

4 miles W of Berwick-upon-Tweed; private house, open part year

Paxton is an object-lesson in Palladian design. It is perfectly symmetrical, with a raised portico at the centre of its entrance front. Matching wings spread out to each side, a 'female' wing for kitchens and a 'male' wing for stables, with further courts and service blocks beyond. All is proportioned, with ornament kept dignified and plain. Orderly, hierarchical and morally superior to the Catholic excesses of European Baroque, this is the Age of Reason set in stone.

Palladian style dominated British taste for more than half a century. All too often it is dignified and rather dull, but Paxton is enchanting. Perhaps it is the setting, in a gentle wooded landscape high above the River Tweed. Or the soft pink colour of the sandstone – in sunlight Paxton positively glows. Perhaps most importantly, the scale is right. Despite its great portico and spreading wings, Paxton is a relatively modest and manageable country villa such as Andrea Palladio himself might have designed for a Venetian nobleman two centuries before.

It was John Adam, Robert's eldest brother, who drew up the plans in 1758. The client was Patrick Home, scion of a fearsome Borders family that had taken part in almost every battle fought on

Above In 1773, Patrick Home sold Paxton House to his cousin Ninian for £15,000. During the rest of his lifetime – he died in 1795 – Ninian continued to add to Paxton; the drawing room includes some of the fine pieces of Chippendale furniture that he bought for the house. The narrow vertical strips of decoration that run around the room are pieces of rare 18th-century wallpaper that Ninian imported from France shortly before his death.

Scottish soil from Flodden to Sheriffmuir. Patrick was made of gentler stuff. In his early twenties, while at the Prussian court of Frederick the Great, he met and fell in love with Sophie de Brandt. His mother disapproved, threatened disinheritance and the lovers were forced to part; in January 1751 Patrick embarked on a Grand Tour. A few months later, however, his mother was murdered by her butler and Patrick returned to Scotland to take up the running of his estates. Yet he hung onto his dream and had Paxton built as the home he could share with Sophie. Sadly, the marriage never took place and Patrick eventually sold Paxton to his cousin.

The decor of the rooms reflects the whims of fashionable taste. In the entrance hall exquisite Rococo plasterwork from the 1760s celebrates the natural forms of birds, fruit and flowers; just 20 years later, the drawing room and dining room used stylized Roman motifs. Much of the furniture is from Chippendale's workshop of a plain design suited to an unpretentious house. The Georgian kitchen has been restored and is now occasionally used for demonstrations of Georgian cuisine, using charcoal-fuelled hobs of surprising sophistication.

In contrast to this domesticity, the picture gallery comes as an astonishing surprise. Designed for George Home by Robert Reid in 1811, it was one of the first private galleries in Britain and is still one of the most spectacular. With domes and vaults of intricate geometry, it is a wonderful example of neo-classicism at its most palatial. The pictures come from the National Galleries of Scotland, including works by Raeburn, Opie, Reynolds and Nasmyth. In 1988 John Home Robertson gave Paxton to the nation and it is now run by the Paxton Trust. Although no longer lived in, and a touch too neat and tidy to be true, the house remains full of old and odd mementoes that hint at the character of a family home.

Smailholm tower

☆ Fortified tower house built in the 15th century

Near Smailholm, 9 miles N of Jedburgh; Historic Scotland, open all year

The years have not softened Smailholm. Built without concern for beauty or convenience, it rises from a windswept rocky outcrop that provided the rubble for the sturdy walls. Gun-loops guard the approaches; a battlemented walkway hugs the roof. Hundreds of such fortified farmhouses were built throughout the Borders in the 15th and 16th centuries, when feuds and cattle-raiding were a way of life. Few have survived in such unaltered state.

Smailholm was built in the 15th century by the Pringle family, who remained in possession until 1645. A protective wall, known as a barmkin, provided the first line of defence. There are also the remains of a house from the 17th century, and excavations have revealed traces of an older hall and chamber served by a kitchen range across the way. The tower, the compound's inner citadel, is entered through a timber door and iron yett, or portcullis. A vaulted storeroom occupies the ground floor, with a narrow turnpike stair rising to the upper levels. The first floor hall is surprisingly comfortable, with a corbelled fireplace, window seats and an intra-mural latrine. Above this is a more austere chamber, with smaller windows and a modest fire. The top floor has been altered and is therefore harder to interpret, but seems to have consisted of two rooms, possibly the preserve of the laird's wife and children. Outside, on the north wall-walk, there is a seat for a watchman built against a chimney-stack for warmth. From here, the views stretch more than 20 miles across the rolling landscape.

As a child Sir Walter Scott came to stay at nearby Sandyknowe Farm, and in later life he acknowledged the influence that Smailholm had on his imagination. In the upper rooms of the tower there is an exhibition of tiny, intricately modelled figures enacting scenes from Scott's *Border Ballads*. Far from being kitsch, they are distinctly sinister and their eldritch company is quite in keeping with this lonely place.

Thirlestane castle

☆☆☆☆ A 16th-century tower house, turned 17th-century ducal palace, with Victorian additions

Near Lauder, 7 miles NE of Galashiels; private house, open part year

Where would architecture be without men of ruthless ambition? Men like Sir John Maitland, who began to build this house at the heart of his estate at Thirlestane in 1587. Just fourteen years earlier he had been imprisoned for his support of the exiled Mary, Queen of Scots, but he recovered to pursue an extraordinary career, becoming Secretary of State, Keeper of the Seal and, finally, Lord Chancellor of Scotland. He wanted a home in keeping with his lofty position and so created this massive four-and-a-half-storey range. With four corner towers and rows of turrets on each side, Thirlestane could perhaps be described as a tower-house on steroids.

A home of such splendour would have satisfied most families for generations, but the Maitlands were not most families. Sir John's grandson, also John, had an even more spectacular career. Charles II appointed him his High Commissioner in Scotland, with almost regal powers. Married to a wealthy heiress, the Countess of Dysart, and created Duke of Lauderdale in 1672, he seized every prize he set

Above The Grand Bed Chamber is furnished in Victorian style; the great carved bed, on loan from Burghley House in Lincolnshire, was made around 1860. The astonishing plasterwork ceiling, however, dates from the 1st Duke of Lauderdale's transformation of Thirlestane in the 1670s. Such was the Duke's power and influence that he was able to commission Charles II's favourite stuccoist, George Dunsterfield, to come and work for long periods at Thirlestane.

his eyes on by being clever, calculating – and corrupt. The owner of a number of fine houses, he indulged, with insouciant extravagance, his passion for architectural improvement. At Thirlestane he brought in Sir William Bruce, overseer of the King's Works in Scotland, to remodel his grandfather's now somewhat outdated pile. Bruce was at the start of a career that would make him the architect of choice for Scotland's aristocracy and at the time was working under Lauderdale on rebuilding

Holyrood Palace in Edinburgh, assisted by craftsmen brought in at government expense from England and elsewhere. Lauderdale hijacked this talented team, including master mason Robert Mylne, to work on his own home. At a cost of almost £10,000, he ended up with a ducal palace of unmatched quality and style.

When improving their main home in England – Ham House in West London – the Duke and Duchess had ordered the demolition of Jacobean towers to create a fashionably plain façade. No such concessions to English taste were made in remodelling Thirlestane. The entrance front, on the old building's western gable, was made even more extravagant with new towers and a raised forecourt flanked by ogee-roofed pavilion wings. Dutch joiners installed some of the first sash windows seen in Scotland, but the style remained defiantly traditional. The biggest transformation was indoors, where grandiose new apartments were created to cater for the rigid etiquette that pervaded social life in noble households in the late 17th century.

Lauderdale did not long enjoy the fruits of his career. In 1679 failing health combined with his unpopularity to force his resignation; just before his death in 1682 he was stripped of all his offices. Even the dukedom was extinguished since he left no male heir. But this was not the end of the story. Successive Earls of Lauderdale, descendants of the Duke's younger brother, passed their ancestral home down the generations. As respected members of the aristocracy they led quiet, law-abiding lives that revolved around the social calendar rather than affairs of state. The house remained the relic of a vanished age, scarcely changing from the time of Charles II to the coronation of Queen Victoria. Until, in 1840, the 9th Earl commissioned William Burn to turn the gloomy, dilapidated ducal palace into a modern country seat.

As one of Britain's most fashionable architects, Burn had already built or redesigned more than 90 country houses and his work at Thirlestane was typical. The house, already large, was massively extended with new wings to either side of the west front. These included family accommodation (with a private suite for the Earl, a life-long bachelor), bedrooms for guests and a labyrinthine backstairs world of kitchens, servants' quarters, sculleries and service courts. In the older castle, the 17th century apartments were replaced with new reception rooms suited for the entertainment of large house parties, with libraries and turret studies as male retreats.

'... Thirlestane could perhaps be described as a tower-house on steroids.'

Thirlestane is thus a house of many layers in which different ages overlap. Externally, its phases are hard to disentangle as a consistent baronial grandeur unifies the old castle with Bruce's ducal palace and Burn's Victorian mansion. Internally, the lay-out is down to Burn, and the furnishings are also largely 19th century, but there are still rooms where it is apparent that this was once the home of Scotland's uncrowned king. On the first floor, in what was the state apartment culminating in a grand bed chamber, the plasterwork is astonishingly rich. The ceilings, created by the English plasterer George Dunsterfield, almost droop beneath the weight of garlands, swags, animals, foliage and flowers. The woodwork is equally flamboyant. An elaborately carved doorway in the ante-room must have struck a proper sense of awe into those who sought admittance to the privileged and private rooms beyond. For all the Victorian respectability imposed by Burn, Thirlestane exudes older memories of pride and power.

Right In 1738, Charles Stuart, 5th Earl and 11th Laird of Traquair, built a new set of gates at the end of the avenue that lead to his house, each pillar topped with a carved stone bear. The same Earl locked the Bear Gates after a visit by Bonnie Prince Charlie and vowed to open them again only when a Stuart king sat on the British throne once more.

Traquair

☆☆☆☆ Stuart stronghold and reputedly Scotland's oldest inhabited house

Near Innerleithen, 10 miles W of Galashiels; private house, open part year

A carved oak door at the foot of Traquair's main stair depicts a Scottish unicorn impaling an English lion. Dating from 1601, just two years before the Union of the Crowns, this image encapsulates the independent spirit of a quintessentially Scottish house. Its origins predate recorded history. According to tradition the house began as a thatched timber hall, deep in Ettrick Forest, in the mid-10th century. It was a hunting lodge by the time Alexander I signed a charter there in 1107, and it remained a royal residence until the wars of independence in the late 13th century. It passed through several noble families until 1491, when the Earl of Buchan gave it to his son James Stuart, whose descendants live there still. Just possibly, the cellars of the present house rest on the footings of a very ancient incarnation of Traquair – the building certainly incorporates the walls of a medieval tower.

Right A set of servants' bells can still be seen in the entrance hall at Traquair. Each bell had a different note so that illiterate servants could tell which one had rung by the sound it made. Below the bells hangs an oak carving of the Royal Arms of Scotland, presented by Mary, Queen of Scots after her visit in 1566; beneath is a copy of her 1587 death warrant. On the floor under the hall chest are three old curling stones. **Far right** The First Library contains some 3,000 books, amassed by the 4th and 5th Earls between 1710 and 1740. The deep coving that runs around the room is painted with portraits of great philosophers and writers. This decoration is part of the library's cataloguing system; a book marked PLAT 3–12 would be filed as the twelfth book on the third shelf under Plato's portrait.

It is almost impossible to trace the building's architectural development by eye, for it has grown organically with little help from grand designs. Throughout the 16th and 17th centuries it was added to and altered, gradually expanding and gaining extra floors until the old tower was totally absorbed, but the pieces of this jigsaw cannot be seen because the joins are covered over with painted harling. The last alteration was in 1695 when James Smith, the fashionable architect of the day, added new wings to the entrance front and a wrought-iron screen. Since then nothing much has changed. The house was never classicized and neither did it fall prey to the 19th-century passion for battlements and bare stone walls. Instead it has remained true to itself, a genuinely old, unpretentious and hugely characterful home.

Traquair is a reflection of the family who have lived there for the past 500 years. Linked by ancient blood-ties to Scotland's last royal dynasty, many Stuarts of Traquair shared a heroic genius for backing lost causes. The 1st Earl, ennobled by Charles I in 1628, fell foul of the Covenanting Presbyterians, fought against Cromwell in the Civil War and died in poverty just before the Restoration. The 2nd Earl converted to Catholicism at a time when celebrating Mass risked retribution from both mob and law. The 4th was condemned as a Jacobite in 1715 – he was rescued by his wife from the Tower of London on the eve of his execution. The 5th welcomed Bonnie Prince Charlie as a guest in 1745 and spent time in prison. The 7th was a gambler who lost his wealthy wife's fortune. The 8th refused to marry, so the earldom died with him in 1861. Since then the family have lived more sensible lives.

The house is Jacobite and Catholic to its core. Mass is still celebrated in the Chapel and the Priest's Room has a secret stair. The Bear Gates, through which the Bonnie Prince departed in 1745, will remain sealed until a Stuart once again sits on the throne. A heady mix of ritual and legend hangs in the air. Even in the Georgian surroundings of the High Drawing Room there is a sense that a bewigged phantom might at any time appear. The family's unwritten motto, 'Do not disturb', has ensured the preservation of the library, where an early 18th-century collection of 3,000 books has remained intact since the Enlightenment. Next door a second

library contains more recent acquisitions, along with documents from the family archives. Ranging from coded Jacobite correspondence to household accounts, these provide fascinating glimpses of the past. In 1742 a pint of brandy cost 2/6d (12.5p), 100 oysters could be bought for 1/1d (5p) and a goose was 1/4d (6p). At the same time, Teresa Graham was paid 4d (2p) a day to do the laundry.

Traquair's lairds clearly hated to throw anything away. The Museum Room boasts curiosities that would have been the envy of Sir Walter Scott at Abbotsford (see page 154), including a medieval bedstead, a 16th-century calculating machine known as Napier's Bones, and a rosary and crucifix that belonged to Mary, Queen of Scots. One wall is decorated with a beautiful late-medieval mural, uncovered beneath old wallpaper a century ago. Such discoveries, or rediscoveries, are part of Traquair's lore. In 1965 Peter Maxwell Stuart, the 20th laird, found all the equipment from the former brewery of the house buried under rubbish in an outhouse. The brewery was revived and Traquair Ale is now sold worldwide. There is a sense throughout the house that further secrets are buried, waiting to be found.

Glossary

The aim in this book has been to avoid terms not familiar to the lay person. However, some specialist terms in common use in architectural circles may have crept in, for which the following may be helpful.

acanthus – pattern of an exotic Mediterranean flower with large leaves used in classical decoration.
anthemion – a honeysuckle flower pattern used in classical decoration.
Artisan Mannerist – buildings created by masons using pattern books (rather than architects) in the period c.1615–75. Mannerism originated in 16th-century Italy and was characterised by Classical elements used in unusual ways. It was taken up in the Low Countries, then spread to England.
ashlar – block of masonry fashioned into a wall, either load-bearing or to cover brick.
bailey, inner and outer – a fortified enclosure, usually moated and surrounded by a curtain wall, containing a motte (mound) with a keep on top. Walls are topped by battlements, with crenellations which protected defenders from arrows, and machicolations, or floor openings, through which attackers could be fired down on.
baluster – upright post supporting the handrail on stairs.
bargeboard – wooden board protecting the eaves of a roof.
bay – a space of wall between any vertical element, such as an upright beam, pillar or a division into a window or door.
bay window – window projecting out from a flat wall, either canted if the sides are straight, or bowed if curved.
bolection mould – moulding concealing the join of vertical and horizontal surfaces, shaped like an S in cross-section.
Boulle – elaborate inlay work on the surface of furniture, customary in 17th and 18th-century French work.
bow – see bay window
canted – see bay window
cartouche – frame for a picture or statue, often oval and surrounded by a scroll.
caryatid – a column in the shape of a draped female figure.
casements – see sashes
castle of enclosure – a form of early medieval castle in which individual buildings are enclosed within a curtain wall, in contrast to later medieval castles that consisted of a tower with subsidiary buildings in a courtyard to front or rear.
chinoiserie – a style of Rococo with Chinese motifs, often linked with Gothick.
coffering – a ceiling composed of beams enclosing sunken square or round panels.
collars – see roof timbers
corbel – a stone or wood projection in a wall that supports a beam, statue or sill.
cornice – (1) a ledge or projecting upper part of a classical entablature. (2) Moulding at the top of a wall concealing the join with the ceiling.
cottage ornée – late-Georgian/Victorian picturesque cottage, usually with thatched roof and Gothic windows.
crenellation – see bailey
crocket – Gothic decorative device, usually a cusp or curling leaf, at regular intervals on outer edges of spires, pinnacles and gables
cruck – a simple structure of two, usually curved, trunks of wood formed into an inverted V which support the walls and roof of a medieval house.
curtain wall – in castle-building, a wall constructed between defensive projections such as bastions.
dentil – one of a series of small square blocks along the base of a cornice
dorter – a sleeping room or dormitory, especially in a college or monastery.
dressing – a general term for finishings; stone is dressed to either a smooth or ornamental surface.
enfilade – a line of rooms in sequence along one side of a house, usually with interconnecting doors.
entablature – a feature of classical architecture comprising everything above column height, formally composed of architrave, frieze and cornice.
flatwork – decorative plaster or woodwork in low relief.
frontispiece – a decorative bay above a doorway in a Tudor or Jacobean building, customarily composed of Renaissance motifs.
gable – the triangular end of a double-pitched roof, sometimes with stepped or scrolled (Dutch) sides.
garderobe – privy or lavatory, usually discharging into a ditch or moat outside a medieval house.
Great Chamber – see solar
grisaille – monochrome painting, usually a mural and in shades of grey.
grotesque – decorative wall motif of human figures, as found in Roman grottoes.
half-timbering – term for timber-framed house derived from the practice of splitting logs in half to provide beams.
hipped roof – a roof with a sloping end instead of an end gable.
Ho-Ho bird – chinoiserie motif associated with 18th-century Rococo style.
jetty or jettied floor – upper floor extended, or oversailed, beyond the lower one to give more space upstairs and protect lower walls from adverse weather. Jettying also uses the downward thrust of the upper walls to form a cantilever, preventing internal ceiling beams from bowing.
keep – see bailey
king post – see roof timbers
linenfold – a pattern on wall panels imitating folded linen.
louvre – a covered turret above a medieval hall that allowed smoke to escape.
machicolation – see bailey
mannerism – see Artisan Mannerist
mansard – a roof with two separate pitches of slope.
motte – see bailey
mullion – central divider of window, made of metal or stone.
oversail – see jetty
oriel – an upper window projecting from a wall, sometimes (incorrectly) used to indicate a tall medieval window lighting the dais end of the Great Hall.
Palladian – a style of classical architecture, formal and refined outside, often lavish inside, named after Italian architect, Andrea Palladio (1508–80). Moving spirit behind most English classical designers, especially Inigo Jones and, later, Lord Burlington, William Kent and the early Georgians.
parlour – see solar
piano nobile – the main ceremonial floor of a classical building, sitting on the basement or 'rustic' lower floor.
pier-glass – a wall mirror supported by a small table, bracket or console.
pietra dura – literally 'hard stone'; a decorative inlay using highly polished stones such as marble, jasper and porphyry
pilaster – a flat column projecting only slightly from a wall.
pointing – mortar or cement used to seal between bricks.
porte-cochère – a grand porch with a driveway through it, allowing passengers to alight from carriages under cover.
prodigy house – a large, ostentatious house of the Elizabethan/Jacobean period.
putti – unwinged sculptures of chubby boys found in Classical and Baroque decoration.
queen post – see roof timbers
quoins – dressed corner stones.

render – a covering of stucco, cement or limewash on the outside of a building.
Rococo – the final phase of Baroque style in the 18th century, typified by refined painted and plaster decoration, often asymmetrical and with figures.
roof timbers – a tie-beam runs horizontally across the roof space; a king post rises vertically from the tie beam to the apex of the roof; queen posts rise not to the apex but to subsidiary beams known as collars; wind-braces strengthen the roof rafters.
rustic – a name given in Palladian architecture to the lower floor or basement, beneath the piano nobile.
rustication – treatment of ashlar by deep-cutting joints so they look stronger or cruder.
sashes – windows opening by rising on sash ropes or cords, as opposed to casements which open on side hinges.
scagliola – composition of artificial stone that imitates appearance of grained marble.
screens passage – accessed from the main door of a medieval building and built into one end of a Great Hall to shield it from draughts. Door ors arches lead from the passage into the hall on one side and kitchens on other. Above is usually a minstrels' gallery.
Serlian – motifs derived from pattern books of the Italian Renaissance architect, Sebastiano Serlio (1475–1554).
sgraffito – plaster decoration scratched to reveal another colour beneath.
solar – the upstairs room at the family end of a medieval hall, originally above an undercroft or parlour. Originally accessed by ladder or spiral stairs, it was usually replaced by a Great Chamber in the Tudor era.
strapwork – strap or ribbon-like decorative scrolls in Elizabethan and Jacobean design.
stucco – plaster, usually protective, covering for brick, sometimes fashioned to look like stone.
studding – vertical timbers laid close to each other to strengthen the wall. Close-studding tends to indicate wealth.
tie-beam – see roof timbers
undercroft – a vaulted room or crypt beneath a building, partly or wholly underground
vault – a ceiling, usually of stone composed of arches.
Venetian window – Palladian window composed of three components, the centre one arched.
wind-braces – see roof timbers

Simon Jenkins' sources

The best guides to any house are the people who occupy it. They have felt its walls and sensed its seasons. They stand witness to its ghosts, real and imagined, and have thus become part of its history. As a substitute, guidebooks vary widely from the academic to the plain childish. The best are published by English Heritage, erudite and enjoyable. National Trust guidebooks are at last moving from the scholarly to the accessible, and the Trust's compendium *Guide*, by Lydia Greeves and Michael Trinick, is excellent.

My selection of a thousand properties derives from numerous sources. These include Hudson's *Historic Houses and Gardens*, supplemented by *Museums and Galleries* published by Tomorrow's Guides. The Historic Houses Association website is another invaluable source. Of recent house surveys, the best are John Julius Norwich's *Architecture of Southern England* (1985), John Martin Robinson's *Architecture of Northern England* (1986) and Hugh Montgomery-Massingberd's *Great Houses of England and Wales* (2000). Nigel Nicolson's *Great Houses of Britain* (1978) describes the most prominent. Their lists are not exhaustive and include houses not open to the public. Behind them stands Nikolaus Pevsner's massive 'Buildings of England' series, which deals with houses more generously (with plans) in the newer revised editions.

On English domestic architecture, the classics are hard to beat. They include Olive Cook's *The English House Through Seven Centuries* (1968), Alec Clifton-Taylor's *The Pattern of English Building* (1972), Hugh Braun's *Old English Houses* (1962), Sacheverell Sitwell's *British Architects and Craftsmen* (1964) and Plantagenet Somerset Fry's *Castles of Britain and Ireland* (1980).

On specific periods the best are Mark Girouard's *Robert Smythson and the English Country House* (1983), Giles Worsley's *Classical Architecture in England* (1995), Kerry Downes's *English Baroque Architecture* (1966) and Girouard's *The Victorian Country House* (1971). Joe Mordaunt Crook takes a lively look at the Victorian battle of the styles in *The Dilemma of Style* (1989). Jeremy Musson describes the manorial revival in *The English Manor House* (1999) and Gavin Stamp takes a wider look at the same period in *The English House 1860–1914* (1986). *Edwardian Architecture*, edited by Alastair Service (1975), brings the story into the 20th century and Clive Aslet's *The Last Country Houses* (1982) almost completes it.

On social history, Girouard's *Life in the English Country House* (1978) is incomparable. *Creating Paradise* (2000) by Richard Wilson and Alan Mackley sets the house in its economic context. So does Mordaunt Crook's *The Rise of the Nouveaux Riches* (1999) and David Cannadine's *The Decline and Fall of the British Aristocracy* (1990). Adrian Tinniswood offers a fascinating insight in his *History of Country House Visiting* (1989). The desperate post-war bid to save houses is described in Marcus Binney's *Our Vanishing Heritage* (1984) and John Cornforth's *The Country Houses of England 1948–1998* (1998). Peter Mandler covers the same period in his scholarly *The Fall and Rise of the Stately Home* (1997).

Biographies of architects are too legion to list but Howard Colvin's *Biographical Dictionary of British Architects* (1978) was my bible over disputed dates and attributions. Of a more personal character is James Lees-Milne's delightful account of the National Trust's early acquisitions in *People and Places* (1992). Houses in distress are visited in John Harris's *No Voice from the Hall* (1998). *Writers and their Houses* (1993) is a first-class collection of essays, edited by Kate Marsh.

I am indebted to the many architectural commentaries in *Country Life*, champion of the historic buildings cause for over a century. I do not believe I could have found a thousand houses for my list were it not for its progenitors, Edward Hudson and Christopher Hussey, and their many successors.

Contact details

Note: Readers are advised to check opening times before visiting, either via the websites and addresses below or in Hudson's Historic Houses & Gardens, the annual guide to castles, houses and heritage sites open to the public. Houses sited close to the border of a neighbouring county may have that county given as their postal address.

Abbotsford – Melrose, Roxburghshire, TD6 9BQ www.scottsabbotsford.co.uk Tel 01896 752043 Open late Mar–late Oct, daily 9.30am–5pm (2–5pm on Sun in Mar–May & Oct)
Acorn Bank – Temple Sowerby, Penrith, Cumbria, CA10 1SP www.nationaltrust.org.uk Tel 01768 361893 Gardens open late Mar–late Oct, Wed–Sun 10am–5pm
Alnwick Castle – Alnwick, Northumberland, NE66 1NQ www.alnwickcastle.com Tel 01665 510777/511100 Open early Apr–late Oct, daily 10am–5pm
Appleby Castle – Boroughgate, Appleby, Cumbria, CA16 6XH Exterior can be viewed
Appleby: St Anne's Hospital – Boroughgate, Appleby, Cumbria Tel 01768 351487 Open all year, daily 9am–5pm
Aydon Castle – Corbridge, Northumberland, NE45 5PJ www.english-heritage.org.uk/aydoncastle Tel 01434 632450 Open mid-Apr–late Sep, Thur–Mon 10am–5pm
Ayton Castle – Ayton, Eyemouth, Berwickshire, TD14 5RD Tel 01890 781212 Open mid-May–mid-Sep by prior appointment
Barnard Castle: Blagraves House – 30–32 The Bank, Barnard Castle, Durham, DL12 8PN www.blagraves.com Tel 01833 637668
Barnard Castle: Bowes Museum – Barnard Castle, Durham, DL12 8NP www.thebowesmuseum.org.uk Tel 01833 690606 Open all year, daily 11am–5pm
Barnard Castle: The Castle – Castle House, Barnard Castle, Durham, DL12 9AT www.english-heritage.org.uk/barnardcastle Tel 01833 638212 Open all year, daily (Thur–Mon in Nov–Mar) 10am–6pm (to 4pm in Oct–Mar)
Bamburgh Castle – Bamburgh, Northumberland, NE69 7DF www.bamburghcastle.com Tel 01668 214515 Open mid-Mar–late Oct, daily 11am–5pm
Beamish Museum – Beamish, Durham, DH9 0RG www.beamish.org.uk Tel 0191 370 4000 Open early Jan–early Dec, daily (closed Mon & Fri in late Oct–late Mar) 10am–5pm (10am–4pm in late Oct–late Mar)
Belford Hall – Belford, Northumberland, NE70 7EY Interior communal areas, exterior & grounds open by prior arrangement with Lady Graham (01668 213140) or Mr J H Harris (01668 213576)
Belsay Castle & Belsay Hall – Belsay, Ponteland, Northumberland, NE20 0DX www.english-heritage.org.uk/belsay Tel 01661 881636 Open all year, daily (Thur–Mon in Nov–Mar) 10am–5pm (to 4pm in Oct–Mar)
Bishop Auckland: Auckland Castle – Bishop Auckland, Durham, DL14 7NR www.Auckland-castle.co.uk Tel 01388 601627 Open Easter–Sep, Sun & Mon (also Wed in Aug) 2–5pm
Blackwell – Bowness-on-Windermere, Cumbria, LA23 3JR www.blackwell.org.uk Tel 01539 446139 Open mid-Feb–late Dec, daily 10.30am–5pm (to 4pm Feb–Mar & Nov–Dec)
Bowhill – Bowhill, Selkirk, TD7 5ET www.buccleuch.com OR www.bowhill.org.uk Tel 01750 22204 Open Jul, daily 1–5pm
Brantwood – Coniston, Cumbria, LA21 8AD www.brantwood.org.uk Tel 01539 441396 Open all year, daily (Wed–Sun in mid-Nov–mid-Mar) 11am–5.30pm (to 4.30pm mid-Nov–mid-Mar)
Brough Castle – Church Brough, Brough, Kirkby Stephen, Cumbria, CA17 4EJ www.english-heritage.org.uk/broughcastle Tel 0871 7161945 Open all year, daily, at any reasonable time
Brougham Castle – Penrith, Cumbria, CA10 2AA www.english-heritage.org.uk/broughamcastle Tel 01768 862488 Open Apr–Sep, daily 10am–5pm, and Oct, Thur–Mon 10am–4pm
Brougham Hall – Penrith, Cumbria Tel 01768 868184 Open all year, daily 9am–6pm or dusk if earlier, although may be closed occasionally
Caerlaverock Castle – Glencaple, Dumfries & Galloway, DG1 4RU www.historic-scotland.gov.uk Tel 01387 770244 Open all year, daily 9.30am–6.30pm (to 4.30pm in Oct–Mar)
Carlisle Castle – Carlisle, Cumbria, CA3 8UR www.english-heritage.org.uk/carlisle Tel 01228 591922 Open all year, daily 9.30am–5pm (10am–4pm in Oct–Mar)
Carlisle: Prior's Tower – The Abbey, Carlisle, Cumbria, CA3 8TZ Tel 01228 548151 Open by arrangement with the Chapter of Carlisle Cathedral
Chester-le-Street: Anker's House – Church Chare, Chester le Street, Durham, DH3 3QB Tel 0191 374 4682 Open Apr–Oct, Mon–Sat 10am–3.30pm and by appointment at other times
Chillingham Castle – Northumberland, NE66 5NJ www.chillingham-castle.com Tel 01668 215359 Open Easter & May–Sep, daily (may be closed some Sats) 1–5pm (grounds open 12pm); Oct–Apr, groups by appointment
Chipchase Castle – Wark, Hexham, Northumberland, NE48 3NT Tel 01434 230203 Open June, daily 2–5pm; tours by arrangement at other times. Gardens open Easter–Jul, Thur–Sun & BH Mon 10am–5pm
Cockermouth: Wordsworth House – Main Street, Cockermouth, Cumbria CA13 9RX www.nationaltrust.org.uk Tel 01900 824805 Open late Mar–late Oct, Tue–Sat & BH Mon (also Mon in Jul–Aug) 11am–4.30pm
Conishead Priory – Conishead Priory & Buddhist Temple, Ulverston, Cumbria, LA12 9QQ www.manjushri.org Tel 01229 584029 Open Easter–Oct, Sat, Sun & BHs 2–5pm (closed occasionally and opening times may vary); grounds open all year, daily dawn–dusk
Cragside – Rothbury, Morpeth, Northumberland, NE65 7PX www.nationaltrust.org.uk Tel 01669 620150 Open early Apr–early Nov, Tue–Sun 1–5.30pm (to 4.30pm in early Oct–early Nov)
Croxdale Hall – Croxdale, Durham, DH6 5JP Tel 01833 690100 Open May–mid Jul, Tue & Wed by arrangement
Dalemain – Penrith, Cumbria, CA11 0HB www.dalemain.com Tel 01768 486450 Open late Mar–late Oct, Sun–Thur 11am–4pm; gardens open 10.30am–5pm
Drumlanrig Castle – Thornhill, Dumfries & Galloway, DG3 4AQ www.drumlanrig.com Tel 01848 331555 Open May–Aug, daily, 12–4pm in May & Jun, 11am–4pm in Jul & Aug
Dryburgh Abbey – St Boswells, Melrose, Roxburghshire, TD6 0RQ www.historic-scotland.gov.uk Tel 01835 822381 Open all year, daily 9.30am–5.30pm (to 4.30pm in Oct–Mar)
Durham: Durham Castle – Palace Green, Durham, DH1 3RW www.durhamcastle.com Tel 0191 374 4682 Open all year, daily (Wed, Sat & Sun in Oct–Easter) 10am–4pm (afternoons only Oct–Easter)
Durham: Crook Hall – Sidegate, Durham, DH1 5SZ Tel 0191 384 8028 Open Easter weekend & late May–mid Oct, Wed–Sun & BH Mon 1–5pm
Ecclefechan: Carlyle's Birthplace – The Arched House, High Street, Ecclefechan, Dumfries & Galloway, DG11 3DG www.nts.org.uk Tel 01576 300666 Open Jun–Sep, Fri–Mon 1–5pm
Ellisland Farm – Hollywood Road, Auldgirth, Dumfries & Galloway, DG2 0RP www.ellislandfarm.co.uk Tel 01387 740426 Open all year, daily (Tue–Sat in Oct–Mar) 10am–5pm (to 4pm on Sun)
Ferniehirst Castle – Jedburgh, Roxburghshire, TD8 6NX Tel 01835 862201 Open early Jun–early Aug, Tue–Sun 11am–4pm
Finchale Priory – Brasside, Newton Hall, DH1 5SH www.english-heritage.org.uk/finchale Tel 0191 269 1200 Open by arrangement with key keeper (tel 0191 386 6528)
Floors Castle – Kelso, Roxburghshire, TD5 7SF www.floorscastle.com Tel 01573 223333 Open Easter weekend & May–late Oct, daily 11am–5pm
Grasmere: Dove Cottage – Grasmere, Cumbria, LA22 9SH www.wordsworth.org.uk Tel 01539 435544 Open early Feb–early Jan, daily 9.30am–5.30pm
Harperley Camp – Firtree, Crook, Durham, DL15 8DX www.powcamp.com Tel 01388 767098 Open all year, daily for guided tours 12–2pm
Headlam Hall Hotel – Headlam, Near Gainford, Darlington, Durham, DL2 3HA www.headlamhall.co.uk Tel 01325 730238
Hermitage Castle – Newcastleton, Roxburghshire, TD9 0LU www.historic-scotland.gov.uk Tel 01387 376222 Open Apr–Sep, daily 9.30am–6.30pm
Hill Top – Near Sawrey, Ambleside, Cumbria, LA22 0LF www.nationaltrust.org.uk Tel 01539 436269 Open early Apr–late Oct, Sat–Wed & Good Fri (also Thur in Aug) 10.30am–4.30pm

Holker Hall – Cark-in-Cartmel, Grange-over-Sands, Cumbria, LA11 7PL www.holker-hall.co.uk Tel 01539 558328 Open late Mar–late Oct, Sun–Fri 11am–4pm; gardens open 10.30am–5.30pm

Hutton-in-the-Forest – Penrith, Cumbria, CA11 9TH www.hutton-in-the-forest.co.uk Tel 01768 484449 Open mid-Apr–early Oct, Wed, Thur, Sun & BH Mon 12.30–4pm

Hylton Castle – Craigavon Road, Sunderland, Durham, AR5 3PA www.hyltoncastle.com Can be viewed from Hylton Dene public park all year, daily, at any reasonable time

Isel Hall – Cockermouth, Cumbria, CA13 0QG Tel 01900 821778 Open late Mar–early Oct, Mon 2–4pm and to groups by appointment at other times

Jedburgh Castle Jail – Castlegate, Jedburgh, Roxburghshire, TD8 6QD Tel 01835 864750 Open Apr–Oct daily 10am–4.30pm (1–4pm on Sun)

Jedburgh: Mary, Queen of Scots' House – Queen Street, Jedburgh, Roxburghshire, TD8 6EN Tel 01835 863331 Open early Mar–late Nov, daily 10am–4.30pm (from 11am on Sun)

Kendal: Abbot Hall – Kendal, Cumbria, LA9 5AL www.abbothall.org.uk. Tel 01539 722464 Open mid-Jan–late Dec, Mon–Sat 10.30am–5pm (to 4pm in Jan–Mar & Nov–Dec)

Kirkcudbright: Broughton House – 10–12 High Street, Kirkcudbright, Dumfries & Galloway, DG6 4JX www.nts.org.uk Tel 01557 330437 Open Easter–Oct, daily 12–5pm (10–5pm in Jul–Aug); gardens also open Feb–Easter, daily 11am–4pm

Kirkcudbright: MacLellan's Castle – Castle Street, Kirkcudbright, Dumfries & Galloway, DG6 4JD www.historic-scotland.gov.uk Tel 01557 331856 Open Apr–Sep, daily 9.30am–5.30pm

Langley Castle Hotel – Haydon Bridge, Northumberland, NE47 5LU www.langleycastle.com Tel 01434 688888

Levens Hall – Kendal, Cumbria, LA8 0PD www.levenshall.co.uk Tel 01539 560321 Open early Apr–mid-Oct, Sun–Thur 12–5pm; gardens open 10am–5pm

Lindisfarne Castle – Holy Island, Berwick-upon-Tweed, Northumberland, TD15 2SH www.nationaltrust.org.uk Tel 01289 389244 Open mid-Mar–late Oct, late Dec & mid–late Feb, Tue–Fri (daily in late Dec & mid–late Feb); opening times depend on local tides, contact the castle for further information

Lowther Castle – Estate Office, Lowther, Penrith, Cumbria, CA10 2HG www.lowther.co.uk Tel 01931 712577 Contact for opening information

Lumley Castle Hotel – Chester-le-Street, Durham, DH3 4NX www.lumleycastle.com Tel 0191 389 1111

Manderston – Duns, Berwickshire, TD11 3PP www.manderston.co.uk 01361 883450 Open mid-May–late Sep, Thur & Sun 1.30–5pm; groups by appointment at other times

Mellerstain – Gordon, Berwickshire, TD3 6LG www.mellerstain.com Tel 01573 410225 Open Easter & May–Oct, Sun–Mon & Wed–Thur (Sun only in Oct) 12.30–5pm

Mirehouse – Keswick, Cumbria, CA12 4QE www.mirehouse.com Tel 01768 772287 Open Apr–Oct, Sun & Wed (also Fri in Aug) 2–5pm; gardens open daily 10am–5.30pm

Muncaster Castle – Ravenglass, Cumbria, CA18 1RQ www.muncaster.co.uk Tel 01229 717614 Open mid-Feb–early Nov, Sun–Fri 12–5pm; gardens open Feb–Dec, daily 10.30am–6pm or dusk, if earlier

Neidpath Castle – Peebles, Tweedale, EH45 8NW Tel 01721 720333 Open May–Sep, Wed–Sun & BH Mon 11am–6pm (1–5pm on Sun)

Newcastle-upon-Tyne: Bessie Surtees House – 41–44 Sandhill, Newcastle-upon-Tyne, NE1 3JF www.english-heritage.org.uk/bessiesurtees Tel 0191 269 1200 Open all year, Mon–Fri (but closed BHs) 10am–4pm

Newcastle-upon-Tyne: Castle – Castle Keep, Castle Garth, Newcastle-upon-Tyne, NE1 1RQ www.museums.ncl.ac.uk/keep/ Tel 0191 232 7938 Open all year, daily 9.30am–5.30pm (to 4.30pm in Oct–Mar)

Old Gala House – Scott Grescent, Galashiels, TD1 3JS Tel 01750 20096 Open Apr–Oct, Tue–Sat (daily in Jun–Aug) 10am–4pm (from 1pm on Sun and Tue–Fri in Oct)

Paxton House – Berwick-upon-Tweed, TD15 1SZ www.paxtonhouse.co.uk Tel 01289 386291 Open Apr–Oct, daily 11am–5pm

Preston Hall – Yarm Road, Eaglescliffe, Stockton-on-Tees, Durham, TS18 3RH www.stockton.gov.uk Tel 01642 527375 Open all year, daily 10am–5.30pm (to 4.30pm Mon–Sat and 2–4.30pm on Sun in Oct–Mar)

Preston Tower – Chathill, Northumberland, NE67 5DH Tel 01665 589227 Open mid-Apr–late Sep, Thur–Mon 10am–6pm

Raby Castle – Staindrop, Darlington, Durham, DL2 3AH www.rabycastle.com Tel 01833 660202 Open May, Jun & Sep, Wed & Sun, and Jul–Aug, Sun–Fri (also Sat–Mon on BH weekends, including Easter); 1–5pm. Gardens open May–Sep, Sun–Fri & BH Sat 11am–5.30pm (to 5pm in Sep)

Rammerscales – Lockerbie, Dumfries & Galloway, DG11 1LD Tel 01387 810229 Open last week of Jul & first three weeks of Aug, Sun–Fri 2–5pm

Rokeby Park – Barnard Castle, Durham, DL12 9RZ Tel 01833 637334 Open first May BH, then from second May BH–early Sep, Mon & Tue 2–5pm

Rydal Mount – Rydal, Cumbria, LA22 9LU www.rydalmount.co.uk Tel 01539 433002 Open all year, daily (closed Tue in Nov–Feb) 9.30am–5pm (to 4pm in Nov–Feb)

Seaton Delaval Hall –The Avenue, Seaton Sluice, Whitley Bay, Northumberland, NE26 4QR Tel 0191 237 1493/0786 Open May–Sep, BH Mon in May & Aug, Wed & Sun in Jun–Sep, 2–6pm

Shambellie House – National Museum of Costume, Shambellie House, New Abbey, Dumfries & Galloway, DG2 8HQ www.nms.ac.uk Tel 01387 850375 Open Apr–Oct, daily 10am–5pm

Sizergh Castle – Kendal, Cumbria, LA8 8AE www.nationaltrust.org.uk Tel 01539 560951 Open early Apr–late Oct, Sun–Thur & BH Mon 1–5pm; gardens open 12–5pm

Smailholm Tower – Smailhom, Kelso, Roxburghshire, TD5 7PG www.historic-scotland.gov.uk Tel 01573 4600365 Open all year, daily (Sat–Wed in Oct & Sat–Sun in Nov–Mar) 9.30am–6.30pm (to 4.30pm in Oct–Mar)

Storrs Hall Hotel – Windermere, Cumbria, LA23 3LG Tel 01539 447111

Swarthmoor Hall – Ulverston, Cumbria, LA12 0JQ www.swarthmoorhall.co.uk Tel 01229 583204 Open for tours mid-Mar–mid-Oct, Tue–Fri from 2.30pm; group tours by arrangement at other times

Thirlestane Castle – Lauder, Berwickshire, TD2 6RU www.thirlestanecastle.co.uk Tel 01578 722430 Open mid-Apr–late Sep (also Good Fri, Easter Sun & Mon), Sun, Wed, Thur & BH Mon (Sun–Thur in Jul–Aug) 10am–3pm

Threave Castle – Castle Douglas, Dumfries & Galloway, DG7 1BG www.historic-scotland.gov.uk Tel 07711 223101 Open Apr–Sep, daily 9.30–6.30pm (last ferry to castle at 4.30pm)

Threave House – Castle Douglas, Dumfries & Galloway, DG7 1RX www.nts.org.uk Tel 01556 502575 Open Apr–Oct, Wed–Fri & Sun 11am–3.30pm; garden open all year, daily 9.30am–5pm (to 4.30pm on Fri)

Townend – Troutbeck, Windermere, Cumbria, LA23 1LB www.nationaltrust.org.uk Tel 01539 432628 Open late Mar–late Oct, Wed–Sun & BH Mon 1–5pm or dusk if earlier

Traquair – Innerleithen, Peeblesshire EH44 6PW www.traquair.co.uk Tel 01896 830323 Open Apr–Oct, daily 12–5pm (from 10.30am in Jun–Aug and 11am–4pm in Oct), and weekends in Nov, 11am–3pm

Wallington Hall – Cambo, Morpeth, Northumberland, NE61 4AR www.nationaltrust.org.uk Tel 01670 773600 Open mid-Mar–early Nov, Wed–Mon 1–5.30pm (to 4.30pm in early Sep–early Nov); garden open all year, daily 10am–7pm (to 6pm in Oct, to 4pm in Nov–Mar)

Warkworth Castle & Hermitage – Warkworth, Alnwick, Northumberland, NE66 0UJ www.english-heritage.org.uk/warkworth Tel 01665 711423 Castle open all year, daily (Sat–Mon in Nov–Mar) 10am–5pm (to 4pm in Oct–Mar); Hermitage open Apr–Sep, Wed, Sun & BHs, 11am–5pm

Washington: Old Hall – The Avenue, Washington Village, Washington, Tyne & Wear, NE38 7LE www.nationaltrust.org.uk Tel 0191 416 6879 Open early Apr–late Oct, Sun–Wed 11am–5pm; gardens open 10am–5pm

Witton Castle –Witton-le-Wear, Bishop Auckland, Durham, DL14 0DE www.witton-castle.co.uk Tel 01388 488230 Castle can be viewed as part of a holiday complex

Workington Hall – Curwen Park, Workington, Cumbria Sited in a public park so exterior can be viewed; occasional entry can be arranged with Allerdale Borough Council (01900 326253)

Wray Castle – Low Wray, Ambleside, Cumbria, www.english-heritage.org.uk & www.nationaltrust.org.uk Tel 01539 436269 Entrance hall, music room, drawing room and fern house open July & Aug, Sat–Wed 2–4pm (and on Heritage open days); grounds open all year

Index

Main entries for houses are in **bold**

A

Abbot Hall 44
Abbotsford 154-6
Acorn Bank 16
Adam, John 177
Adam, Robert 101, 172, 173, 174
Adam, William 162, 172-3
Addison, Edward 40
Allan Bank 34
Allies and Morrison 20
almshouses 18, 77
Alnwick Castle 100-3
Ambleside 54
anchorage 77
Anker's House 77
Appleby 17-18
Appleby Castle 17-18
Armstrong, Lord 106, 116
Art Nouveau 20, 42
Arts and Crafts 19, 20, 42
Atkinson, William 154
Attlee, Clement 130
Auckland Castle 74-6
Auldgirth 143
Aydon Castle 104-5
Ayton Castle 157

B

Bacon, Francis 51
Baillie Scott, M. H. 19-20, 21
Bamburgh Castle 106-7
Barnard Castle 68-9
Barnard Castle (town) 66-9, 94
Bates, Cadwallader 120
Beamish Museum 70-3
Bear Gates 183, 184
Beaumont, Gilles 46
Belcamp, Jan van 44
Belford Hall 108
Bellingham, James 45, 47, 48
Belsay Castle 109
Belsay Hall 110-11
Berwick-upon-Tweed 177
Bessie Surtees House 123
Bevan, Aneurin 130
Bishop Auckland 74, 84
Blackwell 19-21
Blagraves House 66
Bonnar & Carfrae 157
Bonnard, Pierre 163
Bowes Museum 67-8
Bowhill 158-9
Bowness-on-Windermere 19
Boyd, Thomas 143
Brantwood Hall 22-3
Brough Castle 24
Brougham Castle 25
Brougham Hall 26
Broughton House 144-5
Brown, Ford Madox 116
Brown, Lancelot (Capability) 101
Browne, George 60, 61
Browning, Robert 54
Bruce, Sir William 181-2
Brueghel, Jan 106
Bryce, David 148, 157
Buddhist community 31
Bulletti, Anton 102
Bullock, George 156
Burkett, Mary 43
Burn, William 91, 93, 159, 182
Burne-Jones, Sir Edward 116, 119
Burns, Robert 54, 143

C

Caerlaverock Castle 136-7
Cambo 128
Cameron, Julia Margaret 51
Canaletto 68, 102, 158
Canina, Luigi 101, 102
Canova, Antonio 53
Canute, King 90
Cark-in-Cartmel 38
Carlisle 27-9
Carlisle Castle 28-9
Carlyle, Thomas 51, 142
Carlyle's Birthplace 142
Carr, John 44, 62, 78, 91, 95
Castle Douglas 149, 150
Castle of Newcastle upon Tyne 124-5
Chantrey, Sir Francis 155
Charles II 141, 180
Chester-le-Street 77, 88
Chillingham Castle 112-14
Chillingham wild cattle 112, 113
Chipchase Castle 115
Chippendale, Thomas 178
Claude Lorrain 158
Clifford, Lady Anne 17-18, 24, 25, 33, 44
Cockermouth 30, 34, 43
Coleridge, Samuel Taylor 35
Conishead Priory 31
Coniston 22
Cortese, Giuseppe 78
Cosway, Maria 78
Crace, J. G. 38, 95
Cragside 116-19
Cripps, Sir Stafford 130
Cromwell, Oliver 17, 66
Crook Hall 79
Croxdale Hall 78
Cumbria 14-63
Cuyp, Aelbert 48

D

Dalemain 32-3
Darlington 86
de Hooch, Pieter 91
de Laszlo, Philip Alexius 53, 102
de Morgan, William 116
Dentists's house, Beamish Museum 70
Devis, Arthur 33
Dobson, John 108, 130
Dobson, William 103
Dove Cottage 34-5
Drumlanrig Castle 138-41
Dryburgh Abbey 160
Dumfries 136, 138, 147, 148
Dumfries & Galloway 134-51
Duns 168
Dunsterfield, George 181, 182
Durham (city) 79-83
Durham (county) 64-97
Durham Castle 80-2

E

Ecclefechan 142
Edward I 113, 136
Edward II 160
Eldon, Lord 123
Elizabeth I 47, 121, 158
Elliott, Archibald 166
Ellisland Farm 143
Emmerson, Henry Hetherington 119
English Civil War 28

F

Ferguson, C. J. 106
Ferneley, John 56
Ferniehurst Castle 161
Finchale Priory 83
Firtree 84
Floors Castle 162-3
Fowler, John 131
Fox, George 59

G

Gainsborough, Thomas 53, 131, 158
Gaitskell, Hugh 130
Galashiels 154, 158, 172, 176
Gandy, J. M. 58
Garrett, David 129
Gill, Macdonald 121
Gillespie Graham, James 157
Gillow of Lancaster 44, 48
Giordano, Luca 93
Girtin, Thomas 44
Glasgow Boys 145
Gothick 31, 75, 76, 78, 87, 93
Goya, Francisco 68
Grasmere 34, 35
Greek style 110
Guardi, Francesco 158

H

Harperley Camp 84-5
Hawkshead 34
Haydon Bridge 120
Hazlitt, William 35
Headlam Hall 86
Hedges, Nathaniel 33
Henry I 28
Henry II 28, 124
Henry VI 52
hermitage 133
Hermitage Castle 164-5
Herring, John Frederick 91
Hexham 104
Hill Top 36-7
Hodgson, J. 120
Hogarth, William 44
Holbein, Hans 141
Holker Hall 38-9
Holland, Jools 97
Holy Island 121
Home, George 178
Hornel, E. A. 144, 145
Horner, H. P. 63
Hudson, Edward 121
Hutton-in-the-Forest 40-2
Hylton Castle 87

I, J

Inman, Henry 54
Innerleithen 183
Isel Hall 43
James I (James VI of Scotland) 47, 112, 114, 161, 165
James II 159
James II of Scotland 151
Jedburgh 161, 166-7
Jedburgh Castle Jail 166
Jekyll, Gertrude 122
John, Augustus 114, 122

K

Kelso 162
Kendal 44, 45, 55
Keppie, John 145
Keswick 50
Kinross, John 168, 169
Kirkcudbright 144-6
Kneller, Sir Godfrey 53, 140
Koeck van Aelst, Pieter 46

L

La Tour, Georges de 89
Lafranchini, Pietro 131
Lamb, Charles 35
Langley Castle 120

Larkin, William 44
Lauder 180
Lauderdale, 1st Duke of 180-2
Laurence, Samuel 51
Lawrence, Sir Thomas 53
Lely, Sir Peter 47, 53, 91, 93, 103, 141
Leonardo da Vinci 141
Lethaby, W. R. 119
Levens Hall 45-8
Lindisfarne Castle 121-2
Longmire, William 61
Lowther Castle 49
Lumley Castle 88
Lutyens, Sir Edwin 121, 122

M

Macdonald, William Bell 147
MacLellan's Castle 146
Maitland, Sir John 180
Malfatti, Luigi 102
Manderston 168-71
Marshall, Benjamin 91
Mary, Queen of Scots 28, 165, 167, 184, 185
Mary, Queen of Scots' House 167
Matisse, Henri 163
medicinal and culinary herbs 16
Mee, Arthur 69
Mellerstain 172-4
Merton, John 141
Miller, Sir James 168, 169, 171
Mirehouse 50-1
Monck, Sir Charles 110
Montiroli, Giovanni 102
Morris, William 19, 42, 119
Morritt, Anne 95
Mounsey, Dr James 147
Muncaster Castle 52-3
Munnings, Sir Alfred 53, 91
Munro, Alexander 131
Music teacher's house, Beamish Museum 71
Mylne, Robert 182

N,O

Napoleon Bonaparte 47-8
Nash, Joseph 46
Nasmyth, Alexander 174, 178
Near Sawrey 36
Neidpath Castle 175
Newcastle upon Tyne 123-5
Nollekens, Joseph 76
Northumberland 98-133
Nucci, Giuseppe 102
Old Gala House 176
Opie, John 178
Oudry, Jacques-Charles 38

P

Paine, James 91, 108
Paley & Austin 38
Palladianism 94, 108, 129, 177
Palma Vecchio 102
Paxton House 177-8
Peddie & Kinnear 149
Peebles 175
Peel, John 42
pele towers 27, 32, 33, 40, 43, 45-6, 52, 55, 56, 62, 109, 112, 113, 115, 125
Pellechet, Jules 67
Penrith 16, 25, 26, 32, 49
Penshaw Monument 87
Percy family 101, 132
Pevsner, Nikolaus 49, 78, 97
Picturesque style 25, 109
Pit cottages, Beamish Museum 72
Playfair, William 162, 163
Pockerley Manor, Beamish Museum 73
Potter, Beatrix 36-7, 63
Pre-Raphaelites 129, 131
Preston Hall 89
Preston Tower 125
Prince Bishops of Durham 74, 81
Prior's Tower 27
prisoner-of-war camp 84-5
Prout, Samuel 23
Puiset, Hugh de 82

Q

Quakerism 59
Queensberry, 4th Duke of 138, 175
Quincy, Thomas de 35

R

Raby Castle 90-3
Raeburn, Sir Henry 158, 178
Raine, James 79
Rammerscales 147
Raphael 103
Ratcliffe, Dorothy Una 16
Ravenglass 52
Rembrandt van Rijn 141
Renaissance style 141, 162
Reni, Guido 103
Reynolds, Sir Joshua 44, 53, 93, 95, 131, 158, 178
Richard III 28
Rising of the North 68-9, 90, 93
Robbia, Luca della 23
Robert Bruce 138
Robinson, Sir Thomas 74, 94, 95
Rococo 33, 76, 78, 88, 91, 95, 115, 131, 178
Rokeby Park 94-5
Rokeby Venus 94
Rombouts, Theodore 107
Romney, George 44, 131
Rose, Joseph 42
Rothbury 116
Rubens, Peter Paul 47
Ruskin, John 22-3, 44, 130, 131
Rydal Mount 54

S

St Anne's Hospital 18
St Boswells 160
St Godric 83
Salvin, Anthony 40, 42, 52, 53, 78, 101, 103, 132
Scots-baronial 148, 149, 157
Scott, Sir Walter 35, 58, 68, 154-6, 160, 165, 179
Scott, William Bell 130
Scottish Borders 152-85
Seaton Delaval Hall 126-7
Sebastiano del Piombo 102
Shambellie House 148
Shaw, Richard Norman 19, 116, 118, 119
Simpson & Brown 161
Sitwell, Sacheverell 126
Sizergh Castle 55-7
Skelton, Tom 53
Smailholm Tower 179
Smirke, Robert 49
Smith, James 141, 184
Southey, Robert 35, 58
Spedding, James 51
Spedding, Tom 51
Spencer-Stanhope, John Roddam 116
Staindrop 90
Stockton-on-Tees 89
Storrs Hall 58
Stuart, Prince Charles Edward (Bonnie Prince Charlie) 28, 140, 183, 184
Stuart, Prince James Francis Edward (Old Pretender) 57
Suggia, Guilhermina 122
Sunderland 87
Swarthmoor Hall 59

T

Taccalozzi, Giovanni 102
Temple Sowerby 16
Teniers, David 91
Tennyson, Alfred, Lord 51
Thirlestane Castle 180-2
Threave Castle 150-1
Threave House 149
Titian 102
topiary garden 46
Townend 60-1
Traquair 183-5
Trevelyan, Sir Charles 130
Trevelyan, Lady Pauline 129, 130
Troutbeck 60
Turner, J. M. W. 23, 44, 103

U, V

Ulverston 31, 59
Unthank 40
van Dyck, Anthony 32, 39, 102, 103
Vanbrugh, John 88, 126, 127
Velasquez, Diego 94
Victoria, Queen 155
Vos, Cornelis de 93

W,Z

Wallington Hall 128-31
Wardrop, James 157
Wark 115
Warkworth Castle 132
Warkworth Hermitage 133
Wars of the Roses 106
Wars of Scottish Independence 164
Washington, George 96
Washington Old Hall 96
Webster, George 31, 38, 40, 42
Wellington, Duke of 48
West, Benjamin 95
Westmorland and Cumberland Yeomanry 33
Wilkins, William 110
Windermere 58, 63
Witton Castle 97
Witton-le-Wear 97
Woolner, Thomas 130, 131
Wootton, John 91
Wordsworth, Dorothy 25, 30, 34, 35, 54
Wordsworth, William 25, 30, 34-5, 51, 54, 58, 63, 138
Wordsworth House 30
Workington Hall 62
Worsnop, Thomas 107
Wray Castle 63
Wright, Joseph 44
Wyatt, James 74, 75, 76
Wyatt, Philip 31
Zoffany, Johann 33
Zucchi, Antonio 173
Zurbarán, Francisco 75-6

T=top TL=top left TR=top right B=bottom BL=bottom left BR=bottom right L=left R=right C=centre CL=centre left CR=centre right

Front Cover Lakeland Arts Trust/(Interior of Blackwell, Bowness-on-Windermere) **Back Cover** Thirlestane Castle Trust/(Thirlestane Castle) **Endpapers** The National Trust/Andreas von Einsiedel (wallpaper, Cragside) **1** The Interior Archive/Christopher Simon Sykes **2-3** Heritage House Group Limited **4-7** European Map Graphics Ltd. **8** Quintin Wright **11** Artist, Roger Hutchins **12** Tyne & Wear Museums/Laing Art Gallery (portrait of John Dobson attributed to William Dixon) **14-15** The National Trust/Joe Cornish **16** The National Trust/Clive Boursnell **17** Simon Ledingham **18** Jerry Hardman-Jones **19-21** Lakeland Arts Trust **22 T** Collections/Liz Stares **BL** Courtesy of the Brantwood Trust, Coniston **23** Courtesy of the Brantwood Trust, Coniston **24** David Lyons **25** English Heritage/Jonathan Bailey **26-27** Jerry Hardman-Jones **28** Collections/Roy Stedall-Humphryes **29** English Heritage **30 TL** Collections/Simon Warner **TR** The National Trust/Nadia Mackenzie **31** New Kadampa Tradition **32** Collections/Simon Warner **32-33 T** Courtesy of Dalemain Estates **33 B** Collections/Quintin Wright **34** The Wordsworth Trust, Dove Cottage. **36** The National Trust/Geoffrey Frosh **37** The National Trust/Joe Cornish **37 inset** The National Trust **38** Collections/Quintin Wright **39** Courtesy of Holker Hall **40-42** Collections/Quintin Wright **43** Jerry Hardman-Jones **44** Lakeland Arts Trust **45** Collections/Jill Swainson **46** Collections/Quintin Wright **47** Courtesy of Levens Hall & Gardens **48** Collections/Quintin Wright **49** Collections/Simon Warner **50-51** Jerry Hardman-Jones **52 T, B** Heritage House Group Limited **52-53** Collections/Quintin Wright **54 TL** Collections/Jill Swainson **TR** Rydal Mount and Gardens **55** The National Trust/Alasdair Ogilvie **56-57** The National Trust/Andreas von Einsiedel **58** Courtesy of English Lakes Hotels **59** Geoff Harris, 2nd Image Photography **60** The National Trust/Matthew Antrobus **61 T** The National Trust/© Talbot & Whiteman **CR** The National Trust/John Parry **62** Jerry Hardman-Jones **63** John Moffat **64-65** www.lastrefuge.co.uk **66** Peter Wood GVS photography/www.virtualteesdale.com **67** Collections/Graeme Peacock **68 BL** The Bowes Museum **68-69** Collections/Graeme Peacock **70-73** Beamish North of England Open Air Museum **74-75** Country Life/Paul Barker **75 TR** Collections/Quintin Wright **76** Country Life/Paul Barker **77** Mike Rutter **78** English Heritage **79** Courtesy of Crook Hall **80-81** Collections/Roy Stedall-Humphryes **82** Collections/Roy Stedall-Humphryes **83** English Heritage/Jonathan Bailey **84-85** North News and Pictures **85 B** PA Photos **86** Courtesy of Headlam Hall **87** English Heritage/Jonathan Bailey **88** Collections/Graeme Peacock **89** Stockton Museum Service **90-91** Collections/Roy Stedall-Humphryes **92** Collections/Quintin Wright **93** Heritage House Group Limited **94-95** Courtesy of The Right Honourable Sir Andrew Morritt **96** The National Trust/Joe Cornish **97** www.in4link.co.uk **98-99** Collections/Graeme Peacock **100-1** John Parker **102** His Grace the Duke of Northumberland **102-3** Heritage House Group Limited **104** Collections/Graeme Peacock **105** Collections/Quintin Wright **106-7** Collections/David Taylor **107 inset** Courtesy of Bamburgh Castle **108** Smiths Gore, Corbridge **109** John Parker **110** Collections/Philip Nixon **111** English Heritage/Paul Highnam **112-13** The Interior Archive/Christopher Simon Sykes **114** Heritage House Group Limited **115** Don Brownlow/Borders Photography **116-17** John Parker **118 T** The National Trust/Andreas von Einsiedel **B** The National Trust/Nadia Mackenzie **119** The National Trust/Nadia Mackenzie **120** Collections/Roy Stedall-Humphryes **121** John Parker **122** The National Trust/Andreas von Einsiedel **123 L** Newcastle Document Services **R** Collections/McQuillan & Brown 124-125 Collections/Graeme Peacock **125-7** John Parker **128-9** Don Brownlow/Borders Photography **130-1** The National Trust/Colin Dixon. **132** English Heritage/Paul Highnam **133** English Heritage/Bob Skingle **134-5** The Interior Archive/Fritz von der Schulenberg **136-7** Collections/Alan Barnes **139** Collections/Allan Devlin **140 T** The Interior Archive/Christopher Simon Sykes **B** The Interior Archive/Fritz von der Schulenburg **141** The Interior Archive/Fritz von der Schulenburg **142** Reproduced by kind permission of The National Trust for Scotland **143** Scottish Viewpoint/VisitScotland **144-5** Reproduced by kind permission of The National Trust for Scotland **146** Scottish Viewpoint/Allan Devlin **147** Courtesy of Malcolm Bell Macdonald **148** © Trustees of the National Museums of Scotland **149** Scottish Viewpoint/VisitScotland **150-1** Collections/Allan Devlin **152-3** Scottish Viewpoint/Paul Tomkins/STB **154** The Interior Archive/Christopher Simon Sykes **155** Collections/Michael Jenner **156 T** The Interior Archive/Christopher Simon Sykes **B** Collections/Dennis Barnes **157** Collections/Malcolm Crowther **158-9** The Interior Archive/Christopher Simon Sykes **160** Derek Jackson/www.borderprints.co.uk **161** Charles Denoon **162-3** Courtesy of The Roxburghe Estates **164-5** David Lyons **166** Derek Jackson/www.borderprints.co.uk **167** Scottish Viewpoint/John Pringle **168-74** The Interior Archive/Christopher Simon Sykes **175** Scottish Viewpoint/VisitScotland **176** Scottish Borders Council **177-8** Jarrold Publishing and Paxton House, reproduced by kind permission of the publisher. **179** David Lyons **180-1** Thirlestane Castle Trust **183**The Interior Archive/Christopher Simon Sykes **184-5** The Interior Archive/Fritz von der Schulenburg

Discover Britain's Historic Houses: The Borders

Reader's Digest Project Team
Series editor Christine Noble
Project editor Lisa Thomas
Art editor Jane McKenna
Picture researcher Christine Hinze
Caption writer/copy editor Caroline Smith
Proofreader Ron Pankhurst
Indexer Marie Lorimer
Product production manager Claudette Bramble
Production controller Katherine Bunn

Reader's Digest General Books
Editorial director Julian Browne
Art director Anne-Marie Bulat
Managing editor Alastair Holmes
Picture resource manager Sarah Stewart-Richardson
Pre-press account managers Sandra Fuller, Penelope Grose

Colour origination Colour Systems Limited, London
Printed and bound in Europe by Arvato, Iberia

We are committed to both the quality of our products and the service we provide to our customers. We value your comments, so please feel free to contact us on **08705 113366** or via our web site at **www.readersdigest.co.uk**

If you have any comments or suggestions about the content of our books, you can contact us at: **gbeditorial@readersdigest.co.uk**

All rights reserved. No part of this book may be reproduced, stored in a retrieval system, or transmitted in any form or by any means, electronic, electrostatic, magnetic tape, mechanical, photocopying, recording or otherwise, without permission in writing from the publishers.

Published by The Reader's Digest Association Limited, 11 Westferry Circus, Canary Wharf, London E14 4HE

© The Reader's Digest Association Limited 2007

www.readersdigest.co.uk

® Reader's Digest, The Digest and the Pegasus logo are registered trademarks of the Reader's Digest Association, Inc., of Pleasantville, New York, USA.

This book was designed, edited and produced by The Reader's Digest Association Limited based on material from *England's Thousand Best Houses* by Simon Jenkins, first published by Allen Lane, the Penguin Press, a publishing division of Penguin Books Ltd.

Copyright © Simon Jenkins 2003

Concept code UK0149/L/S
Book code 634-006 UP0000-1
ISBN 978 0 276 44248 3
Oracle code 356600006H.00.24